P9-CPY-324

Company's Coming®

Baking
Simple to
Sensational

Our
100th
cookbook

Photo Legend front and back cover:

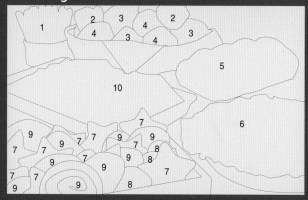

1. Cheese Sticks, page 134
2. Cranberry Brie Muffins, page 91
3. Smoked Cheese Apple Muffins, page 96
4. Red Pepper Jalapeño Muffins, page 91
5. Mixed Grain Loaf, page 11
6. Cran-Berry Pie, page 118
7. Gingerbread Stars, page 150
8. Cranberry Macadamia Mounds, page 165
9. Almond Jelly Swirls, page 75
10. Sugar-Capped Rhubarb Loaf, page 110

Baking—Simple to Sensational
Copyright © Company's Coming Publishing Limited

All rights reserved worldwide. No part of this book may be reproduced, stored in a retrieval system or transmitted in any form by any means without written permission in advance from the publisher.

In the case of photocopying or other reprographic copying, a license may be purchased from the Canadian Copyright Licensing Agency (Access Copyright). Visit www.accesscopyright.ca or call toll free 1-800-893-5777. In the United States, please contact the Copyright Clearance Centre at www.copyright.com or call 978-646-8600.

Brief portions of this book may be reproduced for review purposes, provided credit is given to the source. Reviewers are invited to contact the publisher for additional information.

First Printing September 2004

National Library of Canada Cataloguing in Publication

Paré, Jean.
    Baking : simple to sensational / Jean Paré.

(Special occasion series)
Includes index.
ISBN 1-896891-86-1

    1. Baking. I. Title. II. Series: Paré, Jean   Special occasion series.

TX765.P36 2004   641.7'1   C2004-900747-5

Published by
Company's Coming Publishing Limited
2311 – 96 Street
Edmonton, Alberta, Canada T6N 1G3
Tel: 780-450-6223   Fax: 780-450-1857
www.companyscoming.com

Company's Coming is a registered trademark owned by Company's Coming Publishing Limited

Printed in China

Pictured at left: Pecan Tart, page 160

Baking—Simple to Sensational was created
thanks to the dedicated efforts of the people
and organizations listed below.

COMPANY'S COMING PUBLISHING LIMITED

Author	Jean Paré
President	Grant Lovig
Production Manager	Derrick Sorochan
Design Director	Jaclyn Draker
Publishing Coordinator	Shelly Willsey
Senior Designer	Zoë Henry

THE RECIPE FACTORY

Research & Development Manager	Nora Prokop
Editor	Laurel Hoffmann
Editorial Assistant	Kari Christie
Associate Editors	Audrey Carroll
	Joan McManners
Copywriters	Debbie Dixon
	Kari Christie
Proofreaders	Pam Phillips
	Connie Townsend
	Audrey Dahl
Senior Food Editor	Lynda Elsenheimer
Food Editor	Jessica Assaly
Recipe Editors	Mary Anne Korn
	Lovoni Walker
Kitchen Services Manager	Jill Corbett
Test Kitchen Staff	James Bullock
	Sandra Clydesdale
Photo Editor	Patricia Meili-Bullock
Photography	Stephe Tate Photo
Photographer's Assistant	Ron Checora
Food Stylist	Ashley Billey
Prep Kitchen Coordinator	Audrey Smetaniuk
Prep Assistant	Linda Dobos
Prop Stylist	Paula Bertamini
Registered Dietitian	Margaret Ng

We gratefully acknowledge the following suppliers for their
generous support of our Test Kitchen and Photo Studio:

Broil King Barbecues
Corelle®
Hamilton Beach®
Lagostina®
Proctor Silex®
Tupperware®

Our special thanks to the following businesses for providing
extensive props for photography:

Anchor Hocking Canada	La Cache
Baker's Secret®	Linens 'N Things
Browne & Co. Ltd.	Michaels The Arts And Crafts Store
Canhome Global	Mikasa Home Store
Casa Bugatti	Pfaltzgraff Canada
Cherison Enterprises Inc.	Pier 1 Imports
Danesco Inc.	The Bay
Dansk Gifts	Tupperware
Island Pottery Inc.	Winners
Klass Works	

Table of Contents

Sweet and savoury breads await your cravings. Choose a spicy flatbread or cheesy loaf, a fruity pull-apart or sticky buns. Filled with grains, herbs, spices, fruits, nuts, cheese and more—all sensational! How-to photos for braiding, shaping, cutting and rolling.

Wispy chiffon plays on your tongue but a ginger spice cake lingers… or if you'd rather, try something with mango, coconut, walnuts or figs. And don't forget the decadent cheesecake! Choose from blueberry, banana, raspberry and chocolate.

How easy it is to lose count when there are so many delectable cookies to eat! Give in to something chewy, melting, cream-filled or chocolate-infused. Or rather than round, choose square—squares, that is. Dream of date meringues, awaken your senses with chocolate and nuts, or stick to caramel.

Try a wide variety of muffins, biscuits and loaves rich with chocolate, hot with jalapeño or sweet with mango, apple, raspberry, cranberry or apricot. Twenty-three simple reasons to enjoy the moment!

Irresistible flaky goodness with so much variety. Anticipate tasting the expected—tarts, pies and strudel. Then prepare for the unexpected— profiteroles, spirals, triangles and more. Surprise yourself, as well as your guests!

Offer these homemade treats to your family and friends. Bake crunchy biscotti, melt-in-your-mouth shortbread or try a new twist on an old favourite— mini fruitcakes—just right for wrapping in showy cellophane or filling a decorative tin or gift box.

Find family favourites or try tempting new recipes—fancy cookies, holiday buns, cakes, pies, squares, and even some savoury breads. Make traditional babka and paska, or classic fruitcake and shortbread. Or plan to be different this year and tuck mincemeat inside puff pastry—wow!

Foreword

Baking has always been a part of my life. When I was catering, so many people asked for my baking recipes, particularly sweeter delicacies like cakes, cookies, squares and pies, that the first cookbook I chose to write was *150 Delicious Squares*. I took inspiration from my parents, both of whom loved and appreciated the art of baking. Now, more than 23 years later, *Baking—Simple to Sensational* is my 100th cookbook!

Today you might think the popularity of baking from scratch is slowly fading. After all, can't we find practically anything in the grocery store to make our baking experience easier? Just add water, an egg or two and voilà, instant treat! It's true that we're often starved for time, but I'm delighted to see there's a renewed interest in home baking. Maybe we have fond childhood memories of helping Mom or Dad in the kitchen. Or maybe we find that baking is the perfect way to unwind from the stress in our lives. Whatever the reason, the reward is always worth the effort—and I'm not just talking about the food. When you serve or make a gift of freshly baked bread or a piping hot pie, it's a moment when you can feel good about all you've accomplished.

Now, as we put the finishing touches on *Baking—Simple to Sensational*, I feel we're helping to bring the art of baking home where it belongs. A broad assortment of recipes was created especially for this book, from simple coffee cakes to sensational cheesecakes. Every recipe has been carefully tested in our Company's Coming kitchen, then photographed in scrumptious colour.

What makes this book particularly useful is that every chapter features a different baking style for any time of the day, week or year. It could be a special occasion, a simple afternoon impulse, or part of a planned gift exchange. You might even just want to stock your freezer for last minute entertaining, because most baked goods freeze beautifully. Pies, tarts, cakes, cookies, bread, squares… you'll find them all here.

If you'd like to practice your baking skills or learn a few new tricks, there are illustrated how-to steps throughout the book. Looking for a perfectly delicious gift to give? A special collection of recipes has been assembled in one chapter, chosen because they can be easily wrapped and delivered.

Of course, baking for the holiday season is still my real passion; I simply love the many colourful ways to create such welcome treats. You'll find all kinds of festive recipe ideas in the chapter on holiday entertaining, including some special large-quantity recipes that are particularly appropriate for events like baking exchanges. No more calculators, finger counting or mistaken measurements as you try to double or triple a recipe!

Breathe some new life into your home cooking. Keep *Baking—Simple to Sensational* within easy reach, and reach for it often. Treat the family to homemade muffins for breakfast. Bake your own unique cake for that next birthday celebration. Chase off blustery, wet days with a fresh batch of warm cookies, made with a little help from the kids. And remember, it doesn't matter when or how often you bake; the home-baked goodness that comes from your kitchen will tell everyone that you cared enough to make them something from your heart.

Jean Paré

Each recipe has been analyzed using the most up-to-date version of the Canadian Nutrient File from Health Canada, which is based on the United States Department of Agriculture (USDA) Nutrient Data Base. If more than one ingredient is listed (such as "hard margarine or butter"), or a range is given (1 – 2 tsp., 5 – 10 mL) then the first ingredient or amount is used in the analysis. Where an ingredient reads "sprinkle," "optional," or "for garnish," it is not included as part of the nutrition information. Milk, unless stated otherwise, is 1% and cooking oil, unless stated otherwise, is canola.

Margaret Ng, B.Sc. (Hon), M.A.
Registered Dietitian

Glossary

The following are brief descriptions of some ingredients, terms
and tools used throughout the recipes in this book.
Before getting started, review these descriptions
to familiarize yourself with them.

Ingredients

Bulgur:
Wheat kernels that have been steamed, dried and crushed until tender and chewy. Often used in Middle Eastern cooking and as a main ingredient in the popular *tabbouleh* or wheat salad but also adds texture and bulk to grain breads.

Cracked Buckwheat:
Hulled, crushed seeds from an herb plant that commonly grows in cooler climates. Often mistaken for a cereal grain. Its pungent flavour comes from a quality amino acid content that makes it nutritionally superior to most cereal grains.

Cream of Tartar:
White powdered acidic ingredient often added to egg whites for stability and volume when being beaten.

Crystallized Ginger:
Gingerroot that is shaved, cooked in a sugar syrup, then coated with coarse sugar. Pinkish in colour. Can be purchased in minced form in jars for use in cakes and other baking, or in shaved form in jars for use as a garnish.

Sanding (coarse) Sugar:
Coarse-grained granulated sugar used for decorating the tops of pastries and cookies for a shiny, sugary crust. Comes in white and various colours and is available at specialty kitchen stores.

Sweetened Condensed Milk:
Sugar and milk heated until much of the liquid is evaporated to make a thick, sticky, sweet milk. Comes in a can. Used in baked goods and desserts. Not to be mistaken for the common canned evaporated milk.

Terms

Dragée: pronounced dra-ZHAY
Tiny round, hard candies used for decorating that are usually silver or gold.

Ganache: pronounced gah-NAHSH
A glaze made of chocolate and whipping cream used to coat cakes or desserts in a smooth, almost shiny, thin layer.

Parchment Paper (also known as silicone paper):
A moisture-resistant, non-stick paper used for lining baking pans and making disposable piping bags. Also reusable—clean by wiping with damp cloth. Discard when it becomes dark or heavily soiled. Available in large rolls/sheets that can be cut to fit any pan size.

Tools & Pans

Brioche Mold:
Special pan for making large brioche. Available in some specialty kitchen stores.

Bundt Pan:
A tube pan with fluted sides used for baking cakes.

Springform Pan:
A round metal pan with a high, straight expandable side, equipped with a spring-loaded hinge. The bottom is easily removed from the side by releasing the hinge, making it simple to remove cakes, tortes and cheesecakes. Available in at least 3 different sizes: 8 inch (20 cm); 9 inch (22 cm); 10 inch (25 cm).

Tart Pan:
A metal baking pan with a removable bottom and low, fluted sides.

Breads

Remember the smell of freshly baked bread,
wafting through the house, luring you into the kitchen?
Savour the taste and re-live the memories
with these homemade savoury and sweet creations.

Mixed Grain Loaf

Braiding makes this an attractive presentation.

Cracked buckwheat (see Glossary, page 9)	1/3 cup	75 mL
Bulgur (see Glossary, page 9)	1/3 cup	75 mL
Boiling water	2 cups	500 mL
Milk	3/4 cup	175 mL
Water	1/4 cup	60 mL
Granulated sugar	2 tsp.	10 mL
Envelope of active dry yeast (or 2 1/4 tsp., 11 mL)	1/4 oz.	8 g
All-purpose flour	2 3/4 cups	675 mL
Whole wheat flour	1/2 cup	125 mL
Shelled sunflower seeds, toasted (see Tip, page 80)	1/3 cup	75 mL
Salt	2 tsp.	10 mL
Olive (or cooking) oil	1 tbsp.	15 mL
Large egg, fork-beaten	1	1
All-purpose flour, approximately	1/4 cup	60 mL
Milk	1 tbsp.	15 mL
Poppy seeds	1 tbsp.	15 mL
Sesame seeds	1 tbsp.	15 mL

Combine buckwheat and bulgur in medium bowl. Cover with boiling water. Let stand for 30 minutes. Drain well.

Measure first amount of milk, water and sugar into small saucepan. Heat and stir on medium until warm and sugar is dissolved. Pour into small bowl. Let stand for 5 minutes.

Sprinkle yeast over top. Let stand for 10 minutes. Stir until yeast is dissolved.

Combine next 4 ingredients in extra-large bowl. Make a well in centre.

Add olive oil, egg, buckwheat mixture and yeast mixture to well. Mix until soft dough forms.

Turn out dough onto lightly floured surface. Knead for 5 to 10 minutes, adding second amount of flour, 1 tbsp. (15 mL) at a time if necessary to prevent sticking, until smooth and elastic. Place in greased extra-large bowl, turning once to grease top. Cover with greased waxed paper and tea towel. Let stand in oven with light on and door closed for about 1 hour until doubled in bulk. Punch dough down. Turn out onto lightly floured surface. Knead for 1 minute. Divide dough into 3 portions. Divide each portion in half, for a total of 6 pieces. Roll each piece into 12 inch (30 cm) rope.

Lay 3 ropes, side by side, along length of work surface. Pinch ropes together at one end.

Braid ropes. Pinch together at opposite end.

Place in greased 9 x 5 x 3 inch (22 x 12.5 x 7.5 cm) loaf pan, tucking ends under.

Cover with greased waxed paper and tea towel. Repeat with remaining ropes, placing in second greased loaf pan. Cover with greased waxed paper and tea towel. Let both loaves stand in oven with light on and door closed for about 30 minutes until almost doubled in size.

Brush loaves with second amount of milk. Divide and sprinkle poppy seeds and sesame seeds over top of each. Bake in 375°F (190°C) oven for about 30 minutes until golden brown and hollow sounding when tapped. Let stand in pans for 5 minutes before removing to wire racks to cool. Makes 2 loaves. Each loaf cuts into 16 slices, for a total of 32 slices.

1 slice: 86 Calories; 2 g Total Fat (0.7 g Mono, 0.9 g Poly, 0.3 g Sat); 7 mg Cholesterol; 14 g Carbohydrate; 1 g Fibre; 3 g Protein; 154 mg Sodium

Pictured on front cover.

Olive Bread

For those who love olives. A great partner to your favourite pasta.

Milk	1 1/4 cups	300 mL
Granulated sugar	2 tsp.	10 mL
Envelope of active dry yeast (or 2 1/4 tsp., 11 mL)	1/4 oz.	8 g
All-purpose flour	3 cups	750 mL
Salt	1 tsp.	5 mL
Olive (or cooking) oil	1/4 cup	60 mL
All-purpose flour, approximately	1/2 cup	125 mL
Chopped black Italian olives	1 cup	250 mL
Chopped fresh basil (or 2 1/4 tsp., 11 mL, dried)	3 tbsp.	50 mL
All-purpose flour	1 tbsp.	15 mL

Combine milk and sugar in small heavy saucepan. Heat and stir on medium until warm and sugar is dissolved. Pour into small bowl. Let stand for 5 minutes.

Sprinkle yeast over top. Let stand for 10 minutes. Stir until yeast is dissolved.

Measure first amount of flour and salt into large bowl. Stir. Make a well in centre. Add olive oil and yeast mixture to well. Mix until stiff dough forms.

Turn out dough onto lightly floured surface. Knead for 5 to 10 minutes, adding second amount of flour, 1 tbsp. (15 mL) at a time if necessary to prevent sticking, until smooth and elastic. Place in greased large bowl, turning once to grease top. Cover with greased waxed paper and tea towel. Let stand in oven with light on and door closed for about 1 hour until doubled in bulk. Punch dough down. Turn out onto lightly floured surface. Knead for 1 minute.

Roll out dough to 9 x 11 inch (22 x 28 cm) rectangle. Sprinkle olives and basil evenly over top, leaving 3/4 inch (2 cm) edge on each side. Roll up, jelly roll-style, from long side. Place loaf, seam-side down, on greased baking sheet, tucking ends under.

Sprinkle with third amount of flour. Cut 6 slashes across top of loaf, about 1/2 inch (12 mm) deep, using knife. Let stand, uncovered, in oven with light on and door closed for about 1 hour until doubled in size. Bake in 375°F (190°C) oven for about 35 minutes until bread is golden brown and hollow sounding when tapped. Let stand on baking sheet for 5 minutes before removing to wire rack to cool. Cuts into 30 slices.

1 slice: 76 Calories; 2.5 g Total Fat (1.7 g Mono, 0.3 g Poly, 0.4 g Sat);
   0 mg Cholesterol; 11 g Carbohydrate; 1 g Fibre; 2 g Protein; 110 mg Sodium

Pictured on pages 12/13.

Left: Olive Bread, above
Top Right: Cheesy Hot Pepper
Pull-Aparts, page 14

Cheesy Hot Pepper Pull-Aparts

Delightfully airy rolls that will spice up any meal.

Water	2/3 cup	150 mL
Milk	2/3 cup	150 mL
Butter (or hard margarine)	3 tbsp.	50 mL
Granulated sugar	3 tbsp.	50 mL
Salt	1 tsp.	5 mL
All-purpose flour	1 1/2 cups	375 mL
Envelope of instant yeast (or 2 1/4 tsp.,11 mL)	1/4 oz.	8 g
Large egg, fork-beaten	1	1
All-purpose flour	2 cups	500 mL
Grated sharp Cheddar cheese	1 1/2 cups	375 mL
Pickled pepper rings, drained and finely diced	1/4 cup	60 mL
Dried chives	1 tbsp.	15 mL
Garlic powder (optional)	1/2 tsp.	2 mL
Pepper	3/4 tsp.	4 mL
All-purpose flour, approximately	1/4 cup	60 mL
Butter (or hard margarine), melted (optional)	2 tsp.	10 mL

Combine first 5 ingredients in small saucepan. Heat and stir on medium until warm and sugar is dissolved and butter is almost melted. Pour into large bowl. Stir until butter is melted. Let stand for 5 minutes.

Measure first amount of flour and yeast into small bowl. Stir. Add to warm milk mixture. Stir until smooth. Add egg. Stir.

Combine next 6 ingredients in medium bowl. Stir. Add to yeast mixture. Stir until soft, slightly sticky dough forms.

Turn out dough onto lightly floured surface. Knead for 5 to 10 minutes, adding third amount of flour, 1 tbsp. (15 mL) at a time if necessary to prevent sticking, until smooth and elastic. Divide dough in half. Divide each half into 8 portions, for a total of 16 portions. Roll each into ball. Place 8 balls in each of 2 greased 9 inch (22 cm) round pans. Cover with greased waxed paper and tea towel. Let stand in oven with light on and door closed for about 1 hour until doubled in size. Bake in 375°F (190°C) oven for about 20 minutes until golden brown. Let stand in pans for 5 minutes before removing to wire racks to cool.

Brush top of rolls with melted butter. Makes 16 pull-aparts.

1 pull-apart: 231 Calories; 7.6 g Total Fat (2.2 g Mono, 0.4 g Poly, 4.5 g Sat); 36 mg Cholesterol; 32 g Carbohydrate; 1 g Fibre; 8 g Protein; 286 mg Sodium

Pictured on page 13.

Mushroom Garlic Pizza Bread

A spicy, savoury pizza. Great to serve as an appetizer too.

BREAD BASE		
Warm water	3/4 cup	175 mL
Granulated sugar	2 tsp.	10 mL
Envelope of active dry yeast (or 2 1/4 tsp., 11 mL)	1/4 oz.	8 g
All-purpose flour	2 cups	500 mL
Salt	1 1/2 tsp.	7 mL
Olive (or cooking) oil	2 tbsp.	30 mL
All-purpose flour, approximately	1/2 cup	125 mL
ROASTED TOMATO SAUCE		
Roma (plum) tomatoes, halved lengthwise	6	6
Granulated sugar	2 tsp.	10 mL
Dried crushed chilies	1/2 tsp.	2 mL
Salt	1/2 tsp.	2 mL
Pepper	1/4 tsp.	1 mL
Olive (or cooking) oil	1 tbsp.	15 mL
Finely chopped onion	1/2 cup	125 mL
Garlic cloves, minced (or 1/2 tsp., 2 mL, powder)	2	2
TOPPING		
Butter (or hard margarine)	1 1/2 tbsp.	25 mL
Olive (or cooking) oil	2 tsp.	10 mL
Sliced mixed mushrooms (such as white, brown, shiitake, oyster)	3 cups	750 mL
Garlic cloves, minced (or 1/2 tsp., 2 mL, powder)	2	2
Crumbled feta cheese (about 2 1/2 oz., 70 g)	1/2 cup	125 mL
Finely grated fresh Parmesan cheese	1/2 cup	125 mL
Torn fresh basil	2 tbsp.	30 mL

Bread Base: Stir warm water and sugar in small bowl until sugar is dissolved. Sprinkle yeast over top. Let stand for 10 minutes. Stir until yeast is dissolved.

Combine first amount of flour and salt in large bowl. Make a well in centre. Add olive oil and yeast mixture to well. Mix until dough pulls away from side of bowl and is no longer sticky.

Turn out dough onto lightly floured surface. Knead for 5 to 10 minutes, adding second amount of flour, 1 tbsp. (15 mL) at a time if necessary to prevent sticking, until smooth and elastic. Place in greased large bowl, turning once to grease top. Cover with greased waxed paper and tea towel. Let stand in oven with light on and door closed for about 1 hour until dough is doubled in bulk. Punch dough down. Turn out onto lightly floured surface. Knead for 1 minute. Roll out and press dough into greased 12 inch (30 cm) pizza pan, forming rim around edge.

Roasted Tomato Sauce: Place tomatoes, cut-side up, on wire rack in baking sheet with sides.

Combine next 4 ingredients in small cup. Divide and sprinkle over top of each tomato half. Bake in 375°F (190°C) oven for about 45 minutes until browned and wilted. Cool slightly.

Heat olive oil in small frying pan on medium. Add onion and garlic. Cook for 5 to 10 minutes, stirring often, until onion is softened. Cool slightly. Transfer to blender or food processor. Add tomatoes. Process until smooth. Makes 1 3/4 cups (425 mL) sauce.

Topping: Heat butter and olive oil in large frying pan on medium-high. Add mushrooms. Cook for 5 to 10 minutes, stirring occasionally, until mushrooms are browned and liquid is evaporated.

Add garlic. Heat and stir until fragrant. Remove from heat.

Combine feta cheese, Parmesan cheese and basil in small bowl. Spread sauce evenly over dough, leaving 1/2 inch (12 mm) edge. Spoon topping evenly over sauce. Sprinkle with cheese mixture. Bake on lowest rack in 475°F (240°C) oven for about 15 minutes until bottom of crust is golden brown. Cuts into 8 wedges.

1 wedge: 326 Calories; 13.6 g Total Fat (6.4 g Mono, 1.1 g Poly, 5.1 g Sat);
    20 mg Cholesterol; 42 g Carbohydrate; 3 g Fibre; 11 g Protein;
    866 mg Sodium

Pictured above.

Pita Bread

*Soft and chewy. Cut into wedges and serve
with hummus or your favourite dip.*

Milk	1 1/3 cups	325 mL
Granulated sugar	1 tsp.	5 mL
Envelope of active dry yeast (or 2 1/4 tsp., 11 mL)	1/4 oz.	8 g
All-purpose flour	4 cups	1 L
Salt	2 tsp.	10 mL
Plain yogurt, room temperature	1/2 cup	125 mL
Warm water	1/3 cup	75 mL
Large egg, room temperature	1	1
Olive (or cooking) oil	1 tbsp.	15 mL
All-purpose flour, approximately	1 cup	250 mL

Combine milk and sugar in small heavy saucepan. Heat and stir on medium until warm and sugar is dissolved. Pour into small bowl. Let stand for 5 minutes.

Sprinkle yeast over top. Let stand for 10 minutes. Stir until yeast is dissolved.

Measure first amount of flour and salt into extra-large bowl. Stir. Make a well in centre.

Combine next 4 ingredients in separate small bowl. Add to well. Add yeast mixture. Mix until soft, sticky dough forms.

Work in second amount of flour as needed until dough pulls away from side of bowl and is no longer sticky. Turn out onto lightly floured surface. Knead for 5 to 10 minutes, adding more flour if necessary to prevent sticking, until smooth and elastic. Place in greased extra-large bowl, turning once to grease top. Cover with greased waxed paper and tea towel. Let stand in oven with light on and door closed for about 1 hour until doubled in bulk. Punch dough down. Turn out onto lightly floured surface. Knead for 1 minute. Divide dough into 12 portions. Roll each portion into ball. Arrange balls, evenly spaced apart, on lightly floured baking sheet. Cover with greased waxed paper and tea towel. Let stand in oven with light on and door closed for 20 minutes. Remove from oven. Heat separate ungreased baking sheet on second rack from top in 475°F (240°C) oven until hot. Roll out 2 balls into thin 6 inch (15 cm) rounds. Keep remaining balls covered to prevent drying. Place rounds on hot baking sheet. Bake for about 5 minutes until bread is puffed and lightly browned. Remove to wire rack to cool slightly. Wrap warm bread in tea towel to keep soft. Repeat 5 more times with remaining balls. Makes 12 pita breads.

1 pita bread: 238 Calories; 2.7 g Total Fat (1.3 g Mono, 0.4 g Poly, 0.7 g Sat); 20 mg Cholesterol; 44 g Carbohydrate; 2 g Fibre; 8 g Protein; 419 mg Sodium

Pictured on page 19.

Savoury Cheese Rolls

*Tender, attractive rolls are perfect for a
quick lunch—just add your favourite filling.*

Warm water	1 1/2 cups	375 mL
Granulated sugar	1 tsp.	5 mL
Envelopes of active dry yeast (1/4 oz., 8 g, each) or 4 1/2 tsp. (22 mL)	2	2
All-purpose flour	5 cups	1.25 L
Granulated sugar	2 tbsp.	30 mL
Salt	2 tsp.	10 mL
Milk	2/3 cup	150 mL
Butter (or hard margarine), melted	3 tbsp.	50 mL
Large egg, fork-beaten	1	1
All-purpose flour, approximately	1/2 cup	125 mL
Milk	1 tbsp.	15 mL
Grated sharp Cheddar cheese	1 1/3 cups	325 mL
Finely chopped bacon slices, cooked almost crisp	8	8

Stir warm water and sugar in small bowl until sugar is dissolved. Sprinkle yeast over top. Let stand for 10 minutes. Stir until yeast is dissolved.

Combine next 3 ingredients in extra-large bowl. Make a well in centre.

Add next 3 ingredients and yeast mixture to well. Mix until dough pulls away from side of bowl and is no longer sticky.

Turn out dough onto lightly floured surface. Knead for 5 to 10 minutes, adding second amount of flour, 1 tbsp. (15 mL) at a time if necessary to prevent sticking, until smooth and elastic. Place in greased extra-large bowl, turning once to grease top. Cover with greased waxed paper and tea towel. Let stand in oven with light on and door closed for about 30 minutes until doubled in bulk. Punch dough down. Turn out onto lightly floured surface. Knead for 1 minute. Divide dough into 4 portions. Divide each portion into 4 pieces, for a total of 16 pieces. Roll each into 2 x 4 inch (5 x 10 cm) oval roll. Arrange rolls, evenly spaced apart, on 2 greased baking sheets. Cover with greased waxed paper and tea towel. Let stand in oven with light on and door closed for 15 to 20 minutes until almost doubled in size.

rush rolls with second amount of milk. Divide and sprinkle heese and bacon over top of each. Bake on separate racks in 75° F (190°C) oven for 25 to 30 minutes, switching position of ans halfway through baking time, until golden brown and ollow sounding when tapped. Let stand on baking sheets for minutes before removing to wire racks to cool. Makes 16 rolls.

roll: 263 Calories; 8 g Total Fat (2.5 g Mono, 0.6 g Poly, 4.3 g Sat);
    33 mg Cholesterol; 38 g Carbohydrate; 2 g Fibre; 9 g Protein; 442 mg Sodium

ctured on page 19.

Potato Bread

*Nicely textured, moist bread with
a wonderful buttery flavour.*

Medium potato, peeled and cut into 1 inch (2.5 cm) cubes	1	1
Water		
Salt	1/2 tsp.	2 mL
Milk	2 cups	500 mL
Butter (or hard margarine)	1/4 cup	60 mL
Granulated sugar	1/4 cup	60 mL
Envelope of active dry yeast (or 2 1/4 tsp., 11 mL)	1/4 oz.	8 g
All-purpose flour	3 1/2 cups	875 mL
Salt	2 tsp.	10 mL
All-purpose flour, approximately	1 1/2 cups	375 mL

Cook potato in water and salt in small saucepan for about 5 minutes until very tender. Drain. Mash well or press through potato ricer or food mill into medium bowl. Cover to keep warm.

Combine next 3 ingredients in separate small heavy saucepan. Heat and stir on medium until sugar is dissolved and butter is almost melted. Pour into extra-large bowl. Stir until butter is melted. Let stand for 5 minutes.

Sprinkle yeast over top. Let stand for 10 minutes. Stir until yeast is dissolved.

Add first amount of flour, salt and potato. Mix until soft dough forms.

Work in enough of second amount of flour until dough pulls away from side of bowl and is no longer sticky. Turn out onto lightly floured surface. Knead for 5 to 10 minutes, adding flour if necessary to prevent sticking, until smooth and elastic. Place in greased large bowl, turning once to grease top. Cover with greased waxed paper and tea towel. Let stand in oven with light on and door closed for about 1 hour until doubled in bulk. Punch dough down. Turn out onto lightly floured surface. Knead for 1 minute. Divide into 2 equal portions.

Flatten 1 portion of dough into rectangle. Roll up tightly, tucking in ends and stretching if necessary to fit pan. Place, seam-side down, in greased 9 × 5 × 3 inch (22 × 12.5 × 7.5 cm) loaf pan.

Cover with greased waxed paper and tea towel. Repeat with remaining dough. Let both loaves stand in oven with light on and door closed for about 1 hour until dough rises to top of pans. Bake in 400°F (205°C) oven for 10 minutes. Reduce temperature to 375°F (190°C). Bake for about 20 minutes until golden brown and hollow sounding when tapped. Let stand in pans for 5 minutes before removing to wire racks to cool. Makes 2 loaves. Each loaf cuts into 16 slices, for a total of 32 slices.

1 slice: 98 Calories; 1.9 g Total Fat (0.5 g Mono, 0.2 g Poly, 1.1 g Sat);
    5 mg Cholesterol; 18 g Carbohydrate; trace Fibre; 3 g Protein; 173 mg Sodium

Pictured on page 18.

Photo Legend next page:
Top Left: Potato Bread, this page
Top Right: Savoury Cheese Rolls, page 16
Bottom Left: Artichoke Pepper Focaccia,
    page 20
Bottom Right: Pita Bread, page 16

Artichoke Pepper Focaccia

Something a little out of the ordinary.
Serve this savoury bread any time.

Warm water	3/4 cup	175 mL
Granulated sugar	1 tsp.	5 mL
Envelope of active dry yeast (or 2 1/4 tsp., 11 mL)	1/4 oz.	8 g
All-purpose flour	2 cups	500 mL
Salt	1 1/2 tsp.	7 mL
Olive (or cooking) oil	3 tbsp.	50 mL
All-purpose flour, approximately	1/2 cup	125 mL
TOPPING		
Basil pesto	2 tbsp.	30 mL
Thinly sliced red pepper	1/2 cup	125 mL
Marinated artichoke hearts, drained and chopped (about 1/2 of 6 oz., 170 mL, jar)	1/3 cup	75 mL
Finely grated fresh Parmesan cheese	1/3 cup	75 mL

Stir warm water and sugar in small bowl until sugar is dissolved. Sprinkle yeast over top. Let stand for 10 minutes. Stir until yeast is dissolved.

Combine first amount of flour and salt in large bowl. Make a well in centre. Add olive oil and yeast mixture to well. Mix until soft, slightly sticky dough forms.

Turn out dough onto lightly floured surface. Knead for 5 to 10 minutes, adding second amount of flour, 1 tbsp. (15 mL) at a time if necessary to prevent sticking, until smooth and elastic. Place in greased large bowl, turning once to grease top. Cover with greased waxed paper and tea towel. Let stand in oven with light on and door closed for about 1 hour until doubled in bulk. Punch dough down. Turn out onto lightly floured surface. Knead for 1 minute. Roll out to 10 inch (25 cm) round. Place on greased baking sheet. Let stand, uncovered, in oven with light on and door closed for 20 minutes.

Topping: Spread pesto evenly over dough, leaving 1/2 inch (12 mm) edge. Scatter red pepper and artichoke over top. Sprinkle with Parmesan cheese. Bake in 350°F (175°C) oven for about 30 minutes until cheese is golden and crust is lightly browned. Let stand on baking sheet for 5 minutes before removing to wire rack to cool. Cuts into 12 wedges.

1 wedge: 155 Calories; 5 g Total Fat (3.1 g Mono, 0.6 g Poly, 1.1 g Sat); 2 mg Cholesterol; 23 g Carbohydrate; 1 g Fibre; 5 g Protein; 368 mg Sodium

Pictured on page 18.

Cheese And Walnut Rolls

Plan to make this recipe ahead, as it takes a little more time than most. These pungent, crusty rolls are definitely worth the wait.

Water	1 cup	250 mL
Milk	1 cup	250 mL
Granulated sugar	1 tsp.	5 mL
Active dry yeast	1 1/4 tsp.	6 mL
All-purpose flour	2 cups	500 mL
Active dry yeast	1 tsp.	5 mL
Warm water	1 cup	250 mL
Salt	1 tbsp.	15 mL
All-purpose flour, approximately	5 cups	1.25 L
Chopped walnuts, toasted (see Tip, page 80)	1 1/2 cups	375 mL
Grated Gruyère (or Swiss) cheese	1 1/2 cups	375 mL
Crumbled blue cheese (about 2 oz., 57 g)	1/2 cup	125 mL
Yellow cornmeal	2 tbsp.	30 mL

All-purpose flour, for dusting

Combine first amount of water, milk and sugar in small saucepan. Heat and stir on medium until warm and sugar is dissolved. Pour into large bowl. Let stand for 5 minutes.

Sprinkle first amount of yeast over top. Let stand for 10 minutes. Stir until yeast is dissolved.

Add first amount of flour. Stir until smooth. Cover bowl with greased waxed paper and tea towel. Let stand in oven with light on and door closed for at least 8 hours or overnight. Mixture will be bubbly.

Sprinkle second amount of yeast over batter. Add warm water. Stir until smooth. Add salt. Stir.

Work in enough of second amount of flour, 1/2 cup (125 mL) at a time, until dough pulls away from side of bowl and is no longer sticky. Turn out onto lightly floured surface. Knead for 5 to 10 minutes, adding flour if necessary to prevent sticking, until smooth and elastic. Cover dough with inverted bowl. Let stand for 10 minutes. Knead for 5 minutes. Do not add extra flour. Place in greased extra-large bowl, turning once to grease top. Cover with greased waxed paper and tea towel. Let stand in oven with light on and door closed for about 1 hour until doubled in bulk. Punch dough down. Turn dough in bowl. Cover with greased waxed paper and tea towel. Let stand in oven with light on and door closed for about 1 hour until doubled in bulk. Punch dough down.

Turn out dough onto lightly floured surface. Knead for 1 minute. Roll out to 12 x 15 inch (30 x 38 cm) rectangle. Sprinkle walnuts, Gruyère cheese and blue cheese over top. Press down lightly. Fold dough in half to enclose filling. Knead for about 3 minutes until evenly combined. Divide dough in half. Divide each half into 10 portions, for a total of 20 portions. Roll each into ball.

Divide and sprinkle cornmeal on 2 greased baking sheets. Arrange rolls, 1 to 1 1/2 inches (2.5 to 3.8 cm) apart, on baking sheets. Cover with greased waxed paper and tea towel. Let stand in oven with light on and door closed for 30 minutes.

Dust each roll with flour. Bake on separate racks in 400°F (205°C) oven for 30 minutes, switching position of pans halfway through baking time, until golden brown and hollow sounding when tapped. Let stand on baking sheets for 5 minutes before removing to wire racks to cool. Makes 20 rolls.

1 roll: 287 Calories; 10 g Total Fat (2.5 g Mono, 4.1 g Poly, 2.8 g Sat); 13 mg Cholesterol; 38 g Carbohydrate; 2 g Fibre; 11 g Protein; 440 mg Sodium

Pictured above.

Roasted Pepper And Onion Bread

Be sure to let your guests see the beautiful red pepper top before serving!

PEPPER AND ONION TOPPING

Red medium peppers, seeds and ribs removed, quartered (see Note)	2	2
Olive (or cooking) oil	1 tbsp.	15 mL
Thinly sliced red onion	1 cup	250 mL
Garlic cloves, minced (or 1/2 tsp., 2 mL, powder)	2	2
Chopped fresh basil (or 1 1/2 tsp., 7 mL, dried)	2 tbsp.	30 mL
Finely grated fresh Parmesan cheese	2 tbsp.	30 mL
Salt	1/4 tsp.	1 mL
Pepper, sprinkle		

BREAD

All-purpose flour	2 2/3 cups	650 mL
Granulated sugar	1 1/2 tbsp.	25 mL
Envelope of instant yeast (or 2 1/4 tsp., 11 mL)	1/4 oz.	8 g
Salt	2 tsp.	10 mL
Milk	1 cup	250 mL
Olive (or cooking) oil	2 tbsp.	30 mL
All-purpose flour, approximately	1/3 cup	75 mL
Yellow cornmeal	1 tbsp.	15 mL
Large egg, fork-beaten	1	1

Pepper And Onion Topping: Arrange pepper pieces, skin-side up, on ungreased baking sheet. Broil 5 inches (12.5 cm) from heat for about 10 minutes, rearranging as necessary, until skins are blistered and blackened. Remove to small bowl. Cover with plastic wrap. Let sweat for about 15 minutes until cool enough to handle. Peel and discard skins. Chop finely. Set aside.

Heat olive oil in medium frying pan on medium. Add onion. Cook for 5 to 10 minutes, stirring often, until onion is softened.

Add garlic. Heat and stir for about 1 minute until fragrant.

Add next 4 ingredients and roasted pepper. Stir. Remove from heat. Cool. Makes 1 1/2 cups (375 mL) topping.

Bread: Combine first 4 ingredients in large bowl. Make a well in centre.

Heat and stir milk in small heavy saucepan on medium until very warm. Add warm milk, olive oil and 1/2 cup (125 mL) topping to well. Mix until soft dough forms.

Turn out dough onto lightly floured surface. Knead for 5 to 10 minutes, adding second amount of flour, 1 tbsp. (15 mL) at a time if necessary to prevent sticking, until smooth and elastic. Place in greased large bowl, turning once to grease top. Cover with greased waxed paper and tea towel. Let stand in oven with light on and door closed for about 1 hour until almost doubled in bulk. Punch dough down.

Turn out onto lightly floured surface. Knead for 1 minute. Roll out to 10 inch (25 cm) round. Sprinkle cornmeal on ungreased baking sheet. Place dough on cornmeal.

Cut '+' on top of loaf, about 8 inches (20 cm) long and 1/2 inch (12 mm) deep.

Spread slashes apart to make space for topping. Spoon remaining topping into slashes.

Let stand, uncovered, in oven with light on and door closed for about 45 minutes until almost doubled in size.

Brush dough with egg. Bake in 350°F (175°C) oven for about 35 minutes, covering loaf with foil if necessary to prevent over-browning, until golden brown and hollow sounding when tapped. Let stand on baking sheet for 5 minutes before removing to wire rack to cool. Cuts into 16 slices.

1 slice: 146 Calories; 3.6 g Total Fat (2.2 g Mono, 0.4 g Poly, 0.8 g Sat); 15 mg Cholesterol; 24 g Carbohydrate; 1 g Fibre; 4 g Protein; 362 mg Sodium

Pictured on page 23.

Note: To speed preparation time, purchase a jar of roasted red peppers. Use 1 1/3 cups (325 mL), drained, blotted dry and finely chopped; and omit first paragraph in method.

Herb And Garlic Focaccia

Great for dipping into olive oil and balsamic vinegar.
Serve as an appetizer, or with soup or salad.

Milk	1 1/3 cups	325 mL
Granulated sugar	1 tsp.	5 mL
Envelope of active dry yeast (or 2 1/4 tsp., 11 mL)	1/4 oz.	8 g
All-purpose flour	1 1/4 cups	300 mL
Salt	2 tsp.	10 mL
Olive (or cooking) oil	2 tbsp.	30 mL
All-purpose flour, approximately	2 cups	500 mL
HERB AND GARLIC TOPPING		
Olive (not cooking) oil	1/4 cup	60 mL
Garlic cloves, thinly sliced	2	2
Chopped fresh basil (not dried)	1/4 cup	60 mL
Chopped fresh rosemary leaves (not dried)	1 tsp.	5 mL
Yellow cornmeal	1 tbsp.	15 mL
Coarse sea salt	1/2 tsp.	2 mL

Combine milk and sugar in small heavy saucepan. Heat and stir on medium until warm and sugar is dissolved. Pour into small bowl. Let stand for 5 minutes.

Sprinkle yeast over top. Let stand for 10 minutes. Stir until yeast is dissolved.

Combine first amount of flour and salt in extra-large bowl. Make a well in centre. Add olive oil and yeast mixture to well. Mix until smooth batter forms.

Work in enough of second amount of flour until dough pulls away from side of bowl and is slightly sticky. Turn out onto lightly floured surface. Knead for 3 to 5 minutes, adding flour if necessary to prevent sticking, until smooth. Place in greased extra-large bowl, turning once to grease top. Cover with greased waxed paper and tea towel. Let stand in oven with light on and door closed for about 2 hours until tripled in bulk.

Herb And Garlic Topping: Heat olive oil in small saucepan on low. Add garlic. Heat and stir for 2 to 3 minutes until fragrant. Remove from heat.

Add basil and rosemary. Stir. Let stand for 30 minutes to blend flavours.

Sprinkle cornmeal on bottom of greased 10 x 15 inch (25 x 38 cm) jelly roll pan. Punch dough down. Turn out onto lightly floured surface. Knead for 1 minute. Gently roll out or press into 10 x 15 inch (25 x 38 cm) rectangle, 1/4 inch (6 mm) thick. Transfer to prepared pan. Stretch and shape dough to evenly cover bottom of pan. Cover with greased waxed paper and tea towel. Let stand in oven with light on and door closed for about 45 minutes until doubled in size. Poke indentations over surface of dough with fingers or wooden spoon handle, about 1/4 inch (6 mm) deep and 1 1/2 inches (3.8 cm) apart. Drizzle topping evenly over dough. Oil will pool in indentations.

Sprinkle with coarse sea salt. Bake in 425°F (220°C) oven for about 20 minutes until golden brown. Let stand in pan for 5 minutes before removing to wire rack to cool. Cuts into 30 pieces.

1 piece: 85 Calories; 3.1 g Total Fat (2.1 g Mono, 0.3 g Poly, 0.5 g Sat); 1 mg Cholesterol; 12 g Carbohydrate; 1 g Fibre; 2 g Protein; 204 mg Sodium

Pictured on page 25.

Parmesan Garlic Flatbread

Rich-flavoured and tender with a little bit of crunch.

Warm water	1 1/3 cups	325 mL
Granulated sugar	1/2 tsp.	2 mL
Envelope of active dry yeast (or 2 1/4 tsp., 11 mL)	1/4 oz.	8 g
All-purpose flour	1 cup	250 mL
Salt	1 tsp.	5 mL
Olive (or cooking) oil	3 tbsp.	50 mL
All-purpose flour, approximately	2 3/4 cups	675 mL
Finely grated fresh Parmesan cheese	2/3 cup	150 mL
Chopped fresh oregano leaves (or 1/2 tsp., 2 mL, dried)	2 tsp.	10 mL
Garlic cloves, minced (or 3/4 tsp., 4 mL, powder)	3	3
Olive (or cooking) oil	1 tbsp.	15 mL
Finely grated fresh Parmesan cheese	1/3 cup	75 mL
Coarse sea salt	1/4 tsp.	1 mL

Stir warm water and sugar in small bowl until sugar is dissolved. Sprinkle yeast over top. Let stand for 10 minutes. Stir until yeast is dissolved.

Combine first amount of flour and salt in extra-large bowl. Make a well in centre. Add first amount of olive oil and yeast mixture to well. Mix until sticky batter forms.

Work in enough of second amount of flour until dough pulls away from side of bowl and is still slightly sticky. Turn out onto lightly floured surface. Knead for 3 to 5 minutes, adding flour if necessary to prevent sticking, until smooth. Place in greased extra-large bowl, turning once to grease top. Cover with greased waxed paper and tea towel. Let stand in oven with light on and door closed for about 1 1/2 hours until tripled in bulk. Punch dough down.

Turn out dough onto lightly floured surface. Knead for 1 minute. Shape into ball. Flatten slightly. Sprinkle with first amount of Parmesan cheese, oregano and garlic. Press down lightly. Fold dough in half to enclose filling. Knead for about 3 minutes until evenly combined. Roll out or press into greased 12 inch (30 cm) pizza pan. Cover with greased waxed paper and tea towel. Let stand in oven with light on and door closed for about 45 minutes until doubled in size. Poke indentations over surface of dough with fingers or wooden spoon handle, about 1/4 inch (6 mm) deep and 1 1/2 inches (3.8 cm) apart.

Drizzle second amount of olive oil evenly over dough. Oil will pool in indentations. Sprinkle with second amount of Parmesan cheese and coarse sea salt. Bake in 425°F (220°C) oven for about 20 minutes until golden brown. Let stand in pan for 5 minutes before removing to wire rack to cool. Cuts into 12 wedges.

1 wedge: 235 Calories; 7.7 g Total Fat (4.2 g Mono, 0.6 g Poly, 2.4 g Sat);
    7 mg Cholesterol; 33 g Carbohydrate; 1 g Fibre; 8 g Protein; 412 mg Sodium

Pictured below.

Left: Parmesan Garlic Flatbread, page 24

Right: Herb And Garlic Focaccia, page 24

Cornmeal Garlic Rolls

*Subtle garlic flavour makes these rolls perfect
with deli meats for lunch.*

Milk	1 cup	250 mL
Granulated sugar	1 tsp.	5 mL
Envelope of active dry yeast (or 2 1/4 tsp., 11 mL)	1/4 oz.	8 g
All-purpose flour	3 3/4 cups	925 mL
Yellow cornmeal	1/3 cup	75 mL
Salt	2 tsp.	10 mL
Milk	3/4 cup	75 mL
Butter (or hard margarine), melted	3 tbsp.	50 mL
Olive (or cooking) oil	2 tbsp.	30 mL
Garlic cloves, minced (or 3/4 tsp., 4 mL, powder)	3	3
All-purpose flour, approximately	1/4 cup	60 mL
Yellow cornmeal	2 tbsp.	30 mL

Combine milk and sugar in small heavy saucepan. Heat and stir on medium until warm and sugar is dissolved. Pour into small bowl. Let stand for 5 minutes. Sprinkle yeast over top. Let stand for 10 minutes. Stir until yeast is dissolved.

Combine first amount of flour, cornmeal and salt in extra-large bowl. Make a well in centre.

Add next 4 ingredients and yeast mixture to well. Mix until dough pulls away from side of bowl and is no longer sticky.

Turn out dough onto lightly floured surface. Knead for 5 to 10 minutes, adding second amount of flour, 1 tbsp. (15 mL) at a time if necessary to prevent sticking, until smooth and elastic. Place in greased extra-large bowl, turning once to grease top. Cover with greased waxed paper and tea towel. Let stand in oven with light on and door closed for about 1 hour until doubled in bulk. Punch dough down. Turn out onto lightly floured surface. Knead for 1 minute. Roll into 12 inch (30 cm) rope. Cut into 12 portions. Roll each portion into 5 inch (12.5 cm) length, narrower on ends and thicker in centre.

Sprinkle 1/2 tbsp. (7 mL) cornmeal onto each of 2 baking sheets. Arrange 6 rolls, evenly spaced, on each baking sheet. Divide and sprinkle remaining cornmeal over rolls. Cut 3 diagonal slashes across each roll, about 1/2 inch (12 mm) deep. Let stand, uncovered, in oven with light on and door closed for about 25 minutes until almost doubled in size. Bake on separate racks in 375°F (190°C) oven for about 30 minutes, switching position of pans halfway through baking time, until golden brown and hollow sounding when tapped. Let stand on baking sheets for 5 minutes before removing to wire racks to cool. Makes 12 rolls.

1 roll: 243 Calories; 6.1 g Total Fat (2.7 g Mono, 0.5 g Poly, 2.4 g Sat);
    9 mg Cholesterol; 40 g Carbohydrate; 2 g Fibre; 6 g Protein; 441 mg Sodium

Pictured on page 27.

Pagnotta

*Italian pagnotta (pan-YAH-tah) is baked starting
in a cold oven. Crisp outside, moist inside.*

Warm water	1/2 cup	125 mL
Granulated sugar	1/2 tsp.	2 mL
Envelope of active dry yeast (or 2 1/4 tsp., 11 mL)	1/4 oz.	8 g
All-purpose flour	3 cups	750 mL
Salt	1 tsp.	5 mL
Water	3/4 cup	175 mL
Olive (or cooking) oil	2 tbsp.	30 mL
All-purpose flour, approximately	1/4 cup	60 mL
All-purpose flour, for dusting	1 1/2 tbsp.	25 mL

Stir warm water and sugar in small bowl until sugar is dissolved. Sprinkle yeast over top. Let stand for 10 minutes. Stir until yeast is dissolved.

Combine first amount of flour and salt in large bowl. Make a well in centre. Add water, olive oil and yeast mixture to well. Mix until dough pulls away from side of bowl and is slightly sticky. Place in greased large bowl, turning once to grease top. Cover with greased waxed paper and tea towel. Let stand in oven with light on and door closed for about 40 minutes until almost doubled in bulk. Punch dough down.

Turn out dough onto lightly floured surface. Knead for 5 to 10 minutes, adding as little of second amount of flour as possible, until smooth and elastic. Shape into 6 inch (15 cm) round, about 2 inches (5 cm) thick. Place on greased baking sheet.

Dust top with third amount of flour.

Cut circular slash around dough, about 1 inch (2.5 cm) deep and 1 1/2 inches (3.8 cm) from edge.

Place in cold oven. Turn oven to 375°F (190°C). Bake for 45 to 50 minutes, from time oven is turned on, until golden brown and hollow sounding when tapped. Let stand on baking sheet for 5 minutes before removing to wire rack to cool. Cuts into 10 slices.

1 slice: 176 Calories; 3.2 g Total Fat (2.1 g Mono, 0.4 g Poly, 0.4 g Sat);
    0 mg Cholesterol; 32 g Carbohydrate; 1 g Fibre; 5 g Protein; 239 mg Sodium

Pictured on page 27.

Top: Cornmeal Garlic Rolls, this page
Bottom: Pagnotta, above

Grissini

*These thick, tender Italian bread sticks
are great with a salad.*

Warm water	1 1/3 cups	325 mL
Granulated sugar	1 tsp.	5 mL
Envelope of active dry yeast (or 2 1/4 tsp., 11 mL)	1/4 oz.	8 g
All-purpose flour	3 cups	750 mL
Salt	1 1/2 tsp.	7 mL
Olive (or cooking) oil	1/3 cup	75 mL
All-purpose flour, approximately	2 tbsp.	30 mL
Chopped fresh basil (optional)	1/2 cup	125 mL
Garlic cloves, minced	4	4
Water		
Coarse sea salt	1 tsp.	5 mL
Finely grated fresh Parmesan cheese	3 tbsp.	50 mL

Stir warm water and sugar in small bowl until sugar is dissolved. Sprinkle yeast over top. Let stand for 10 minutes. Stir until yeast is dissolved.

Combine first amount of flour and salt in extra-large bowl. Make a well in centre. Add olive oil and yeast mixture to well. Mix until soft dough forms.

Turn out dough onto lightly floured surface. Knead for 5 to 10 minutes, adding second amount of flour, 1 tbsp. (15 mL) at a time if necessary to prevent sticking, until smooth and elastic.

Roll out dough to 10 inch (25 cm) round. Sprinkle with basil and garlic. Fold dough in half to enclose filling. Knead for about 3 minutes until evenly combined. Place in greased extra-large bowl, turning once to grease top. Cover with greased waxed paper and tea towel. Let stand in oven with light on and door closed for about 1 hour until doubled in bulk. Punch dough down. Turn out onto lightly floured surface. Knead for 1 minute. Divide dough into 2 equal portions. Roll 1 portion into 12 inch (30 cm) rope. Cut into 12 pieces. Roll each piece into 6 inch (15 cm) stick. Repeat with second portion of dough. Place sticks, 3/4 inch (2 cm) apart, on 2 greased baking sheets.

Brush sticks with second amount of water. Sprinkle coarse sea salt and Parmesan cheese over each. Bake on separate racks in 450°F (230°C) oven for about 15 minutes, switching position of pans halfway through baking time, until golden brown and crisp. Let stand on baking sheets for 5 minutes before removing to wire racks to cool. Makes 24 bread sticks.

1 bread stick: 96 Calories; 3.6 g Total Fat (2.4 g Mono, 0.3 g Poly, 0.6 g Sat); 1 mg Cholesterol; 14 g Carbohydrate; 1 g Fibre; 2 g Protein; 263 mg Sodium

Pictured on page 30.

Variation: Omit fresh basil and garlic. Substitute 1 cup (250 mL) finely grated fresh Parmesan cheese and 2 tsp. (10 mL) paprika.

Ciabatta

Pronounced chuh-BAH-tah. Italian bread named for its slipper shape. Versatile golden loaf with a crusty, chewy texture. Great for sandwiches or simply dip slices into a mixture of olive oil and balsamic vinegar.

STARTER		
Warm water	1 cup	250 mL
Active dry yeast	1 tsp.	5 mL
All-purpose flour	3/4 cup	175 mL
DOUGH		
Warm water	1/4 cup	60 mL
Envelope of active dry yeast (or 2 1/4 tsp., 11 mL)	1/4 oz.	8 g
Warm water	1 cup	250 mL
Olive (or cooking) oil	2 tbsp.	30 mL
Salt	2 1/2 tsp.	12 mL
All-purpose flour	3 cups	750 mL
All-purpose flour	1/2 cup	125 mL

Starter: Combine warm water and yeast in small bowl. Stir.

Measure flour into large bowl. Make a well in centre. Add yeast mixture to well. Mix until smooth batter forms. Cover with greased waxed paper and tea towel. Heat oven on lowest temperature for 1 minute to create necessary warmth for starter to rise. Turn oven off. Leave batter in warm oven with door closed for 12 to 18 hours until doubled in bulk and collapsed.

Dough: Combine first amount of warm water and yeast in small bowl. Let stand for 10 minutes. Stir until yeast is dissolved.

Combine next 3 ingredients, yeast mixture and starter in large bowl.

Work in enough of first amount of flour until very soft, sticky dough forms. Place in greased large bowl, turning once to grease top. Cover with greased waxed paper and tea towel. Let stand in oven with light on and door closed for about 1 1/2 hours until dough has more than doubled in bulk. Do not punch down. Turn out dough onto lightly floured surface. Divide into 2 equal portions.

sprinkle about 2 tbsp. (30 mL) of second amount of flour on each of 2 ungreased baking sheets. Place 1 portion of dough on each baking sheet. Shape each diagonally across baking sheet into flat loaf, about 12 inches (30 cm) long and 5 inches (12.5 cm) wide. Dust loaves liberally with remaining flour. Let stand in oven with light on and door closed for 30 minutes. Bake on separate racks in 425°F (220°C) oven for about 30 minutes, switching position of pans halfway through baking time, until golden brown and hollow sounding when tapped. Lightly spray water into oven about 3 times at start of baking to produce steam to develop nice crust on bread. Repeat twice during baking. Let stand on baking sheets for 5 minutes before removing to wire racks to cool. Makes 2 loaves. Each loaf cuts into 12 slices, for a total of 24 slices.

1 slice: 89 Calories; 1.4 g Total Fat (0.9 g Mono, 0.2 g Poly, 0.2 g Sat); 0 mg Cholesterol; 16.5 g Carbohydrate; 1 g Fibre; 3 g Protein; 248 mg Sodium

Pictured on page 30.

Herb Bread Ring

Lovely, golden-crusted ring of bread.
Great served with soup or salad.

Milk	1 1/4 cups	300 mL
Granulated sugar	1/2 tsp.	2 mL
Envelope of active dry yeast (or 2 1/4 tsp., 11 mL)	1/4 oz.	8 g
All-purpose flour	3 cups	750 mL
Chopped fresh basil (or 2 1/4 tsp., 11 mL, dried)	3 tbsp.	50 mL
Chopped fresh parsley (or 2 1/4 tsp., 11 mL, flakes)	3 tbsp.	50 mL
Chopped fresh rosemary leaves (or 1/2 tsp., 2 mL, dried)	2 tsp.	10 mL
Salt	1 tsp.	5 mL
Olive (or cooking) oil	1 tbsp.	15 mL
All-purpose flour, approximately	1/2 cup	125 mL
Olive (or cooking) oil	2 tsp.	10 mL
Coarse sea salt	1/2 tsp.	2 mL

Combine milk and sugar in small heavy saucepan. Heat and stir on medium until warm and sugar is dissolved. Pour into small bowl. Let stand for 5 minutes.

Sprinkle yeast over top. Let stand for 10 minutes. Stir until yeast is dissolved.

Combine next 5 ingredients in large bowl. Make a well in centre. Add first amount of olive oil and yeast mixture to well. Mix until soft dough forms.

Turn out onto lightly floured surface. Knead for 5 to 10 minutes, adding second amount of flour, 1 tbsp. (15 mL) at a time if necessary to prevent sticking, until smooth and elastic. Place in greased large bowl, turning once to grease top. Cover with greased waxed paper and tea towel. Let stand in oven with light on and door closed for about 1 hour until doubled in bulk. Punch dough down. Turn out onto lightly floured surface. Knead for 1 minute. Divide into 2 equal portions. Roll each into 24 inch (60 cm) rope. Lay ropes side by side along length of greased baking sheet. Pinch ropes together at one end.

Twist ropes around each other. Pinch together at opposite end. Shape twisted rope into ring. Pinch ends together to seal. Cover with greased waxed paper and tea towel. Let stand in oven with light on and door closed for about 45 minutes until almost doubled in size.

Brush ring with second amount of olive oil. Sprinkle with coarse sea salt. Bake in 425°F (220°C) oven for about 20 minutes until golden brown and hollow sounding when tapped. Let stand on baking sheet for 5 minutes before removing to wire rack to cool. Cuts into 10 pieces.

1 piece: 207 Calories; 3.2 g Total Fat (1.9 g Mono, 0.4 g Poly, 0.6 g Sat); 1 mg Cholesterol; 38 g Carbohydrate; 2 g Fibre; 6 g Protein; 374 mg Sodium

Pictured on page 31.

Photo Legend next page:
Top Left: Grissini, page 28
Centre Right: Herb Bread Ring, this page
Bottom Left: Ciabatta, page 28

Coffee-Glazed Cinnamon Rolls

Cinnamon-filled rolls drizzled with a sweet coffee glaze.

All-purpose flour	2 1/4 cups	550 mL
Envelope of instant yeast (or 2 1/4 tsp., 11 mL)	1/4 oz.	8 g
Milk	1 cup	250 mL
Butter (or hard margarine)	1/3 cup	75 mL
Granulated sugar	1/3 cup	75 mL
Salt	1/2 tsp.	2 mL
Large eggs, fork-beaten	3	3
All-purpose flour, approximately	2 1/4 cups	550 mL
CINNAMON FILLING		
Brown sugar, packed	1 cup	250 mL
All-purpose flour	1/3 cup	75 mL
Butter (or hard margarine), softened	1/4 cup	60 mL
Ground cinnamon	1 tbsp.	15 mL
Milk	2 tbsp.	30 mL
COFFEE GLAZE		
Icing (confectioner's) sugar	2 cups	500 mL
Hot prepared strong coffee, approximately	3 tbsp.	50 mL
Chopped pecans, toasted (see Tip, page 80)	1/2 cup	125 mL

Measure first amount of flour and yeast into extra-large bowl. Stir. Make a well in centre.

Combine next 4 ingredients in small heavy saucepan. Heat and stir on medium until sugar is dissolved and butter is almost melted. Remove from heat. Stir until butter is melted. Let stand for 5 minutes.

Add eggs and warm milk mixture to well in flour mixture. Stir until soft, sticky dough forms.

Work in enough of second amount of flour until dough pulls away from side of bowl and is no longer sticky. Turn out onto lightly floured surface. Knead for 3 to 5 minutes, adding flour if necessary to prevent sticking, until smooth. Place in greased extra-large bowl, turning once to grease top. Cover with greased waxed paper and tea towel. Let stand in oven with light on and door closed for about 1 hour until doubled in bulk. Punch dough down. Turn out onto lightly floured surface. Knead for 1 minute. Divide into 2 equal portions. Roll out 1 portion to 8 x 12 inch (20 x 30 cm) rectangle.

Cinnamon Filling: Combine first 4 ingredients in medium bowl. Makes 1 3/4 cups (425 mL) filling. Divide and sprinkle 1/2 of filling evenly over rectangle. Press down lightly. Roll up, jelly roll-style, from long side. Press seam against roll to seal. Cut into 12 slices. Arrange cut-side up, about 1 1/2 inches (3.8 cm) apart, on greased baking sheet with sides. Cover with greased waxed paper and tea towel. Repeat with remaining dough and filling. Let stand in oven with light on and door closed for 30 minutes.

Brush rolls with milk. Bake, 1 baking sheet at a time, on centre rack in 375°F (190°C) oven for about 18 minutes until golden brown. Let stand on baking sheet for 5 minutes before removing to wire rack to cool.

Coffee Glaze: Measure icing sugar into small bowl. Stir in enough coffee until barely pourable consistency. Makes about 3/4 cup (175 mL) glaze.

Sprinkle rolls with pecans. Drizzle or pipe glaze over rolls. Makes 24 rolls.

1 roll: 260 Calories; 7.4 g Total Fat (2.7 g Mono, 0.8 g Poly, 3.4 g Sat); 40 mg Cholesterol; 45 g Carbohydrate; 1 g Fibre; 4 g Protein; 116 mg Sodium

Pictured on page 33.

Rum Baba

Tender, light yeast cakes saturated with sweet, rum-flavoured syrup. Serve with fresh fruit.

Milk	1/3 cup	75 mL
All-purpose flour	1/3 cup	75 mL
Envelope of active dry yeast (or 2 1/4 tsp., 11 mL)	1/4 oz.	8 g
All-purpose flour	3/4 cup	175 mL
Granulated sugar	3 tbsp.	50 mL
Salt	1/2 tsp.	2 mL
Large eggs, fork-beaten	2	2
Butter (or hard margarine), melted	3 tbsp.	50 mL
RUM SYRUP		
Granulated sugar	1 1/2 cups	375 mL
Water	1 cup	250 mL
Amber (or dark) rum	3 tbsp.	50 mL

Heat milk in small heavy saucepan on medium until warm. Remove from heat. Add first amount of flour. Stir until smooth. Let stand for 5 minutes.

Top Left: Coffee-Glazed Cinnamon Rolls, page 32

Bottom Right: Rum Baba, page 32

Sprinkle yeast over top. Let stand for 10 minutes. Stir until yeast is dissolved.

Combine second amount of flour, sugar and salt in large bowl. Make a well in centre.

Add eggs, butter and yeast mixture to well. Mix until sticky batter forms. Cover with greased waxed paper and tea towel. Let stand in oven with light on and door closed for about 45 minutes until doubled in bulk. Stir. Divide batter among 6 greased 1/2 cup (125 mL) ramekins or molds. Let stand, uncovered, on baking sheet with sides in oven with light on and door closed for about 20 minutes until batter rises to top of ramekins. Bake in 375°F (190°C) oven for about 15 minutes until tops are golden brown and wooden pick inserted in centre of cake comes out clean. Let stand on wire rack for 3 minutes. Run knife around inside edge of each ramekin to loosen. Remove to 9 inch (22 cm) round pan.

Rum Syrup: Combine sugar and water in medium saucepan. Heat and stir on medium for about 2 minutes until sugar is dissolved. Bring to a boil on medium-high. Boil, without stirring, for 3 minutes. Remove from heat.

Add rum. Stir. Makes 1 1/2 cups (375 mL) syrup. Slowly pour over hot babas. Let stand in pan for about 10 minutes until most of syrup has been absorbed. Serves 6.

1 serving: 418 Calories; 8 g Total Fat (2.4 g Mono, 0.6 g Poly, 4.3 g Sat);
    88 mg Cholesterol; 79 g Carbohydrate; 1 g Fibre; 6 g Protein; 287 mg Sodium

Pictured above.

Breads ▪ 33

Walnut Coffee Kugelhupf

Pronounced KOO-guhl-hopf. Spicy walnut filling spirals beautifully through this sweet, golden Austrian yeast cake.

Milk	1/2 cup	125 mL
Granulated sugar	2 tsp.	10 mL
Envelope of active dry yeast (or 2 1/4 tsp., 11 mL)	1/4 oz.	8 g
All-purpose flour	2/3 cup	150 mL
Butter (or hard margarine), softened	2/3 cup	150 mL
Granulated sugar	1/2 cup	125 mL
Vanilla	1 tsp.	5 mL
Large eggs	3	3
Finely grated orange zest	1 tsp.	5 mL
All-purpose flour	2 1/2 cups	625 mL
Salt	3/4 tsp.	4 mL
All-purpose flour, approximately	1/4 cup	60 mL
WALNUT COFFEE FILLING		
Butter (or hard margarine)	2 tbsp.	30 mL
Milk	2 tbsp.	30 mL
Instant coffee granules	1 1/2 tsp.	7 mL
Chopped walnuts, toasted (see Tip, page 80)	1 cup	250 mL
Brown sugar, packed	1/3 cup	75 mL
Day-old bread, processed into crumbs	3 tbsp.	50 mL
Ground cinnamon	1/2 tsp.	2 mL
Ground ginger	1/2 tsp.	2 mL
Ground cloves	1/8 tsp.	0.5 mL
Icing (confectioner's) sugar, for dusting	1 tbsp.	15 mL

Combine milk and first amount of sugar in small heavy saucepan. Heat and stir on medium until warm and sugar is dissolved. Pour into small bowl. Let stand for 5 minutes.

Sprinkle yeast over top. Let stand for 10 minutes. Stir until yeast is dissolved.

Add first amount of flour. Stir until smooth. Cover with greased waxed paper and tea towel. Let stand in oven with light on and door closed for about 45 minutes until doubled in bulk.

Beat butter, second amount of sugar and vanilla in medium bowl until light and creamy. Add eggs, 1 at a time, beating well after each addition. Add orange zest. Beat well.

Measure second amount of flour and salt into extra-large bowl. Stir. Make a well in centre. Add yeast mixture and butter mixture to well. Mix until soft dough forms.

Turn out dough onto lightly floured surface. Knead for 5 to 10 minutes, adding remaining amount of flour, 1 tbsp. (15 mL) at a time if necessary to prevent sticking, until smooth and elastic. Place in greased extra-large bowl, turning once to grease top. Cover with greased waxed paper and tea towel. Let stand in oven with light on and door closed for about 1 1/2 hours until doubled in bulk.

Walnut Coffee Filling: Heat and stir butter, milk and coffee granules in medium saucepan on medium until butter is melted. Remove from heat.

Add next 6 ingredients. Stir well. Punch dough down. Turn out onto lightly floured surface. Knead for 1 minute. Roll out to 8 x 15 inch (20 x 38 cm) rectangle. Spread filling evenly over dough, leaving 1/2 inch (12 mm) edge.

Roll up, jelly roll-style, from long side. Press seam against roll to seal.

Place, seam-side facing in, in greased 12 cup (2.7 L) bundt pan. Gently press roll into pan.

Cover with greased waxed paper and tea towel. Let stand in oven with light on and door closed for about 1 hour until dough rises to about 1/2 inch (12 mm) from top of pan. Bake in 375°F (190°C) oven for 15 minutes. Reduce heat to 350°F (175°C). Bake for 20 minutes until golden brown and hollow sounding when tapped. Let stand in pan for 5 minutes before inverting onto wire rack to cool.

Dust with icing sugar. Cuts into 16 wedges.

1 wedge: 312 Calories; 15.7 g Total Fat (4.3 g Mono, 3.7 g Poly, 6.7 g Sat); 67 mg Cholesterol; 37 g Carbohydrate; 2 g Fibre; 7 g Protein; 240 mg Sodium

Pictured on page 35.

Fruit Bread

Raisin bread with a twist! Serve with a cup of your favourite tea to brighten a winter day.

Milk	1 cup	250 mL
Granulated sugar	1/4 cup	60 mL
Envelope of active dry yeast (or 2 1/4 tsp., 11 mL)	1/4 oz.	8 g
All-purpose flour	1 cup	250 mL
Large egg, fork-beaten	1	1
Finely grated orange zest	1 tsp.	5 mL
Butter (or hard margarine), melted	1/2 cup	125 mL
Dried cranberries	1/3 cup	75 mL
Golden raisins	1/3 cup	75 mL
Currants	1/3 cup	75 mL
Chopped walnuts, toasted (see Tip, page 80)	1/3 cup	75 mL
Salt	1/2 tsp.	2 mL
Ground cinnamon	1/2 tsp.	2 mL
Ground nutmeg	1/4 tsp.	1 mL
All-purpose flour, approximately	2 cups	500 mL
Egg yolk (large), fork-beaten	1	1
Sanding (decorating) sugar (see Glossary, page 9)	1 tbsp.	15 mL

Combine milk and sugar in small heavy saucepan. Heat and stir on medium until warm and sugar is dissolved. Pour into extra-large bowl. Let stand for 5 minutes.

Sprinkle yeast over top. Let stand for 10 minutes. Stir until yeast is dissolved.

Add first amount of flour. Stir until smooth. Cover with greased waxed paper and tea towel. Let stand in oven with light on and door closed for about 30 minutes until mixture forms a foamy domed surface.

Add egg and orange zest. Stir until well combined.

Add next 8 ingredients. Mix well.

Add second amount of flour, 1/2 cup (125 mL) at a time, mixing until soft dough forms. Turn out onto lightly floured surface. Knead for 5 to 10 minutes, adding flour if necessary to prevent sticking, until smooth and elastic. Place in greased extra-large bowl, turning once to grease top. Cover with greased waxed paper and tea towel. Let stand in oven with light on and door closed for about 1 hour until doubled in bulk. Punch dough down. Turn out onto lightly floured surface. Knead for 1 minute. Shape into loaf. Place in greased 9 x 5 x 3 inch (22 x 12.5 x 7.5 cm) loaf pan. Cover with greased waxed paper and tea towel. Let stand in oven with light on and door closed for about 30 minutes until almost doubled in size.

Brush top of loaf with egg yolk. Sprinkle with sanding sugar. Bake in 375°F (190°C) oven for 10 minutes. Reduce heat to 350°F (175°C). Bake for about 30 minutes until golden brown and hollow sounding when tapped. Let stand in pan for 5 minutes before removing to wire rack to cool. Cuts into 16 slices.

1 slice: 217 Calories; 8.8 g Total Fat (2.4 g Mono, 1.5 g Poly, 4.2 g Sat); 44 mg Cholesterol; 31 g Carbohydrate; 2 g Fibre; 5 g Protein; 150 mg Sodium

Pictured on page 37.

Sticky Finger Buns

Fancy buns to serve any time. Sweet and fruity.

Milk	1 cup	250 mL
Water	1/2 cup	125 mL
Liquid honey	3 tbsp.	50 mL
Granulated sugar	2 tbsp.	30 mL
Envelopes of active dry yeast (1/4 oz., 8 g, each) or 4 1/2 tsp. (22 mL)	2	2
All-purpose flour	3 1/2 cups	875 mL
Salt	1/2 tsp.	2 mL
Butter (or hard margarine), cut up	1/3 cup	75 mL
Golden raisins	2/3 cup	150 mL
Diced mixed peel	1/4 cup	60 mL
Vanilla	1 tsp.	5 mL
All-purpose flour, approximately	1/4 cup	60 mL
Apricot jam	1/3 cup	75 mL
PINK ICING		
Icing (confectioner's) sugar	1 1/4 cups	300 mL
Butter (or hard margarine)	1 1/2 tbsp.	25 mL
Milk	4 tsp.	20 mL
Drop of red liquid food colouring	1	1

Heat and stir first 4 ingredients in small saucepan on medium until warm and sugar is dissolved. Pour into small bowl. Let stand for 5 minutes.

Sprinkle yeast over top. Let stand for 10 minutes. Stir until yeast is dissolved.

Measure first amount of flour and salt into extra-large bowl. Stir. Cut in butter until mixture resembles coarse crumbs. Make a well in centre.

Add raisins, peel, vanilla and yeast mixture to well. Mix until soft dough forms. Cover with greased waxed paper and tea towel. Let stand in oven with light on and door closed for about 45 minutes until doubled in bulk. Punch dough down.

Turn out dough onto lightly floured surface. Knead for 3 to 5 minutes, adding second amount of flour, 1 tbsp. (15 mL) at a time if necessary to prevent sticking, until smooth. Divide dough into 4 portions. Divide each portion into 4 pieces for a total of 16 pieces. Shape each piece into 6 inch (15 cm) roll. Arrange rolls, about 2 inches (5 cm) apart, on 2 greased baking sheets. Cover with greased waxed paper and tea towel. Let stand in oven with light on and door closed for about 15 minutes until almost doubled in size. Bake on separate racks in 475°F (240°C) oven for 8 to 10 minutes, switching position of pans halfway through baking time, until golden brown. Let stand on baking sheets for 3 minutes before removing to wire racks until cooled slightly.

Measure jam into small saucepan. Heat and stir on medium-low for about 4 minutes until warm. Brush over tops of hot buns. Let stand on wire racks until cooled completely.

Pink Icing: Heat and stir first 3 ingredients in small saucepan on low until smooth and butter is melted. Remove from heat.

Add food colouring. Stir until colour is even. Makes 1/2 cup (125 mL) icing. Let stand until barely pourable consistency. Drizzle or pipe over tops of cooled buns. Let stand for about 10 minutes until icing is set. Makes 16 buns.

1 bun: 274 Calories; 5.7 g Total Fat (1.6 g Mono, 0.3 g Poly, 3.4 g Sat);
    15 mg Cholesterol; 52 g Carbohydrate; 2 g Fibre; 5 g Protein; 140 mg Sodium

Pictured below.

Top Left and Bottom Right: Fruit Bread, page 36

Top Right: Sticky Finger Buns, page 36

Chelsea Buns

Large, tender pull-apart buns oozing with caramel glaze.
A treat with your morning coffee.

Milk	1 1/2 cups	375 mL
Granulated sugar	1 tsp.	5 mL
All-purpose flour	1 tbsp.	15 mL
Envelopes of active dry yeast (1/4 oz., 8 g, each) or 4 1/2 tsp. (22 mL)	2	2
All-purpose flour	3 1/2 cups	875 mL
Granulated sugar	2 tbsp.	30 mL
Finely grated orange zest	2 tsp.	10 mL
Salt	1 tsp.	5 mL
Ground cinnamon	1/2 tsp.	2 mL
Ground nutmeg	1/2 tsp.	2 mL
Ground ginger	1/2 tsp.	2 mL
Ground cloves	1/4 tsp.	1 mL
Large egg (room temperature), fork-beaten	1	1
Butter (or hard margarine), melted	3 tbsp.	50 mL
All-purpose flour, approximately	1/4 cup	60 mL
Butter (or hard margarine), melted	1 tbsp.	15 mL
Apricot jam	3 tbsp.	50 mL
WALNUT CURRANT FILLING		
Currants (or chopped raisins)	1/2 cup	125 mL
Chopped walnuts, toasted (see Tip, page 80)	1/2 cup	125 mL
Brown sugar, packed	1/3 cup	75 mL
Golden corn syrup, warmed	1 tbsp.	15 mL
CARAMEL GLAZE		
Icing (confectioner's) sugar	1 1/2 cups	375 mL
Caramel ice cream topping	3 tbsp.	50 mL
Butter (or hard margarine), melted	1 tbsp.	15 mL
Milk, approximately	2 tbsp.	30 mL

Combine milk and first amount of sugar in small heavy saucepan. Heat and stir on medium until warm and sugar is dissolved. Remove from heat. Add first amount of flour. Stir until smooth. Let stand for 5 minutes.

Sprinkle yeast over top. Let stand for 10 minutes. Stir until yeast is dissolved.

Combine next 8 ingredients in extra-large bowl. Make a well in centre.

Add egg, first amount of butter and yeast mixture to well. Mix until soft dough forms.

Turn out dough onto lightly floured surface. Knead for 5 to 10 minutes, adding remaining flour, 1 tbsp. (15 mL) at a time if necessary to prevent sticking, until smooth and elastic. Place in greased extra-large bowl, turning once to grease top. Cover with greased waxed paper and tea towel. Let stand in oven with light on and door closed for about 1 hour until doubled in bulk. Punch dough down.

Turn out dough onto lightly floured surface. Knead for 1 minute. Roll out to 9 x 14 inch (22 x 35 cm) rectangle. Brush dough with second amount of butter. Spread jam evenly over top.

Walnut Currant Filling: Combine currants, walnuts and brown sugar in medium bowl. Sprinkle evenly over jam, leaving 1/2 inch (12 mm) border. Press down lightly. Roll up, jelly roll-style, from long side. Press seam against roll to seal. Cut into 12 slices using floured knife. Arrange, cut-side up, in greased 9 x 13 inch (22 x 33 cm) pan. Cover with greased waxed paper and tea towel. Let stand at room temperature for about 30 minutes until doubled in size. Bake in 375°F (190°C) oven for about 30 minutes until golden brown. Let stand in pan for 10 minutes before removing to wire rack to cool slightly.

Brush corn syrup over warm buns.

Caramel Glaze: Stir icing sugar, ice cream topping and butter together in small bowl, adding more milk as needed until barely pourable consistency. Makes about 1 cup (250 mL) glaze. Drizzle or pipe over warm buns. Let stand until glaze is set. Makes 12 buns.

1 bun: 399 Calories; 9.3 g Total Fat (2.5 g Mono, 2.5 g Poly, 3.7 g Sat); 33 mg Cholesterol; 72 g Carbohydrate; 2 g Fibre; 8 g Protein; 297 mg Sodium

Pictured on page 39.

Top Right: Individual Brioche, page 40
Bottom: Chelsea Buns, this page

Individual Brioche

Brioche (BREE-ohsh), a French creation, is made with a rich butter and egg dough. Our variation does not have the classic 'top knot' but each bun glistens with a sprinkling of sanding sugar. Traditionally made in a fluted brioche mold, these are baked in a muffin pan. A heavy-duty mixer with paddle will make mixing easier.

Milk	1 cup	250 mL
Granulated sugar	1 tsp.	5 mL
Envelopes of active dry yeast (1/4 oz., 8 g, each) or 4 1/2 tsp. (22 mL)	2	2
Butter (not margarine), softened	1 cup	250 mL
Granulated sugar	1/3 cup	75 mL
All-purpose flour	3 3/4 – 4 cups	925 mL – 1 L
Salt	1 tsp.	5 mL
Large eggs	4	4
Large egg, fork-beaten	1	1
Sanding (decorating) sugar (see Glossary, page 9)	2 tbsp.	30 mL

Measure milk and first amount of sugar into small heavy saucepan. Heat and stir on medium until warm and until sugar is dissolved. Pour into small bowl. Let stand for 5 minutes.

Sprinkle yeast over top. Let stand for 10 minutes. Stir until yeast is dissolved.

Beat butter and second amount of sugar in small bowl until light and creamy.

Combine next 3 ingredients and yeast mixture in large bowl. Beat with spoon for 5 to 7 minutes until smooth. Add butter mixture, 3 tbsp. (50 mL) at a time, mixing well after each addition, until soft dough forms. Turn out onto lightly floured surface. Knead for 5 to 10 minutes, adding flour if necessary to prevent sticking, until smooth and elastic. Cover bowl with greased waxed paper and tea towel. Chill for at least 8 hours or overnight.

Turn out onto lightly floured surface. Divide dough into 24 portions. Roll each into ball. Grease 24 muffin cups with cooking spray. Place 1 ball in each cup. Brush egg over top of balls. Sprinkle with sanding sugar. Cover with greased waxed paper and tea towel. Let stand in oven with light on and door closed for about 45 minutes until doubled in size. Bake in 400°F (205°C) oven for about 15 minutes until golden brown. Let stand in pans for 5 minutes before removing to wire racks to cool. Makes 24 rolls.

1 roll: 185 Calories; 9.5 g Total Fat (2.8 g Mono, 0.5 g Poly, 5.5 g Sat); 67 mg Cholesterol; 21 g Carbohydrate; 1 g Fibre; 4 g Protein; 201 mg Sodium

Pictured on page 39.

Blueberry Lemon Pull-Aparts

Fragrant lemon and sweet blueberries make these a delightful treat. Just pull apart and enjoy!

Water	3/4 cup	175 mL
Granulated sugar	1/3 cup	75 mL
Butter (or hard margarine), cut up	1/3 cup	75 mL
Salt	1 tsp.	5 mL
Large eggs	2	2
All-purpose flour	1 1/2 cups	375 mL
Envelope of instant yeast (or 2 1/4 tsp., 11 mL)	1/4 oz.	8 g
All-purpose flour	2 1/4 cups	550 mL
All-purpose flour, approximately	3/4 cup	175 mL
Dried blueberries (see Note)	1/2 cup	125 mL
Boiling water	1/2 cup	125 mL
Butter (or hard margarine), melted	1/3 cup	75 mL
Lemon spread (curd)	1/3 cup	75 mL
Granulated sugar	1 cup	250 mL
Ground cinnamon	3/4 tsp.	4 mL
Finely grated lemon peel	2 tsp.	10 mL
Slivered almonds, toasted (see Tip, page 80)	1/2 cup	125 mL

Measure first 4 ingredients into medium saucepan. Heat and stir on medium until sugar is dissolved and butter is almost melted. Remove from heat. Stir until butter is melted. Let stand for 5 minutes.

Beat eggs with fork in large bowl. Slowly add butter mixture to eggs, stirring constantly, until slightly frothy.

Combine first amount of flour and yeast in small bowl. Add to butter mixture. Stir until smooth.

Add second amount of flour, 1/2 cup (125 mL) at a time, mixing until soft dough forms.

Turn out dough onto lightly floured surface. Knead for 5 to 10 minutes, adding third amount of flour, 1 tbsp. (15 mL) at a time if necessary to prevent sticking, until smooth and elastic. Cover dough with inverted bowl. Let stand for 10 minutes. Divide dough into 4 portions. Roll each portion into 10 inch (25 cm) rope. Cut each rope into ten 1 inch (2.5 cm) pieces, for a total of 40 pieces.

Soak blueberries in boiling water in small bowl until cooled to room temperature. Drain. Set aside.

Mix butter and lemon spread in separate small bowl.

Combine second amount of sugar, cinnamon and lemon peel in medium bowl. Dip dough pieces into butter mixture. Roll in sugar mixture until coated.

Arrange 13 dough pieces in single layer in greased 12 cup (2.7 L) bundt pan. Sprinkle with 1/2 of almonds and blueberries.

Arrange another 13 pieces on top to make second layer. Sprinkle with remaining almonds and blueberries. Arrange remaining dough pieces on top. Drizzle with remaining butter mixture. Sprinkle with remaining sugar mixture. Cover with greased waxed paper and tea towel. Let stand in oven with light on and door closed for about 1 1/2 hours until doubled in size. Bake in 350°F (175°C) oven for about 35 minutes until golden brown. Invert onto serving plate, leaving pan in place. Let stand in pan for 15 minutes before removing to wire rack to cool. Serves 8.

1 serving: 613 Calories; 22.9 g Total Fat (8.2 g Mono, 2 g Poly, 11 g Sat); 104 mg Cholesterol; 94 g Carbohydrate; 4 g Fibre; 11 g Protein; 491 mg Sodium

Pictured below.

Note: Dried blueberries are available in the bulk section of large grocery stores or at your local health food or organic food store.

Cakes &
Cheesecakes

A cake or cheesecake for every day of the week
—what a wonderful thought!
You might not want to indulge that often,
but keep this section bookmarked
because you'll find a reason to turn to
these pages more often than you think.

Fig And Macadamia Cake

A satisfying, nutty flavour complements moist figs in this rich cake. Delicious warm or cold.

Chopped dried figs (about 8 oz., 225 g)	1 1/2 cups	375 mL
Water	1 1/2 cups	375 mL
Baking soda	1 tsp.	5 mL
Butter (or hard margarine), softened	1/2 cup	125 mL
Granulated sugar	1 cup	250 mL
Large eggs	3	3
All-purpose flour	1 1/2 cups	375 mL
Baking powder	2 tsp.	10 mL
Finely chopped macadamia nuts, toasted (see Tip, page 80)	2/3 cup	150 mL
Icing (confectioner's) sugar, for dusting	1 tbsp.	15 mL

Combine figs and water in medium saucepan. Bring to a boil. Remove from heat. Add baking soda. Stir. Cover. Let stand for 5 minutes. Process in blender or food processor until smooth. Set aside.

Beat butter and granulated sugar in medium bowl until light and creamy. Add eggs, 1 at a time, beating well after each addition.

Measure flour and baking powder into small bowl. Stir. Add to butter mixture. Stir. Add fig mixture. Stir until well combined.

Add nuts. Stir. Line bottom of greased 9 x 9 inch (22 x 22 cm) pan with waxed paper. Pour batter into pan. Spread evenly. Bake in 350°F (175°C) oven for about 1 hour until wooden pick inserted in centre comes out clean. Let stand in pan on wire rack for 10 minutes. Run knife around inside edges of pan to loosen cake. Remove to wire rack to cool, discarding waxed paper from bottom of cake.

Just before serving, dust with icing sugar. Cuts into 12 pieces.

1 piece: 325 Calories; 15.6 g Total Fat (7.5 g Mono, 0.7 g Poly, 6.4 g Sat); 76 mg Cholesterol; 45 g Carbohydrate; 3 g Fibre; 5 g Protein; 270 mg Sodium

Pictured on page 45.

Lemon Poppy Seed Cake

Lovely, moist cake that looks simple but tastes spectacular! Serve by itself or with whipped cream and fresh berries.

All-purpose flour	1 2/3 cups	400 mL
Granulated sugar	1 cup	250 mL
Poppy seeds	3 tbsp.	50 mL
Baking powder	1 tbsp.	15 mL
Sour cream	1 cup	250 mL
Butter (or hard margarine), melted	1/2 cup	125 mL
Cooking oil	1/3 cup	75 mL
Lemon juice	1/3 cup	75 mL
Large eggs	3	3
Finely grated lemon zest	1 tbsp.	15 mL
LEMON SYRUP		
Granulated sugar	1/2 cup	125 mL
Water	6 tbsp.	100 mL
Lemon juice	1/4 cup	60 mL

Strips of lemon peel, for garnish

Combine first 4 ingredients in large bowl. Make a well in centre.

Beat next 6 ingredients in medium bowl. Add to well. Stir well. Line bottom and side of 9 inch (22 cm) springform pan with parchment (not waxed) paper. Pour batter into pan. Spread evenly. Bake in 350°F (175°C) oven for about 50 minutes until wooden pick inserted in centre comes out clean. Do not remove from pan.

Lemon Syrup: Measure first 3 ingredients into small saucepan. Heat and stir on medium until sugar is dissolved. Boil gently, uncovered, without stirring, for 2 minutes. Makes 1/4 cup (60 mL) syrup. Place cake in pan on wire rack set on baking sheet (in case syrup leaks out). Slowly pour hot syrup evenly over hot cake. Let stand in pan until cool and syrup is absorbed. Run knife around inside edge of pan to loosen cake. Let stand in pan on wire rack until cooled completely.

Remove to serving plate. Garnish with strips of lemon peel. Cuts into 12 wedges.

1 wedge: 362 Calories; 19.8 g Total Fat (7.6 g Mono, 3.2 g Poly, 7.8 g Sat); 84 mg Cholesterol; 43 g Carbohydrate; 1 g Fibre; 5 g Protein; 201 mg Sodium

Pictured on pages 44/45.

Photo Legend next page:
Top Centre and Bottom Right: Lemon Poppy Seed Cake, page 43
Centre Left: Toasted Walnut Cake, page 46
Centre Right: Fig And Macadamia Cake, page 43

Toasted Walnut Cake

Buttery toasted nuts in a delicate cake smothered with a sweet maple glaze.

Butter (or hard margarine), softened	1 cup	250 mL
Granulated sugar	1 cup	250 mL
Brown sugar, packed	1 cup	250 mL
Large eggs	4	4
Vanilla	1 tsp.	5 mL
All-purpose flour	2 1/2 cups	625 mL
Baking powder	2 tsp.	10 mL
Salt	1/2 tsp.	2 mL
Milk	1 cup	250 mL
Chopped walnuts, toasted (see Tip, page 80)	1 cup	250 mL
MAPLE GLAZE		
Icing (confectioner's) sugar	1 cup	250 mL
Butter (or hard margarine), softened	2 tsp.	10 mL
Vanilla	1/4 tsp.	1 mL
Maple (or maple-flavoured) syrup	1/4 cup	60 mL
Chopped walnuts, toasted (see Tip, page 80)	2 tbsp.	30 mL

Beat butter and both sugars in large bowl until light and creamy. Add eggs, 1 at a time, beating well after each addition. Add vanilla. Stir.

Combine flour, baking powder and salt in medium bowl.

Add flour mixture to butter mixture in 3 additions, alternating with milk in 2 additions, beginning and ending with flour mixture.

Fold in walnuts. Pour batter into greased 10 inch (25 cm) angel food tube pan with removable bottom. Spread evenly. Bake in 350°F (175°C) oven for about 1 hour until wooden pick inserted in centre comes out clean. Let stand in pan on wire rack for 30 minutes. Run knife around inside edge of pan to loosen cake. Remove bottom of pan with cake. Run knife around bottom and centre tube of pan to loosen cake. Invert cake onto serving plate.

Maple Glaze: Beat first 4 ingredients in medium bowl until smooth. Makes about 2/3 cup (150 mL) glaze. Immediately drizzle glaze over top of cake, allowing some to drip down side.

Immediately sprinkle with walnuts. Let stand for about 15 minutes until glaze is set. Cuts into 16 wedges.

1 wedge: 420 Calories; 19.5 g Total Fat (5.4 g Mono, 4.2 g Poly, 8.7 g Sat); 89 mg Cholesterol; 57 g Carbohydrate; 1 g Fibre; 7 g Protein; 280 mg Sodium

Pictured on page 44.

Pumpkin Pecan Cake

A moist pumpkin cake with a sweet orange liqueur icing.

All-purpose flour	2 cups	500 mL
Baking powder	1 tbsp.	15 mL
Baking soda	1/2 tsp.	2 mL
Salt	1/4 tsp.	1 mL
Large eggs	3	3
Brown sugar, packed	1 1/2 cups	375 mL
Can of pure pumpkin (no spices)	14 oz.	398 mL
Cooking oil	1/2 cup	125 mL
Sour cream	1/3 cup	75 mL
Finely grated orange zest	2 tsp.	10 mL
Vanilla	1 tsp.	5 mL
Chopped pecans, toasted (see Tip, page 80)	1 cup	250 mL
ORANGE ICING		
Icing (confectioner's) sugar	1 3/4 cups	425 mL
Butter (or hard margarine), melted	3 tbsp.	50 mL
Orange-flavoured liqueur (such as Grand Marnier), or orange juice	2 tbsp.	30 mL
Pecan halves, toasted (see Tip, page 80)	30	30

Combine first 4 ingredients in large bowl. Make a well in centre.

Beat eggs and brown sugar in medium bowl until thick and pale.

Add next 5 ingredients. Beat well. Add pecans. Stir. Add to well. Stir well. Pour batter into greased 9 x 13 inch (22 x 33 cm) pan. Spread evenly. Bake in 350°F (175°C) oven for 25 to 30 minutes until wooden pick inserted in centre comes out clean. Let stand in pan on wire rack for 15 minutes to cool slightly.

Orange Icing: Stir first 3 ingredients in small bowl until smooth. Icing will be stiff. Makes 1 cup (250 mL) icing. Spread evenly over warm cake in pan.

Arrange pecan halves on icing in evenly spaced rows, 5 lengthwise and 6 crosswise. Press lightly into icing. Let stand until cake is cooled completely and icing is set. Cuts into 30 pieces.

1 piece: 206 Calories; 9.9 g Total Fat (5.3 g Mono, 2.3 g Poly, 1.7 g Sat); 26 mg Cholesterol; 28 g Carbohydrate; 1 g Fibre; 2 g Protein; 103 mg Sodium

Pictured on page 47.

Left: Pumpkin Pecan Cake, page 46

Right: Nutmeg Cake, this page

Nutmeg Cake

Delicious cake flavoured with nutmeg and topped with walnuts.

All-purpose flour	2 1/4 cups	550 mL
Baking powder	2 tsp.	10 mL
Ground nutmeg	1 1/2 – 2 tsp.	7 – 10 mL
Cold butter (or hard margarine), cut up	1/2 cup	125 mL
Brown sugar, packed	1 1/2 cups	375 mL
Large egg	1	1
Milk	1 cup	250 mL
Baking soda	1 tsp.	5 mL
Chopped walnuts	2/3 cup	150 mL

Combine first 3 ingredients in large bowl. Cut in butter until mixture resembles coarse crumbs.

Add brown sugar. Stir well. Line bottom of greased 9 x 9 inch (22 x 22 cm) pan with waxed paper. Press 1 1/2 cups (375 mL) brown sugar mixture into bottom of pan. Set aside remaining brown sugar mixture.

Beat egg in small bowl. Add milk and baking soda. Stir. Add to reserved brown sugar mixture. Stir until well combined. Pour over brown sugar mixture in pan. Spread evenly.

Sprinkle walnuts over top. Bake in 350°F (175°C) oven for about 35 minutes until wooden pick inserted in centre comes out clean. Let stand in pan on wire rack for 10 minutes. Run knife around inside edges of pan to loosen cake. Remove to wire rack to cool, discarding waxed paper from bottom of cake. Cuts into 12 pieces.

1 piece: 333 Calories; 13.3 g Total Fat (3.5 g Mono, 3.2 g Poly, 5.7 g Sat); 41 mg Cholesterol; 49 g Carbohydrate; 1 g Fibre; 6 g Protein; 279 mg Sodium

Pictured above.

Burnt Sugar Chiffon Cake

Enjoy the sweet burnt sugar flavour in this caramel-coloured cake with golden icing.

BURNT SUGAR SYRUP

Granulated sugar	3/4 cup	175 mL
Water	6 tbsp.	100 mL
Water	1 cup	250 mL

CAKE

Sifted cake flour (see Note)	2 cups	500 mL
Granulated sugar	1 3/4 cups	425 mL
Baking powder	1 tbsp.	15 mL
Salt	1 tsp.	5 mL
Cooking oil	1/2 cup	125 mL
Water	1/4 cup	60 mL
Egg yolks (large)	7	7
Vanilla	1 tsp.	5 mL
Egg whites (large), room temperature	7	7
Cream of tartar (see Glossary, page 9)	1/2 tsp.	2 mL

BURNT SUGAR ICING

Icing (confectioner's) sugar	4 cups	1 L
Butter (or hard margarine), softened	1/2 cup	125 mL
Vanilla	1 tsp.	5 mL
Water		

Coarse brown sugar (such as
Sugar in the Raw), for garnish

Burnt Sugar Syrup: Heat and stir sugar and first amount of water in large heavy saucepan on medium-low until sugar is dissolved. Brush inside edge of saucepan with damp pastry brush to dissolve any sugar crystals. Boil, uncovered, without stirring, on medium-high until dark butterscotch colour. Remove from heat.

Slowly and carefully add second amount of water. Sugar mixture will sputter furiously. Return to heat. Stir for about 10 seconds until smooth and sugar crystals are dissolved. Colour should be deep golden brown; if too dark, syrup will taste scorched. Cool completely. Makes 3/4 cup (175 mL) syrup. Set aside.

Cake: Measure first 4 ingredients into flour sifter over large bowl. Sift into bowl. Make a well in centre.

Add next 4 ingredients to well. Do not stir. Add 1/2 cup (125 mL) reserved syrup to well. Do not stir.

Beat egg whites and cream of tartar in separate large bowl until stiff peaks form. Using same beaters, beat egg yolk mixture until smooth and light. Fold about 1/4 of egg white mixture into egg yolk mixture to lighten. Add egg yolk mixture to remaining egg white mixture in 2 batches, gently folding after each addition, until no white streaks remain. Pour batter into ungreased 10 inch (25 cm) angel food tube pan with removable bottom. Spread evenly. Bake in 325°F (160°C) oven for 55 minutes. Increase oven temperature to 350°F (175°C). Bake for about 15 minutes until wooden pick inserted in centre of cake comes out clean. Cake top will be quite dark. Invert cake in pan onto neck of glass bottle to cool. Turn upright. Run knife around inside edge of pan to loosen cake. Remove bottom of pan with cake. Run knife around bottom and centre tube of pan to loosen cake. Invert onto serving plate.

Burnt Sugar Icing: Beat first 3 ingredients and remaining syrup in medium bowl, adding enough water until smooth spreading consistency. Makes about 2 cups (500 mL) icing. Spread over cake.

Garnish with brown sugar. Cuts into 20 wedges.

1 wedge: 365 Calories; 12.5 g Total Fat (5.5 g Mono, 2.2 g Poly, 4 g Sat);
89 mg Cholesterol; 61 g Carbohydrate; 0 g Fibre; 3 g Protein; 247 mg Sodium

Pictured on page 49.

Note: In a pinch, you can use 7/8 cup (200 mL) all-purpose flour in place of each 1 cup (250 mL) cake flour.

Top: Hummingbird Cake, page 50
Bottom: Burnt Sugar Chiffon Cake, this page

Hummingbird Cake

A classic cake recipe passed down through generations. Moist and delicious.

All-purpose flour	1 2/3 cups	400 mL
Granulated sugar	1 cup	250 mL
Pecan pieces	1 cup	250 mL
Ground cinnamon	3/4 tsp.	4 mL
Baking soda	1/2 tsp.	2 mL
Salt	1/4 tsp.	1 mL
Can of crushed pineapple, well drained	14 oz.	398 mL
Mashed banana (about 2 1/2 medium bananas)	1 cup	250 mL
Cooking oil	3/4 cup	175 mL
Large eggs	3	3
CREAM CHEESE ICING		
Block of cream cheese, softened	4 oz.	125 g
Butter (or hard margarine), softened	3 tbsp.	50 mL
Vanilla	1 tsp.	5 mL
Icing (confectioner's) sugar	1 1/2 cups	375 mL
Pecan halves, for garnish	1/4 cup	60 mL

Combine first 6 ingredients in large bowl. Make a well in centre.

Beat next 4 ingredients in medium bowl. Pour into well. Stir until just combined. Line bottom of greased 9 x 9 inch (22 x 22 cm) pan with waxed paper. Pour batter into pan. Spread evenly. Bake in 350°F (175°C) oven for about 1 hour until wooden pick inserted in centre comes out clean. Let stand in pan on wire rack for 10 minutes. Run knife around inside edges of pan to loosen cake. Remove to wire rack to cool completely, discarding waxed paper from bottom of cake. Transfer to serving plate.

Cream Cheese Icing: Beat cream cheese and butter in small bowl until light and creamy. Add vanilla. Beat.

Add icing sugar, 1/4 cup (60 mL) at a time while beating, until spreading consistency. Makes 1 3/4 cups (425 mL) icing. Spread over cake.

Arrange pecan halves around edge of cake. Cuts into 12 pieces.

1 piece: 499 Calories; 29 g Total Fat (14.9 g Mono, 6.4 g Poly, 6.1 g Sat); 73 mg Cholesterol; 57 g Carbohydrate; 2 g Fibre; 5 g Protein; 181 mg Sodium

Pictured on page 49.

Chocolate Sour Cream Cake

Thick, rich chocolate cake—sure to be a favourite!

Semi-sweet chocolate baking squares (1 oz., 28 g, each), chopped	4	4
Water	2/3 cup	150 mL
Butter (or hard margarine), softened	3/4 cup	175 mL
Brown sugar, packed	1 1/2 cups	375 mL
Large eggs	3	3
All-purpose flour	2 1/2 cups	625 mL
Baking powder	1 tbsp.	15 mL
Salt	1/4 tsp.	1 mL
Sour cream	2/3 cup	150 mL
CHOCOLATE SOUR CREAM ICING		
Semi-sweet chocolate baking squares (1 oz., 28 g, each), chopped	8	8
Icing (confectioner's) sugar	1 1/2 cups	375 mL
Sour cream, room temperature	3/4 cup	175 mL

Heat and stir chocolate and water in small heavy saucepan on lowest heat until chocolate is almost melted. Do not overheat. Remove from heat. Stir until smooth.

Beat butter and brown sugar in large bowl until light and creamy. Add eggs, 1 at a time, beating well after each addition.

Combine flour, baking powder and salt in small bowl. Add to butter mixture. Stir. Add sour cream and chocolate mixture. Stir well. Line bottoms of 2 greased 8 inch (20 cm) round pans with waxed paper. Divide and pour batter into pans. Spread evenly. Bake in 350°F (175°C) oven for about 30 minutes until wooden pick inserted in centre comes out clean. Let stand in pans on wire racks for 10 minutes. Run knife around inside edge of pans to loosen cakes. Remove to wire racks to cool completely, discarding waxed paper from bottoms of cakes.

Chocolate Sour Cream Icing: Heat and stir chocolate in small heavy saucepan on lowest heat until chocolate is almost melted. Do not overheat. Remove from heat. Stir until smooth. Transfer to medium bowl.

Add icing sugar and sour cream. Stir until smooth. Makes 2 cups (500 mL) icing. Cut each cake layer in half horizontally, using serrated knife, for a total of 4 layers. Place 1 layer on serving plate. Spread top with 1/3 cup (75 mL) icing. Repeat with second and third layers, spreading 1/3 cup (75 mL) icing on top of each. Place remaining layer on top. Cover top and side of cake with remaining icing. Cuts into 12 wedges.

1 wedge: 576 Calories; 26.2 g Total Fat (8 g Mono, 1.2 g Poly, 15.5 g Sat); 98 mg Cholesterol; 84 g Carbohydrate; 3 g Fibre; 7 g Protein; 310 mg Sodium

Pictured on page 51.

Mango Coconut Chiffon Roll

Toasted coconut roll with a sweet mango flavour.

All-purpose flour	1 1/3 cups	325 mL
Granulated sugar	3/4 cup	175 mL
Baking powder	2 tsp.	10 mL
Salt	1/2 tsp.	2 mL
Cooking oil	1/3 cup	75 mL
Egg yolks (large)	4	4
Medium unsweetened coconut, toasted (see Tip, page 80)	1/2 cup	125 mL
Can of sliced mango with syrup, drained and syrup reserved	14 oz.	398 mL
Egg whites (large), room temperature	4	4
Cream of tartar (see Glossary, page 9)	1/2 tsp.	2 mL
Granulated sugar	3 tbsp.	50 mL
Medium unsweetened coconut, toasted (see Tip, page 80)	3 tbsp.	50 mL
Icing (confectioner's) sugar	1 tbsp.	15 mL
MANGO FILLING		
Granulated sugar	3 tbsp.	50 mL
Cornstarch	4 tsp.	20 mL
Whipping cream	1/2 cup	125 mL
Icing (confectioner's) sugar, for dusting	1 tbsp.	15 mL

Line bottom of greased 11 × 17 inch (28 × 43 cm) baking sheet with sides with waxed paper. Measure first 4 ingredients into flour sifter over large bowl. Sift into bowl. Make a well in centre.

Add cooking oil, egg yolks and first amount of coconut to well. Do not stir.

Process mango in blender until puréed. Transfer to 2 cup (500 mL) liquid measure. Add enough mango syrup to equal 1 1/2 cups (375 mL). Stir. Add 3/4 cup (175 mL) mango mixture to well. Beat on medium for about 30 seconds until smooth. Add remaining mango syrup to remaining puréed mango. Stir. Set aside for filling.

Beat egg whites and cream of tartar in separate large bowl with clean beaters until soft peaks form. Add second amount of granulated sugar, 1 tbsp. (15 mL) at a time while beating, until stiff peaks form and sugar is dissolved. Fold about 1/4 of egg white mixture into egg yolk mixture to lighten. Add egg yolk mixture to egg white mixture in 2 batches, gently folding after each addition, until no white streaks remain. Pour batter into prepared pan. Spread evenly. Bake in 325°F (160°C) oven for about 20 minutes until wooden pick inserted in centre comes out clean. Let stand in pan on wire rack for 5 minutes. Run knife around inside edges of pan to loosen cake.

Spread large tea towel on work surface. Cover with sheet of waxed paper. Combine second amount of coconut and icing sugar in small bowl. Sprinkle over waxed paper. Invert cake onto coconut mixture. Carefully peel off and discard waxed paper from bottom of cake. Roll up cake from short end, using towel and waxed paper as guide. Let stand until cool.

Mango Filling: Combine granulated sugar and cornstarch in small saucepan. Add reserved puréed mango. Heat and stir on medium for about 5 minutes until boiling and thickened. Pour into small bowl. Cover. Chill until cold.

Beat whipping cream in separate small bowl until stiff peaks form. Fold into cold mango mixture. Makes about 2 cups (500 mL) filling. Unroll cake. Spread with filling, leaving 1 inch (2.5 cm) edge. Roll up gently, using tea towel as guide and discarding waxed paper. Place roll, seam-side down, on serving plate.

Dust with icing sugar. Cuts into 14 slices.

1 slice: 259 Calories; 12.9 g Total Fat (4.8 g Mono, 2 g Poly, 5.3 g Sat);
    72 mg Cholesterol; 33 g Carbohydrate; 1 g Fibre; 4 g Protein; 162 mg Sodium

Pictured above.

Chocolate Buttercream Roll

*Rich, moist chocolate sponge roll filled
with creamy butterscotch.*

CHOCOLATE ROLL

Egg whites (large), room temperature	5	5
Egg yolks (large)	5	5
Vanilla	1 tsp.	5 mL
Icing (confectioner's) sugar	1 cup	250 mL
All-purpose flour	1/4 cup	60 mL
Cocoa, sifted if lumpy	3 tbsp.	50 mL
Salt	1/2 tsp.	2 mL
Icing (confectioner's) sugar (or cocoa)	1/3 cup	75 mL

EASY BUTTERCREAM FILLING

Butterscotch (or vanilla) pudding powder (not instant), 6 serving size	1	1
Milk	1 cup	250 mL
Butter (not margarine), softened	1 cup	250 mL
Granulated sugar	1/2 cup	125 mL

Chocolate Roll: Line bottom and sides of greased 10 x 15 inch (25 x 38 cm) jelly roll pan with parchment (not waxed) paper, extending paper 2 inches (5 cm) over long sides. Beat egg whites in large bowl until stiff (not dry) peaks form. Set aside.

Using same beaters, beat egg yolks and vanilla in medium bowl for about 3 minutes until thick and pale.

Add next 4 ingredients to egg yolk mixture. Beat until smooth. Fold in egg whites until no white streaks remain. Pour batter into prepared pan. Spread evenly. Bake in 350°F (175°C) oven for 15 to 20 minutes until wooden pick inserted in centre comes out clean. Let stand in pan on wire rack for 5 minutes. Run knife around inside edges of pan to loosen cake.

Spread large tea towel on work surface. Cover with sheet of waxed paper. Sift icing sugar onto waxed paper. Invert cake onto icing sugar. Carefully peel off and discard waxed paper from bottom of cake. Roll up cake from short end, using towel and waxed paper as guide. Let stand until cool.

Easy Buttercream Filling: Stir pudding powder and milk in medium saucepan until smooth. Heat and stir on medium until boiling and thickened. Remove from heat. Stir with whisk until smooth. Cover with plastic wrap directly on surface to prevent skin from forming. Cool to room temperature.

Beat butter in medium bowl on high for about 5 minutes until light. Add sugar, 1 tbsp. (15 mL) at a time while beating constantly. Add cooled pudding. Beat well, scraping down side of bowl once or twice, until light and creamy and sugar is dissolved. Makes 2 3/4 cups (675 mL) filling. Reserve 3/4 cup (175 mL) filling. Unroll cake. Spread remaining filling evenly over cake, leaving 1/2 inch (12 mm) edge.

Roll up gently, discarding waxed paper. Place roll, seam-side down, on serving plate. Decorate with reserved buttercream. Chill until firm. Cuts into 12 slices.

1 slice: 328 Calories; 18.8 g Total Fat (5.6 g Mono, 0.9 g Poly, 11 g Sat); 134 mg Cholesterol; 37 g Carbohydrate; trace Fibre; 4 g Protein; 386 mg Sodium

Pictured on page 55.

Apple Almond Cake

Apples, toasted nuts and spice cake make this dessert simply sensational!

Butter (or hard margarine), softened	1/2 cup	125 mL
Granulated sugar	2/3 cup	150 mL
Large eggs	2	2
All-purpose flour	1 1/2 cups	375 mL
Baking powder	2 tsp.	10 mL
Ground cinnamon	1 tsp.	5 mL
Salt	1/4 tsp.	1 mL
Buttermilk (or reconstituted from powder)	1/2 cup	125 mL
Large tart cooking apple (such as Granny Smith), peeled, cored and grated	1	1
Sliced almonds, toasted (see Tip, page 80)	1/3 cup	75 mL

Beat butter and sugar in medium bowl until light and creamy. Add eggs, 1 at a time, beating well after each addition.

Combine next 4 ingredients in small bowl.

Add flour mixture to butter mixture in 3 additions, alternating with buttermilk in 2 additions, beginning and ending with flour mixture. Beat well. Line bottom of greased 8 inch (20 cm) springform pan with waxed paper. Pour batter into pan. Spread evenly.

Combine apple and almonds in separate small bowl. Spoon evenly over top of batter. Bake in 350°F (175°C) oven for about 1 hour until wooden pick inserted in centre comes out clean. Let stand in pan on wire rack for 10 minutes. Run knife around inside edge of pan to loosen cake. Let stand in pan on wire rack until cooled completely. Remove to serving plate, discarding waxed paper from bottom of cake. Cuts into 8 wedges.

1 wedge: 330 Calories; 16.3 g Total Fat (5.6 g Mono, 1.3 g Poly, 8.3 g Sat); 87 mg Cholesterol; 42 g Carbohydrate; 2 g Fibre; 6 g Protein; 325 mg Sodium

Pictured on page 57.

Honey Walnut Cake

Honey and nut-flavoured cake with a creamy, sweet icing—so good!

Liquid honey	1 cup	250 mL
Plain yogurt (not low-fat)	1/2 cup	125 mL
Butter (or hard margarine), softened	3/4 cup	175 mL
Granulated sugar	1/2 cup	125 mL
Large eggs	3	3
All-purpose flour	1 3/4 cups	425 mL
Baking powder	2 tsp.	10 mL
Baking soda	1/4 tsp.	1 mL
Salt	1/4 tsp.	1 mL
Chopped walnuts, toasted (see Tip, page 80)	1 cup	250 mL
HONEY ICING		
Butter (or hard margarine), softened	1/4 cup	60 mL
Liquid honey	3 tbsp.	50 mL
Icing (confectioner's) sugar	1 1/3 cups	325 mL

Combine honey and yogurt in small bowl.

Beat butter and sugar in large bowl until light and creamy. Add eggs, 1 at a time, beating well after each addition.

Combine next 4 ingredients in separate small bowl. Add to butter mixture. Stir. Add honey mixture. Stir until well combined.

Add walnuts. Stir. Line bottom of greased 9 x 9 inch (22 x 22 cm) pan with waxed paper. Pour batter into pan. Spread evenly. Bake in 350°F (175°C) oven for about 1 hour until wooden pick inserted in centre comes out clean. Let stand in pan on wire rack for 10 minutes. Run knife around inside edges of pan to loosen cake. Remove to wire rack to cool completely, discarding waxed paper from bottom of cake.

Honey Icing: Beat butter and honey in medium bowl until smooth. Add icing sugar, 1/4 cup (60 mL) at a time while beating, until spreading consistency. Makes 1 2/3 cups (400 mL) icing. Spread on top of cooled cake. Cuts into 12 pieces.

1 piece: 518 Calories; 24.1 g Total Fat (6.6 g Mono, 5 g Poly, 11.1 g Sat); 98 mg Cholesterol; 73 g Carbohydrate; 1 g Fibre; 7 g Protein; 329 mg Sodium

Pictured on page 57.

Top: Apple Almond Cake, this page
Bottom: Honey Walnut Cake, above

Amaretto Cherry Chiffon

This tall, pink cake is filled with bits of cherry and toasted almonds in a light chiffon texture. Delightful. Serve with whipped cream and cherries.

All-purpose flour	2 cups	500 mL
Granulated sugar	1 1/4 cups	300 mL
Baking powder	1 tbsp.	15 mL
Salt	1 tsp.	5 mL

Cooking oil	1/2 cup	125 mL
Almond-flavoured liqueur (such as Amaretto)	1/2 cup	125 mL
Maraschino cherry syrup	1/4 cup	60 mL
Egg yolks (large)	6	6
Finely chopped maraschino cherries, drained	1/2 cup	125 mL
Finely chopped sliced almonds, toasted (see Tip, page 80)	1/3 cup	75 mL
Egg whites (large), room temperature	8	8
Cream of tartar (see Glossary, page 9)	1/2 tsp.	2 mL
Granulated sugar	1/4 cup	60 mL
Icing (confectioner's) sugar, for dusting	1 tbsp.	15 mL

Measure first 4 ingredients into flour sifter over large bowl. Sift into bowl. Make a well in centre.

Add next 4 ingredients to well. Beat on medium for about 1 minute until smooth.

Add cherries and almonds. Stir.

Beat egg whites and cream of tartar in separate large bowl with clean beaters until soft peaks form. Add second amount of sugar, 1 tbsp. (15 mL) at a time while beating, until stiff peaks form and sugar is dissolved. Fold about 1/4 of egg white mixture into egg yolk mixture to lighten. Add egg yolk mixture to remaining egg white mixture in 2 batches, gently folding after each addition until no white streaks remain. Pour into ungreased 10 inch (25 cm) angel food tube pan with removable bottom. Spread evenly. Cut through batter with knife to remove large air spaces. Do not tap pan or press down batter. Bake on bottom rack in 325°F (160°C) oven for 60 to 65 minutes until cake springs back when lightly pressed and wooden pick inserted in centre of cake comes out clean. Invert cake in pan onto neck of glass bottle to cool. Turn upright. Run knife around inside edge of pan to loosen cake. Remove bottom of pan with cake. Run knife around bottom and centre tube of pan to loosen cake. Invert onto serving plate.

Dust with icing sugar. Cuts into 20 wedges.

1 wedge: 235 Calories; 8.4 g Total Fat (4.6 g Mono, 2.2 g Poly, 1 g Sat); 65 mg Cholesterol; 33 g Carbohydrate; 1 g Fibre; 4 g Protein; 199 mg Sodium

Pictured on this page.

Chocolate Banana Cake

Dense and moist with a rich chocolate glaze. Garnish with chocolate curls.

Semi-sweet chocolate baking squares (1 oz., 28 g, each), chopped	4	4
Butter (or hard margarine)	1/4 cup	60 mL
All-purpose flour	1 1/2 cups	375 mL
Granulated sugar	3/4 cup	175 mL
Instant coffee granules	2 tsp.	10 mL
Baking powder	2 tsp.	10 mL
Salt	1/2 tsp.	2 mL
Buttermilk (or reconstituted from powder)	1 cup	250 mL
Small banana, mashed	1	1
Large eggs	2	2
CHOCOLATE GLAZE (GANACHE)		
Whipping cream	1/2 cup	125 mL
Semi-sweet chocolate baking squares (1 oz., 28 g, each), chopped	4	4

Heat and stir chocolate and butter in small heavy saucepan on lowest heat for about 5 minutes until chocolate is almost melted. Do not overheat. Remove from heat. Stir until smooth. Set aside.

Combine next 5 ingredients in large bowl. Make a well in centre.

Add buttermilk, banana and eggs to well. Beat until smooth. Add chocolate mixture. Stir. Line bottom of greased 9 inch (22 cm) round pan with waxed paper. Pour batter into pan. Spread evenly. Bake in 350°F (175°C) oven for about 40 minutes until wooden pick inserted in centre comes out clean. Let stand in pan on wire rack for 10 minutes. Run knife around inside edge of pan to loosen cake. Remove to wire rack, discarding waxed paper from bottom of cake. Set rack in waxed paper-lined baking sheet with sides until cake is cooled completely.

Chocolate Glaze: Heat whipping cream in heavy medium saucepan on medium-low until bubbles start to form around edge. Do not boil. Remove from heat. Add chocolate. Stir until chocolate is melted and mixture is smooth. Makes about 1 cup (250 mL) glaze. Let stand for 5 minutes. Pour and spread over cake in even layer until top and sides are covered. Chill for at least 30 minutes. Cuts into 12 wedges.

1 wedge: 298 Calories; 14.3 g Total Fat (4.4 g Mono, 0.6 g Poly, 8.4 g Sat); 60 mg Cholesterol; 41 g Carbohydrate; 2 g Fibre; 5 g Protein; 242 mg Sodium

Pictured below.

Pineapple Coconut Cake

Tropical cake filled with sweet pineapple and decorated with golden coconut.

Butter (or hard margarine), softened	1/2 cup	125 mL
Granulated sugar	1 cup	250 mL
Finely grated lemon zest	1 tsp.	5 mL
Large eggs	2	2
Can of crushed pineapple, with juice	14 oz.	398 mL
Milk	1/3 cup	75 mL
All-purpose flour	2 cups	500 mL
Baking powder	4 tsp.	20 mL
Medium sweetened coconut	3/4 cup	175 mL
PINEAPPLE ICING		
Butter (or hard margarine), softened	3 tbsp.	50 mL
Pineapple juice	1/3 cup	75 mL
Icing (confectioner's) sugar	4 cups	1 L
Medium sweetened coconut, toasted (see Tip, page 80)	1/2 cup	125 mL
Coconut Ribbons, this page, toasted (see Tip, page 80), for garnish		

Beat butter, sugar and lemon zest in large bowl until light and creamy. Add eggs, 1 at a time, beating well after each addition.

Add pineapple with juice and milk. Beat until just combined. Mixture may look curdled, but will come together when flour is added.

Combine flour and baking powder in small bowl. Add to pineapple mixture. Add coconut. Stir well. Line bottoms of 2 greased 8 inch (20 cm) round pans with waxed paper. Divide and pour batter into pans. Spread evenly. Bake in 325°F (160°C) oven for about 45 minutes until wooden pick inserted in centre comes out clean. Let stand in pans on wire racks for 10 minutes. Run knife around inside edge of pans to loosen cakes. Remove to wire racks to cool completely, discarding waxed paper from bottoms of cakes.

Pineapple Icing: Beat butter and pineapple juice in medium bowl until smooth. Add icing sugar, 1/2 cup (125 mL) at a time while beating, until spreading consistency. Makes 1 1/3 cups (325 mL) icing. Place 1 cake layer on serving plate. Spread top with 1/2 cup (125 mL) icing. Place second cake layer on top of icing. Spread remaining icing on top and side of cake.

Sprinkle coconut over top of cake. Lightly press coconut ribbons into icing around side. Chill until ready to serve. Cut into 12 wedges.

1 wedge: 490 Calories; 14.9 g Total Fat (3.7 g Mono, 0.7 g Poly, 9.5 g Sat); 66 mg Cholesterol; 88 g Carbohydrate; 1 g Fibre; 4 g Protein; 272 mg Sodium

Pictured on page 61.

Coconut Ribbons

Pierce Eyes: Pierce holes through eyes of coconut, using metal skewer.

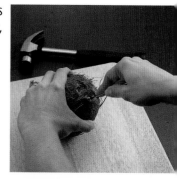

Remove Flesh: Crack coconut with hammer into 3 inch (7.5 cm) pieces. Pry coconut from shell, using dull knife.

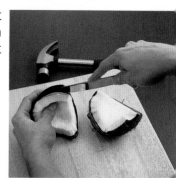

Make Ribbons: Peel coconut into strips, using vegetable peeler.

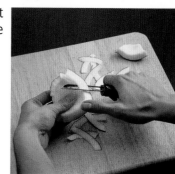

Pictured on page 61.

Apricot Butter Cake

A delicately flavoured cake accented with apricots.

Butter (or hard margarine), softened	3/4 cup	175 mL
Granulated sugar	3/4 cup	175 mL
Finely grated orange zest	2 tsp.	10 mL
Large eggs	3	3
All-purpose flour	1 2/3 cups	400 mL
Baking powder	2 tsp.	10 mL
Salt	1/4 tsp.	1 mL
Milk	1/2 cup	125 mL
Can of apricot halves in light syrup, drained and chopped	14 oz.	398 mL
APRICOT TOPPING		
Unflavoured gelatin	1 tsp.	5 mL
Water	2 tbsp.	30 mL
Apricot jam, warmed and sieved	3 tbsp.	50 mL

Beat butter, sugar and orange zest in medium bowl until light and creamy. Add eggs, 1 at a time, beating well after each addition.

Combine flour, baking powder and salt in small bowl. Add to butter mixture. Add milk. Stir well. Line bottom of greased 9 inch (22 cm) springform pan with waxed paper. Pour batter into pan. Spread evenly.

Sprinkle apricots over top. Bake in 350°F (175°C) oven for about 50 minutes until top is lightly browned and wooden pick inserted in centre comes out clean. Let stand in pan on wire rack for 10 minutes.

Apricot Topping: Sprinkle gelatin over water in small saucepan. Let stand for 1 minute. Heat and stir on medium-low until gelatin is dissolved.

Add jam. Stir well. Makes 1/4 cup (60 mL) topping. Brush warm mixture onto warm cake. Let stand in pan on wire rack until cooled completely. Run knife around inside edge of pan to loosen cake. Remove to serving plate, discarding waxed paper from bottom of cake. Cuts into 8 wedges.

1 wedge: 410 Calories; 20.7 g Total Fat (6.1 g Mono, 1.1 g Poly, 12 g Sat); 131 mg Cholesterol; 50 g Carbohydrate; 2 g Fibre; 7 g Protein; 392 mg Sodium

Pictured on page 63.

PEACH BUTTER CAKE: Substitute 1 can (14 oz., 398 mL) sliced peaches for the apricot.

Ginger Spice Cake

Bundt cake with a dusting of icing sugar. Exploding with flavours of ginger and spice!

Butter (or hard margarine), softened	1/2 cup	125 mL
Brown sugar, packed	3/4 cup	175 mL
Large eggs	2	2
Golden corn syrup	1/3 cup	75 mL
All-purpose flour	2 cups	500 mL
Baking powder	1 tbsp.	15 mL
Ground ginger	1 tsp.	5 mL
Ground cinnamon	3/4 tsp.	4 mL
Baking soda	1/2 tsp.	2 mL
Ground cardamom	1/4 tsp.	1 mL
Salt	1/4 tsp.	1 mL
Milk	3/4 cup	175 mL
Minced crystallized ginger (see Glossary, page 9)	1/2 cup	125 mL
Icing (confectioner's) sugar, for dusting	1 tbsp.	15 mL

Beat butter and brown sugar in medium bowl until light and creamy. Add eggs, 1 at a time, beating well after each addition.

Add corn syrup. Beat until smooth.

Combine next 7 ingredients in small bowl. Add to butter mixture. Do not stir.

Add milk and ginger. Beat until well combined. Grease and lightly flour 12 cup (2.7 L) bundt pan. Pour batter into pan. Spread evenly. Bake in 350°F (175°C) oven for 45 to 50 minutes until wooden pick inserted in centre of cake comes out clean. Let stand in pan on wire rack for 10 minutes before inverting onto wire rack to cool. Transfer cake to serving plate.

Just before serving, dust with icing sugar. Cuts into 16 wedges.

1 wedge: 204 Calories; 7 g Total Fat (2 g Mono, 0.4 g Poly, 4.1 g Sat); 44 mg Cholesterol; 33 g Carbohydrate; 1 g Fibre; 3 g Protein; 239 mg Sodium

Pictured on page 63.

Top: Ginger Spice Cake, above
Bottom: Apricot Butter Cake, this page

Sour Cream Lemon Cake

*Mouth-watering lemon cake with crunchy pistachios
and sweet, tangy icing.*

Butter (or hard margarine)	1/2 cup	125 mL
Milk	1/2 cup	125 mL
Large eggs, room temperature	3	3
Finely grated lemon zest	1 1/2 tbsp.	25 mL
Vanilla	1 tsp.	5 mL
Granulated sugar	1 cup	250 mL
All-purpose flour	1 1/2 cups	375 mL
Baking powder	2 tsp.	10 mL
Salt	1/4 tsp.	1 mL
Sour cream	1/2 cup	125 mL
LEMON ICING		
Butter (or hard margarine), softened	1/2 cup	125 mL
Icing (confectioner's) sugar	1 1/2 cups	375 mL
Lemon juice	2 tsp.	10 mL
Drops of yellow liquid food colouring	1 – 2	1 – 2
Finely chopped pistachios, toasted (see Tip, page 80)	1 cup	250 mL

Heat and stir butter and milk in small saucepan on medium for about 3 minutes until butter is almost melted. Remove from heat. Stir until butter is melted. Cool.

Beat eggs, lemon zest and vanilla in large bowl for about 7 minutes until thick and pale.

Add sugar to egg mixture, 2 tbsp. (30 mL) at a time while beating, until sugar is dissolved.

Combine flour, baking powder and salt in small bowl.

Add flour mixture to egg mixture in 3 additions, alternating with sour cream in 2 additions, beginning and ending with flour mixture. Add cooled milk mixture. Stir until well combined. Line bottom of greased 8 x 8 inch (20 x 20 cm) pan with waxed paper. Pour batter into pan. Spread evenly. Bake in 350°F (175°C) oven for about 45 minutes until wooden pick inserted in centre comes out clean. Let stand in pan on wire rack for 10 minutes. Run knife around inside edges of pan to loosen cake. Remove to wire rack to cool completely, discarding waxed paper from bottom of cake.

Lemon Icing: Beat butter in small bowl for 3 minutes until light and creamy.

Add next 3 ingredients. Beat until smooth. Makes 1 1/3 cups (325 mL) icing. Cut domed top from cake using serrated knife. Reserve for another use. Cut cake into 2 equal rectangles. Place 1 rectangle on serving plate. Spread with about 1/3 cup (75 mL) icing. Place second rectangle on top. Cover top and sides of cake with remaining icing.

Lightly press pistachios into icing around sides. Cuts into 10 slices.

1 slice: 531 Calories; 30.2 g Total Fat (11.6 g Mono, 2.2 g Poly, 14.7 g Sat); 122 mg Cholesterol; 61 g Carbohydrate; 1 g Fibre; 7 g Protein; 364 mg Sodium

Pictured on page 65.

Top: Sour Cream Lemon Cake, this page
Bottom: Blitz Torte, page 66

Blitz Torte

This Swedish delight will become one of your favourites, and it's easy to make. Make the cake ahead and decorate just before serving.

Butter (or hard margarine), softened	1/2 cup	125 mL
Granulated sugar	3/4 cup	175 mL
Egg yolks (large)	4	4
Milk	1/3 cup	75 mL
Vanilla	1 tsp.	5 mL
All-purpose flour	1 cup	250 mL
Baking powder	1 tsp.	5 mL
Egg whites (large), room temperature	4	4
Cream of tartar (see Glossary, page 9)	1/4 tsp.	1 mL
Granulated sugar	3/4 cup	175 mL
Finely chopped walnuts	3/4 cup	175 mL
CUSTARD FILLING		
Milk	1 1/2 cups	375 mL
Vanilla	1/2 tsp.	2 mL
Granulated sugar	1/3 cup	75 mL
All-purpose flour	3 tbsp.	50 mL
Salt	1/8 tsp.	0.5 mL
Milk	1/2 cup	125 mL
Large egg	1	1

Whipped cream (or frozen whipped topping, thawed), for garnish
Fresh berries, for garnish

Beat butter and first amount of sugar in large bowl until light and creamy. Beat in egg yolks, milk and vanilla. Mixture may look curdled, but will come together when flour is added.

Combine flour and baking powder in small bowl. Add to egg yolk mixture. Stir until smooth. Divide and pour batter into 2 greased 9 inch (22 cm) round pans. Spread evenly. Set aside.

Beat egg whites and cream of tartar with clean beaters in medium bowl until soft peaks form. Add second amount of sugar, 1 tbsp. (15 mL) at a time while beating, until stiff peaks form and sugar is dissolved. Fold in walnuts. Divide and spoon over batter in pans. Spread evenly. Bake in 325°F (160°C) oven for about 40 minutes until tops are golden and wooden pick inserted in centre comes out clean. Let stand in pans on wire racks for 10 minutes. Run knife around inside edge of pans to loosen cakes. Remove to wire racks to cool completely.

Custard Filling: Combine first amount of milk and vanilla in medium saucepan. Heat on medium-high for about 3 minutes until small bubbles appear around edge. Do not boil. Remove from heat.

Measure sugar, flour and salt into small bowl. Stir. Add second amount of milk. Stir. Add to hot milk mixture. Heat and stir on medium until boiling and thickened.

Beat egg with fork in same small bowl. Slowly stir 1/4 cup (60 mL) hot milk mixture into egg. Slowly stir egg mixture into remaining hot milk mixture. Heat and stir on medium for about 2 minutes until thickened. Remove from heat. Cool completely. Makes 2 cups (500 mL) filling. Place 1 cake layer, meringue-side up, on serving plate. Spread filling evenly over top. Place second cake layer, meringue-side down, on top of filling. Cover with plastic wrap. Chill for at least 6 hours or overnight.

Just before serving, garnish with whipped cream and fresh berries. Cuts into 12 wedges.

1 wedge: 348 Calories; 15.5 g Total Fat (4.4 g Mono, 3.8 g Poly, 6.3 g Sat); 114 mg Cholesterol; 46 g Carbohydrate; 1 g Fibre; 8 g Protein; 191 mg Sodium

Pictured on page 65.

Orange Layer Cake

Refreshing orange flavour in both the cake and the icing.
It's sure to be a hit served at any time.

Butter (or hard margarine), softened	1/2 cup	125 mL
Granulated sugar	1 1/2 cups	375 mL
Finely grated orange zest	2 tsp.	10 mL
Large eggs	2	2
Frozen concentrated orange juice, thawed	1/3 cup	75 mL
All-purpose flour	2 1/4 cups	550 mL
Baking powder	4 tsp.	20 mL
Salt	1/2 tsp.	2 mL
Milk	1 cup	250 mL
CHOCOLATE ORANGE ICING		
Butter (or hard margarine), softened	2/3 cup	150 mL
Icing (confectioner's) sugar	3 3/4 cups	925 mL
Cocoa, sifted if lumpy	3/4 cup	175 mL
Frozen concentrated orange juice, thawed	3 tbsp.	50 mL

Beat butter and sugar in large bowl until light and creamy. Add orange zest. Add eggs, 1 at a time, beating well after each addition. Add concentrated orange juice. Beat.

Combine flour, baking powder and salt in medium bowl.

Add flour mixture to butter mixture in 3 additions, alternating with milk in 2 additions, beginning and ending with flour mixture. Line bottoms of 2 greased 8 inch (20 cm) round pans with waxed paper. Divide and pour batter into pans. Spread evenly. Bake in 350°F (175°C) oven for about 35 minutes until wooden pick inserted in centre comes out clean. Let stand in pans on wire racks for 10 minutes. Run knife around inside edge of pans to loosen cakes. Remove to wire racks to cool completely, discarding waxed paper from bottoms of cakes.

Chocolate Orange Icing: Combine all 4 ingredients in medium bowl. Beat on low for 1 minute. Beat on high, adding more icing sugar or liquid if necessary, until spreading consistency. Makes about 3 cups (750 mL) icing. Place 1 cake layer on serving plate. Spread 3/4 cup (175 mL) icing over top. Place second layer on top. Spread top and side of cake with remaining icing. Cuts into 12 wedges.

1 wedge: 570 Calories; 21.1 g Total Fat (6.2 g Mono, 1 g Poly, 12.7 g Sat); 88 mg Cholesterol; 94 g Carbohydrate; 3 g Fibre; 6 g Protein; 439 mg Sodium

Pictured above.

Blueberry Cheesecake

Creamy, velvety texture.

VANILLA WAFER CRUST

Vanilla wafers (or 2 3/4 cups, 675 mL, wafer crumbs)	4 cups	1 L
Butter (or hard margarine), melted	1/2 cup	125 mL
Ground nutmeg	1/2 tsp.	2 mL

LEMON FILLING

Granulated sugar	2/3 cup	150 mL
Large eggs	4	4
Blocks of cream cheese (8 oz., 250 g, each), chopped and softened	3	3
Sour cream	2/3 cup	150 mL
Lemon juice	1/3 cup	75 mL
Finely grated lemon zest	1 tbsp.	15 mL

BLUEBERRY TOPPING

Fresh (or frozen, thawed) blueberries	2 cups	500 mL
Granulated sugar	1/3 cup	75 mL
Water	1 tsp.	5 mL
Cornstarch	1 tbsp.	15 mL

Vanilla Wafer Crust: Process wafers in blender or food processor until fine crumbs. Combine crumbs, butter and nutmeg in medium bowl. Press evenly in bottom of greased 9 inch (22 cm) springform pan. Chill for 1 hour.

Lemon Filling: Beat sugar and eggs in large bowl until thick and pale.

Add next 4 ingredients. Beat until well combined. Pour over crust. Spread evenly. Bake in 325°F (160°C) oven for 1 to 1 1/4 hours until centre is almost set. Run knife around inside edge of pan to allow cheesecake to settle evenly. Let stand in pan on wire rack until cooled completely.

Blueberry Topping: Combine blueberries and sugar in medium saucepan. Heat and stir on medium for 5 to 7 minutes until sugar is dissolved. Reduce heat to medium-low. Simmer for about 5 minutes until liquid is released from berries.

Stir water into cornstarch in small cup until smooth. Add to blueberry mixture. Stir until thickened. Cool. Makes 1 1/2 cups (375 mL) topping. Pour over top of cheesecake in pan. Smooth top. Cover. Chill for at least 6 hours or overnight. Cuts into 12 wedges.

1 wedge: 547 Calories; 37.9 g Total Fat (11.4 g Mono, 2.4 g Poly, 21.5 g Sat); 184 mg Cholesterol; 46 g Carbohydrate; 1 g Fibre; 9 g Protein; 384 mg Sodium

Pictured on pages 68/69.

Almond Raspberry Cheesecake

This magnificent baked cheesecake has a soft, creamy texture, the citrus kick of lemon and the irresistible temptation of fresh raspberries.

VANILLA WAFER CRUST

Vanilla wafers (or 3/4 cup, 175 mL, wafer crumbs)	1 cup	250 mL
Ground almonds	3/4 cup	175 mL
Butter (or hard margarine), melted	1/4 cup	60 mL

FILLING

Block of cream cheese, softened	8 oz.	250 g
Ricotta cheese	1 cup	250 mL
Granulated sugar	1 cup	250 mL
Sour cream	1 cup	250 mL
Large eggs	4	4
Egg yolk (large)	1	1
All-purpose flour	3 tbsp.	50 mL
Finely grated lemon zest	1 tbsp.	15 mL
Fresh raspberries	1 1/4 cups	300 mL
Sliced almonds with skin	1/3 cup	75 mL
Fresh raspberries, for garnish	14	14

Vanilla Wafer Crust: Process wafers in blender or food processor until fine crumbs. Combine wafer crumbs, almonds and butter in medium bowl. Press evenly in bottom of greased 9 inch (22 cm) springform pan. Chill for 1 hour.

Filling: Beat cream cheese, ricotta cheese and sugar in large bowl until smooth.

Add next 5 ingredients. Beat well. Pour over crust. Spread evenly.

Sprinkle first amount of raspberries and almonds evenly over top. Bake in 350°F (175°C) oven for about 1 hour until centre is almost set. Run knife around inside edge of pan to allow cheesecake to settle evenly. Let stand in pan on wire rack until cooled completely. Chill for at least 6 hours or overnight.

Just before serving, garnish with second amount of raspberries. Cuts into 12 wedges.

1 wedge: 364 Calories; 24.1 g Total Fat (8.6 g Mono, 2 g Poly, 11.9 g Sat); 147 mg Cholesterol; 30 g Carbohydrate; 1 g Fibre; 9 g Protein; 175 mg Sodium

Pictured on pages 72/73.

Banana Caramel Cheesecake

A creamy banana cheesecake with a butterscotch-like sauce.

PASTRY CRUST

All-purpose flour	1 1/4 cups	300 mL
Icing (confectioner's) sugar	1/4 cup	60 mL
Cold butter (or hard margarine)	1/3 cup	75 mL
Egg yolks (large)	3	3
Cold water, approximately	1 tbsp.	15 mL
Dried beans (or uncooked rice)	1 cup	250 mL

FILLING

Blocks of cream cheese (8 oz., 250 g, each), softened	2	2
Granulated sugar	1/2 cup	125 mL
Mashed banana (about 3 medium)	1 1/2 cups	375 mL
Large eggs	3	3
Vanilla	2 tsp.	10 mL
Amber (or dark) rum (or 1 tsp., 5 mL, rum flavouring)	1 1/2 tbsp.	25 mL

CARAMEL SAUCE

Whipping cream	1/2 cup	125 mL
Brown sugar, packed	1/2 cup	125 mL
Butter (or hard margarine), cut up	1/2 cup	125 mL
Whipped cream, for garnish	2 cups	500 mL
Medium banana, sliced, for garnish	1	1

Pastry Crust: Measure flour and icing sugar into flour sifter over large bowl. Sift into bowl. Cut in butter until mixture resembles coarse crumbs.

Add egg yolks. Stir well. Add cold water, 1 tsp. (5 mL) at a time, until soft dough forms. Turn out onto lightly floured surface. Knead for about 1 minute until smooth. Cover with plastic wrap. Chill for 30 minutes. Press pastry in bottom and 1/2 inch (12 mm) up side of greased 9 inch (22 cm) springform pan. Chill for 30 minutes.

Cover pastry with parchment paper, bringing paper over side of pan. Fill with dried beans. Bake in 375°F (190°C) oven for 10 minutes. Carefully remove beans and paper. (These can be kept for the next time you bake pastry.) Bake for about 10 minutes until golden brown. Let stand in pan on wire rack until cool.

Filling: Beat cream cheese and sugar in large bowl until smooth. Add next 4 ingredients. Beat well. Pour over crust. Spread evenly. Bake in 350°F (175°C) oven for about 45 minutes until centre is almost set. Run knife around inside edge of pan to allow cheesecake to settle evenly. Let stand in pan on wire rack until cooled completely. Chill for at least 5 hours or overnight.

Caramel Sauce: Combine first 3 ingredients in medium saucepan. Heat and stir on low until butter is melted. Simmer, uncovered, for 1 minute. Makes about 1 cup (250 mL) sauce. Keep warm.

Garnish individual servings with dollop of whipped cream and banana slices. Drizzle warm sauce over each. Cuts into 12 wedges.

1 wedge: 494 Calories; 34.2 g Total Fat (10 g Mono, 1.6 g Poly, 20.5 g Sat); 202 mg Cholesterol; 40 g Carbohydrate; 1 g Fibre; 7 g Protein; 286 mg Sodium

Pictured on page 72.

Turtle Cheesecake

A scrumptious dessert! Enough to serve a large group.
Can be made ahead and frozen.

PECAN CRUST		
All-purpose flour	1 1/2 cups	375 mL
Granulated sugar	3 tbsp.	50 mL
Butter (or hard margarine), cut up	3/4 cup	175 mL
Finely chopped pecans	3/4 cup	175 mL
CARAMEL LAYER		
Evaporated milk (or light cream)	3 tbsp.	50 mL
Caramels	32	32
Chopped pecans, toasted (see Tip, page 80)	1 cup	250 mL
CHEESE LAYER		
Blocks of cream cheese, softened (8 oz., 250 g, each)	3	3
Brown sugar, packed	1 cup	250 mL
All-purpose flour	2 tbsp.	30 mL
Large eggs	3	3
Creamed cottage cheese, processed in blender or sieved	1 cup	250 mL
Vanilla	1 1/2 tsp.	7 mL

CHOCOLATE GLAZE (GANACHE)		
Whipping cream	1 cup	250 mL
Semi-sweet chocolate baking squares (1 oz., 28 g, each), chopped	7	7
Chopped pecans, toasted (see Tip, page 80), for garnish		

Pecan Crust: Combine flour and sugar in medium bowl. Cut in butter until mixture resembles coarse crumbs. Add pecans. Stir. Press in bottom and 1 inch (2.5 cm) up side of greased 10 inch (25 cm) springform pan. Bake in 350°F (175°C) oven for 15 to 20 minutes until edge starts to brown. Let stand in pan on wire rack for 10 minutes.

Caramel Layer: Heat and stir evaporated milk and caramels in small saucepan on medium-low until caramels are melted. Pour over crust. Spread evenly.

Sprinkle pecans over top.

Cheese Layer: Beat cream cheese and brown sugar in large bowl until smooth. Add flour. Beat. Add eggs, 1 at a time, beating after each addition until just combined. Add cottage cheese and vanilla. Beat on low until just combined. Pour over pecans. Spread evenly. Bake in 350°F (175°C) oven for about 1 hour until centre is almost set. Run knife around inside edge of pan to allow cheesecake to settle evenly. Let stand in pan on wire rack set in baking sheet with sides until cooled completely. Remove side of pan.

Chocolate Glaze: Heat whipping cream in heavy medium saucepan on medium-low until bubbles start to form around edge. Do not boil. Remove from heat. Add chocolate. Stir until chocolate is melted and mixture is smooth. Makes about 1 1/4 cups (300 mL) glaze. Let stand for 5 minutes. Pour over cheesecake, allowing glaze to drip down side in smooth, even coating.

Sprinkle pecans over top. Chill for at least 1 hour. Cuts into 16 wedges.

1 wedge: 649 Calories; 46.6 g Total Fat (16.4 g Mono, 3.7 g Poly, 24 g Sat); 139 mg Cholesterol; 52 g Carbohydrate; 2 g Fibre; 11 g Protein; 355 mg Sodium

Pictured on pages 72 and 73.

Photo Legend next page:
Top Left: Banana Caramel Cheesecake, page 70
Top Right and Centre Left: Turtle Cheesecake, this page
Bottom Right: Almond Raspberry Cheesecake, page 70

Cookies & Squares

The most enchanting thing about cookies and squares is
that "right now" is always the perfect time to indulge.
Still need a reason? Then think of these tidbits
as your own little reward.

Almond Jelly Swirls

Sweet flavour of jelly spiralled in a sugar cookie.
Subtle taste of almonds, too!

Butter (or hard margarine), softened	1/2 cup	125 mL
Granulated sugar	1 cup	250 mL
Large egg	1	1
Milk	3 tbsp.	50 mL
Almond flavouring	1/2 tsp.	2 mL
All-purpose flour	2 2/3 cups	650 mL
Baking powder	1/2 tsp.	2 mL
Salt	1/4 tsp.	1 mL
BLACK CURRANT FILLING		
Black currant jelly (or blackberry jam)	1/2 cup	125 mL
Cornstarch	1 tsp.	5 mL
Finely chopped sliced almonds, toasted (see Tip, page 80)	1/3 cup	75 mL

Beat butter and sugar in large bowl until light and creamy.

Add egg, milk and almond flavouring. Beat well.

Combine flour, baking powder and salt in medium bowl. Add to butter mixture. Stir until smooth. Divide dough into 2 equal portions. Cover each portion with plastic wrap. Chill for at least 3 hours.

Black Currant Filling: Stir jelly into cornstarch in small saucepan. Heat and stir on medium for about 3 minutes until bubbling. Remove from heat. Cover. Let stand until cooled completely.

Roll out 1 portion of cookie dough between 2 sheets of waxed paper to 8 × 12 inch (20 × 30 cm) rectangle. Place on baking sheet. Chill for 30 minutes. Remove top piece of waxed paper. Spread 1/2 of filling evenly over dough to edge. Sprinkle with 1/2 of almonds. Roll up, jelly roll-style, from short end, using waxed paper as guide. Press seam against roll to seal. Wrap tightly with plastic wrap. Repeat with remaining portions of dough, filling and almonds. Chill for at least 6 hours. Cut each roll into 1/4 inch (6 mm) thick slices. Arrange slices, about 2 inches (5 cm) apart, on greased cookie sheets. Bake in 375°F (190°C) oven for 12 to 14 minutes until edges are golden. Let stand on cookie sheets for 5 minutes before removing to wire racks to cool. Makes about 5 dozen (60) cookies.

1 cookie: 61 Calories; 2 g Total Fat (0.6 g Mono, 0.2 g Poly, 1 g Sat); 7 mg Cholesterol; 10 g Carbohydrate; trace Fibre; 1 g Protein; 32 mg Sodium

Pictured on front and back cover and on this page.

Almond Jelly Swirls, this page

Chewy Cookie Clusters

Each cookie has a collage of colour and burst of flavour!

Cornflakes cereal	3 cups	750 mL
Golden raisins	1 1/2 cups	375 mL
Pistachios, toasted (see Tip, page 80)	1 1/2 cups	375 mL
Sliced almonds, toasted (see Tip, page 80)	1 cup	250 mL
Chopped red glazed cherries	1 cup	250 mL
Finely grated orange zest	1/2 tsp.	2 mL
Can of sweetened condensed milk (see Glossary, page 9)	11 oz.	300 mL
Butter (or hard margarine), melted	2 tbsp.	30 mL

Combine first 6 ingredients in large bowl.

Add condensed milk and butter. Stir until ingredients are well coated. Drop, using 2 tbsp. (30 mL), for each, about 1 inch (2.5 cm) apart, onto parchment paper-lined cookie sheets. Bake in 350°F (175°C) oven for about 8 minutes until lightly browned. Let stand on cookie sheets for 5 minutes before removing to wire racks to cool. Makes about 4 dozen (48) cookies.

1 cookie: 103 Calories; 4.7 g Total Fat (2.6 g Mono, 0.6 g Poly, 1.1 g Sat); 4 mg Cholesterol; 15 g Carbohydrate; 1 g Fibre; 2 g Protein; 32 mg Sodium

Pictured on page 76.

Strawberry Cream Cookies

Buttery cookie sandwiches oozing with sweet, creamy filling.

Butter (or hard margarine), softened	3/4 cup	175 mL
Brown sugar, packed	1/2 cup	125 mL
Vanilla	1/2 tsp.	2 mL
Large egg	1	1
All-purpose flour	2 cups	500 mL
Medium unsweetened coconut	1/2 cup	125 mL
Baking powder	2 tsp.	10 mL
Baking soda	1/4 tsp.	1 mL
Salt	1/4 tsp.	1 mL
STRAWBERRY FILLING		
Butter (or hard margarine), softened	1/4 cup	60 mL
Icing (confectioner's) sugar	3/4 cup	175 mL
Strawberry jam	2 tbsp.	30 mL
Strawberry jam	1/3 cup	75 mL

Beat butter, brown sugar and vanilla in large bowl until light and creamy. Add egg. Beat well.

Combine next 5 ingredients in medium bowl. Add to butter mixture. Stir well. Roll into balls, using 2 tsp. (10 mL) for each. Arrange balls, about 1 1/2 inches (3.8 cm) apart, on greased cookie sheets. Flatten each ball with lightly floured fork to 1/4 inch (6 mm) thickness. Bake in 375°F (190°C) oven for 7 to 10 minutes until firm and edges are golden. Let stand on cookie sheets for 5 minutes before removing to wire racks to cool completely. Makes 56 cookies.

Strawberry Filling: Beat butter and icing sugar in small bowl until light and creamy.

Add first amount of jam. Beat well. Makes about 1/2 cup (125 mL) filling. Lay 1/2 of cookies, bottom-side up, on work surface. Spread each with 1 tsp. (5 mL) filling.

Lay remaining cookies, bottom-side up, on work surface. Spread each with 1/2 tsp. (2 mL) of second amount of jam. Sandwich cookies using 1 cookie with filling and 1 cookie with jam. Makes 28 sandwich cookies.

1 sandwich cookie: 152 Calories; 8.4 g Total Fat (2.1 g Mono, 0.3 g Poly, 5.4 g Sat); 27 mg Cholesterol; 19 g Carbohydrate; trace Fibre; 1 g Protein; 137 mg Sodium

Pictured on page 77.

Top Left: Melting Moments, page 78
Bottom Left: Chewy Cookie Clusters, page 75
Bottom Right: Strawberry Cream Cookies, above

Melting Moments

Melt-in-your-mouth cookie sandwiches.
Perfect with coffee or tea.

Butter (not margarine), softened	1 cup	250 mL
Icing (confectioner's) sugar	1/3 cup	75 mL
Vanilla	1/2 tsp.	2 mL
All-purpose flour	1 1/2 cups	375 mL
Cornstarch	1/2 cup	125 mL
CHOCOLATE COFFEE FILLING		
Butter (or hard margarine), softened	1/4 cup	60 mL
Icing (confectioner's) sugar	1/2 cup	125 mL
Instant coffee granules	2 tsp.	10 mL
Hot water	2 tsp.	10 mL
Semi-sweet chocolate baking squares (1 oz., 28 g, each), melted	2	2

Beat butter, icing sugar and vanilla in large bowl until light and creamy.

Combine flour and cornstarch in small bowl. Add to butter mixture. Stir well. Spoon into piping bag fitted with large closed star tip. Pipe 72 one inch (2.5 cm) rosettes, about 1 1/2 inches (3.8 cm) apart, onto greased cookie sheets. Bake in 350°F (175°C) oven for 10 to 15 minutes until golden and slightly dry. Let stand on cookie sheets for 10 minutes before removing to wire racks to cool completely. Makes 72 cookies.

Chocolate Coffee Filling: Beat butter and icing sugar in small bowl until light and creamy.

Combine coffee granules and hot water in separate small bowl. Add to butter mixture. Stir.

Add chocolate. Beat well. Makes about 3/4 cup (175 mL) filling. Lay 36 cookies, bottom-side up, on work surface. Spoon or pipe 1 tsp. (5 mL) filling onto each cookie. Top with remaining cookies. Makes 36 sandwich cookies.

1 sandwich cookie: 106 Calories; 7.3 g Total Fat (2.1 g Mono, 0.3 g Poly, 4.5 g Sat); 18 mg Cholesterol; 10 g Carbohydrate; trace Fibre; 1 g Protein; 69 mg Sodium

Pictured on pages 76/77.

Coconut Lime Macaroons

These light, golden clusters are chewy on the inside and crunchy on the outside.

Egg yolks (large)	2	2
Granulated sugar	2/3 cup	150 mL
Finely grated lime zest	1 tsp.	5 mL
Flake coconut	1 3/4 cups	425 mL
Egg white (large)	1	1

Beat egg yolks, sugar and lime zest in small bowl for about 5 minutes until thick and pale. Transfer to large bowl.

Add coconut. Stir well.

Beat egg white in separate small bowl with clean beaters until stiff (not dry) peaks form. Fold into coconut mixture. Drop, using 2 tsp. (10 mL), for each, about 2 inches (5 cm) apart, onto parchment paper-lined cookie sheets. Bake on centre rack in 300°F (150°C) oven for 20 to 25 minutes until golden and crispy on outside. Let stand on cookie sheets for 5 minutes before removing to wire racks to cool. Makes about 2 1/2 dozen (30) cookies.

1 cookie: 44 Calories; 1.8 g Total Fat (0.2 g Mono, 0.1 g Poly, 1.4 g Sat); 14 mg Cholesterol; 7 g Carbohydrate; trace Fibre; 0 g Protein; 14 mg Sodium

Pictured on page 83.

Hazelnut Cookies

*Golden hazelnut cookies with spirals of icing on top.
Delicious!*

Butter (or hard margarine), softened	1/2 cup	125 mL
Brown sugar, packed	1 cup	250 mL
Vanilla	1/2 tsp.	2 mL
Large egg	1	1
All-purpose flour	2 cups	500 mL
Baking powder	3/4 tsp.	4 mL
Baking soda	3/4 tsp.	4 mL
Salt	1/4 tsp.	1 mL
Sour cream	1/3 cup	75 mL
Coarsely chopped hazelnuts (filberts), toasted (see Tip, page 80)	2/3 cup	150 mL

HAZELNUT ICING

Butter (or hard margarine)	3 tbsp.	50 mL
Hazelnut-flavoured liqueur (such as Frangelico)	2 tbsp.	30 mL
Icing (confectioner's) sugar	1 cup	250 mL

Beat butter and brown sugar in large bowl until light and creamy. Add vanilla and egg. Beat well.

Combine next 4 ingredients in small bowl. Add to butter mixture. Beat.

Add sour cream and hazelnuts. Stir well. Drop, using 2 tsp. (10 mL), for each, about 1 inch (2.5 cm) apart, onto greased cookie sheets. Bake in 375°F (190°C) oven for 10 to 12 minutes until edges are golden. Let stand on cookie sheets for 5 minutes before removing to wire racks to cool completely.

Hazelnut Icing: Heat and stir butter in small saucepan on medium until melted and golden brown. Remove from heat.

Add liqueur. Stir. Add icing sugar, 1/4 cup (60 mL) at a time while beating, until barely pourable consistency. Makes about 1/2 cup (125 mL) icing. Drizzle or pipe icing onto each cookie. Let cookies stand until icing is set. Makes about 6 dozen (72) cookies.

1 cookie: 60 Calories; 2.8 g Total Fat (1.2 g Mono, 0.2 g Poly, 1.4 g Sat);
    9 mg Cholesterol; 8 g Carbohydrate; trace Fibre; 1 g Protein; 47 mg Sodium

Pictured below.

Chocolate Coconut Cookies

Cute chocolate cookie nuggets with lots of crunch.

Butter (or hard margarine), softened	3/4 cup	175 mL
Granulated sugar	1/3 cup	75 mL
All-purpose flour	1 1/2 cups	375 mL
Cocoa, sifted if lumpy	2 tbsp.	30 mL
Salt	1/4 tsp.	1 mL
Cornflakes cereal	1 cup	250 mL
Medium unsweetened coconut, toasted (see Tip, below)	1/3 cup	75 mL

CHOCOLATE ICING

Icing (confectioner's) sugar	1 cup	250 mL
Cocoa, sifted if lumpy	1 tbsp.	15 mL
Butter (or hard margarine), softened	2 tsp.	10 mL
Milk, approximately	1 1/2 tbsp.	25 mL

Beat butter and sugar in large bowl until light and creamy.

Add flour, cocoa and salt. Stir well.

Add cereal and coconut. Stir until well coated. Drop, using 1 tbsp. (15 mL), for each, about 1 inch (2.5 cm) apart, onto greased cookie sheets. Bake in 350°F (175°C) oven for 10 to 12 minutes until firm and bottoms are browned. Let stand on cookie sheets for 5 minutes before removing to wire racks to cool completely.

Chocolate Icing: Combine icing sugar, cocoa and butter in small bowl.

Beat in enough milk until barely pourable consistency. Makes about 1/3 cup (75 mL) icing. Drizzle or pipe icing onto each cookie. Let stand until icing is set. Makes about 2 1/2 dozen (30) cookies.

1 cookie: 107 Calories; 6 g Total Fat (1.5 g Mono, 0.2 g Poly, 3.9 g Sat); 14 mg Cholesterol; 13 g Carbohydrate; trace Fibre; 1 g Protein; 82 mg Sodium

Pictured on page 83.

Sesame Ginger Cookies

Tasty, buttery cookies with ginger and sesame seeds.

Butter (or hard margarine), softened	1/2 cup	125 mL
Brown sugar, packed	1 cup	250 mL
Vanilla	1 tsp.	5 mL
Large egg	1	1
All-purpose flour	1 1/2 cups	375 mL
Sesame seeds, toasted (see Tip, this page)	1/4 cup	60 mL
Baking powder	1 tsp.	5 mL
Ground ginger	1/2 tsp.	2 mL
Salt	1/4 tsp.	1 mL
Sesame seeds, toasted (see Tip, this page)	1/3 cup	75 mL

Beat butter and brown sugar in large bowl until light and creamy.

Add vanilla and egg. Beat well.

Combine next 5 ingredients in small bowl. Add to butter mixture. Stir well. Divide into 4 equal portions. Shape each portion into 4 inch (10 cm) log, about 1 1/4 inches (3 cm) in diameter. Shape each into squared log by flattening all 4 sides and ends.

Put second amount of sesame seeds in shallow dish. Press each log firmly into seeds until 4 sides are coated in thick layer. Wrap each log in waxed paper. Chill for at least 3 hours, or freeze until ready to use. (If frozen, let stand for 30 minutes before slicing.) Cut each log into 16 slices, 1/4 inch (6 mm) thick. Arrange slices, about 1 1/2 inches (3.8 cm) apart, on greased cookie sheets. Bake in 350°F (175°C) oven for about 12 minutes until edges are golden. Let stand on cookie sheets for 5 minutes before removing to wire racks to cool. Makes 64 cookies.

1 cookie: 48 Calories; 2.3 g Total Fat (0.7 g Mono, 0.4 g Poly, 1.1 g Sat); 7 mg Cholesterol; 6 g Carbohydrate; trace Fibre; 1 g Protein; 34 mg Sodium

Pictured on page 82.

■ ■ ■

To toast nuts, seeds, or coconut, spread evenly in ungreased shallow pan. Bake in 350°F (175°C) oven for 5 to 10 minutes, stirring or shaking often, until desired doneness.

Chocolate Macadamia Squares

A rich, nutty square with a smooth chocolate taste and a hint of orange.

Can of sweetened condensed milk (see Glossary, page 9)	11 oz.	300 mL
Butter (or hard margarine)	1/2 cup	125 mL
Cocoa, sifted if lumpy	1/2 cup	125 mL
Milk	1/2 cup	125 mL
Brown sugar, packed	3/4 cup	175 mL
All-purpose flour	3/4 cup	175 mL
Vanilla	1 tsp.	5 mL
Large eggs	2	2
Semi-sweet chocolate baking squares (1 oz., 28 g, each), chopped finely	6	6
Chopped macadamia nuts, toasted (see Tip, page 80)	1/2 cup	125 mL
Finely grated orange zest	1 1/2 tsp.	7 mL

Heat and stir first 4 ingredients in medium saucepan on medium for about 5 minutes until smooth and butter is melted. Remove from heat.

Add brown sugar, flour and vanilla. Stir until smooth. Add eggs, 1 at a time, beating well after each addition.

Add remaining 3 ingredients. Stir. Line bottom and sides of greased 9 x 9 inch (22 x 22 cm) pan with parchment paper. Pour batter into pan. Spread evenly. Bake in 350°F (175°C) oven for about 30 minutes until just firm. Let stand in pan on wire rack until cooled completely. Cuts into 81 squares.

1 square: 59 Calories; 3.1 g Total Fat (1.3 g Mono, 0.1 g Poly, 1.6 g Sat); 10 mg Cholesterol; 7 g Carbohydrate; trace Fibre; 1 g Protein; 22 mg Sodium

Pictured above.

Photo Legend next page:
Left: Sesame Ginger Cookies, page 80
Top Right: Chocolate Coconut Cookies, page 80
Bottom Right: Coconut Lime Macaroons, page 78

Walnut Caramel Squares

Soft bottom layer with a walnut and coconut topping.
Slight taste of cinnamon, too!

BOTTOM LAYER

All-purpose flour	1 cup	250 mL
Medium unsweetened coconut	1 cup	250 mL
Granulated sugar	1/2 cup	125 mL
Baking powder	2 tsp.	10 mL
Ground cinnamon	1/2 tsp.	2 mL
Salt	1/4 tsp.	1 mL
Butter (or hard margarine), melted	1/2 cup	125 mL

TOP LAYER

Large eggs	2	2
Vanilla	1 tsp.	5 mL
Medium unsweetened coconut	1 cup	250 mL
Brown sugar, packed	3/4 cup	175 mL
Chopped walnuts	2/3 cup	150 mL

Bottom Layer: Combine first 6 ingredients in medium bowl.

Add butter. Stir well. Press evenly in bottom of greased 9 × 13 inch (22 × 33 cm) pan. Bake in 350°F (175°C) oven for about 15 minutes until golden. Let stand for about 5 minutes until slightly cooled.

Top Layer: Beat eggs and vanilla with fork in medium bowl.

Add remaining 3 ingredients. Stir. Spoon over warm coconut layer in pan. Spread evenly. Bake for about 15 minutes until golden. Let stand in pan on wire rack until cooled completely. Cuts into 54 squares.

1 square: 77 Calories; 4.9 g Total Fat (0.9 g Mono, 0.7 g Poly, 3.1g Sat); 12 mg Cholesterol; 9 g Carbohydrate; trace Fibre; 2 g Protein; 46 mg Sodium

Pictured on page 85.

Pecan Apricot Points

Sweet triangles filled with chewy pieces of dried apricot and drizzled with white chocolate.

Can of sweetened condensed milk (see Glossary, page 9)	11 oz.	300 mL
Chopped dried apricots	1 cup	250 mL
Semi-sweet chocolate chips	1 cup	250 mL
Pecan pieces, toasted (see Tip, page 80)	1 cup	250 mL
Flake coconut, toasted (see Tip, page 80)	1 cup	250 mL
Salt, sprinkle		
White chocolate baking squares (1 oz., 28 g, each), chopped	3	3

Combine first 6 ingredients in large bowl. Line bottom and sides of greased 9 × 13 inch (22 × 33 cm) pan with parchment (not waxed) paper. Spoon pecan mixture into pan. Spread evenly. Cover with foil. Bake in 350°F (175°C) oven for 20 minutes. Remove foil. Bake for 10 to 15 minutes until firm and golden. Let stand in pan on wire rack until cooled completely. Remove from pan, discarding paper. Place on wire rack set on waxed paper.

Heat and stir white chocolate in small heavy saucepan on lowest heat until chocolate is almost melted. Do not overheat. Remove from heat. Stir until smooth. Drizzle or pipe with melted chocolate. Let stand until chocolate is set. Cut into 8 rows crosswise and 3 rows lengthwise, making 24 rectangles. Cut each rectangle diagonally to make 2 triangles, for a total of 48 triangles.

1 triangle: 89 Calories; 5.2 g Total Fat (1.8 g Mono, 0.5 g Poly, 2.7 g Sat); 3 mg Cholesterol; 11 g Carbohydrate; 1 g Fibre; 1 g Protein; 13 mg Sodium

Pictured on page 85.

Top: Pecan Apricot Points, above
Bottom: Walnut Caramel Squares, this page

Caramel Nut Squares

*Nutty, chewy pecan squares that are
sweet and oh, so sticky.*

BOTTOM LAYER

All-purpose flour	1 cup	250 mL
Finely chopped pecans	1 cup	250 mL
Quick-cooking rolled oats (not instant)	3/4 cup	175 mL
Brown sugar, packed	2/3 cup	150 mL
Baking powder	1/2 tsp.	2 mL
Salt	1/2 tsp.	2 mL
Butter (or hard margarine), softened	1/2 cup	125 mL
Large egg, fork-beaten	1	1

TOP LAYER

Miniature marshmallows	3 cups	750 mL
Caramel ice cream topping	2/3 cup	150 mL
Chopped pecans	1 1/3 cups	325 mL

Bottom Layer: Combine first 6 ingredients in large bowl.

Cut in butter until mixture resembles coarse crumbs. Add egg. Stir well. Press evenly in bottom of greased 9 × 13 inch (22 × 33 cm) pan. Bake in 350°F (175°C) oven for 10 minutes.

Top Layer: Sprinkle marshmallows over hot crust. Drizzle ice cream topping over marshmallows. Sprinkle with second amount of pecans. Bake for 20 to 25 minutes until golden brown. Let stand in pan on wire rack until cooled completely. Cut with hot, wet knife to prevent sticking. Cuts into 54 squares.

1 square: 122 Calories; 7 g Total Fat (3.5 g Mono, 1.2 g Poly, 1.8 g Sat); 11 mg Cholesterol; 15 g Carbohydrate; 1 g Fibre; 1 g Protein; 79 mg Sodium

Pictured on pages 86/87.

Top Left: Caramel Nut Squares, above
Top Right: Orange Raisin Squares, page 88
Bottom Right: Date Meringue Dreams, page 88

Orange Raisin Squares

Rich-tasting squares with the wonderful combination of orange and raisins.

BOTTOM LAYER

All-purpose flour	1 cup	250 mL
Butter (or hard margarine), softened	1/2 cup	125 mL
Granulated sugar	1/4 cup	60 mL
Cocoa, sifted if lumpy	3 tbsp.	50 mL

TOP LAYER

Large eggs	2	2
Coarsely chopped raisins	1 cup	250 mL
Flake coconut	1/3 cup	75 mL
Brown sugar, packed	1/4 cup	60 mL
Orange juice	2 tbsp.	30 mL
All-purpose flour	1 tbsp.	15 mL
Cocoa, sifted if lumpy	1 tbsp.	15 mL
Finely grated orange zest	1 tbsp.	15 mL
Baking powder	1/2 tsp.	2 mL
Salt	1/4 tsp.	1 mL

Bottom Layer: Combine all 4 ingredients in medium bowl until crumbly. Press evenly in bottom of ungreased 9 x 9 inch (22 x 22 cm) pan. Bake in 375°F (190°C) oven for 15 minutes.

Top Layer: Beat eggs in separate medium bowl until frothy.

Add remaining 9 ingredients. Stir well. Spread evenly over bottom layer in pan. Bake for 20 to 25 minutes until firm. Let stand in pan on wire rack until cooled completely. Cuts into 36 squares.

1 square: 74 Calories; 3.7 g Total Fat (0.9 g Mono, 0.2 g Poly, 2.3 g Sat); 19 mg Cholesterol; 10 g Carbohydrate; 1 g Fibre; 1 g Protein; 54 mg Sodium

Pictured on page 87.

Date Meringue Dreams

A tempting treat—nutty meringue over a soft date filling on a delicious almond base.

BOTTOM LAYER

All-purpose flour	1 1/2 cups	375 mL
Brown sugar, packed	1/3 cup	75 mL
Butter (or hard margarine), softened	1/4 cup	60 mL
Baking powder	1 tsp.	5 mL
Salt	1/4 tsp.	1 mL
Sour cream	1/4 cup	60 mL
Egg yolks (large)	2	2
Almond flavouring	1/4 tsp.	1 mL

MIDDLE LAYER

Apricot jam	3 tbsp.	50 mL
Chopped pitted dates, lightly packed	1 1/2 cups	375 mL
Sour cream	3/4 cup	175 mL
Finely grated orange zest	2 tsp.	10 mL

TOP LAYER

Egg whites (large)	2	2
Brown sugar, packed	1 cup	250 mL
Sliced almonds (with skins)	1/4 cup	60 mL

Bottom Layer: Combine first 5 ingredients in medium bowl until crumbly.

Combine sour cream, egg yolks and almond flavouring in small bowl. Add to flour mixture. Stir well. Press evenly in bottom of greased 9 x 9 inch (22 x 22 cm) pan. Bake in 350°F (175°C) oven for about 15 minutes until golden.

Middle Layer: Brush jam over hot crust.

Combine dates, sour cream and orange zest in medium bowl. Spoon over jam. Spread evenly.

Top Layer: Beat egg whites in separate small bowl until soft peaks form. Add brown sugar, 1/4 cup (60 mL) at a time while beating, until stiff peaks form and sugar is dissolved. Spread evenly over date mixture.

Sprinkle almonds over top. Bake for 25 to 30 minutes until golden. Let stand in pan on wire rack until cooled completely. Cut into 9 squares. Cut each square diagonally to make 2 triangles, for a total of 18 triangles.

1 triangle: 219 Calories; 6.2 g Total Fat (3.1 g Mono, 0.6 g Poly, 2 g Sat); 29 mg Cholesterol; 40 g Carbohydrate; 2 g Fibre; 3 g Protein; 107 mg Sodium

Pictured on page 87.

Chocolate-Filled Squares

A sure favourite for any chocolate lover! Distinctly layered square with a shortbread base.

BOTTOM LAYER

All-purpose flour	1 cup	250 mL
Butter (or hard margarine), softened	6 tbsp.	100 mL
Brown sugar, packed	3 tbsp.	50 mL
Baking powder	1/2 tsp.	2 mL
Large egg	1	1
Vanilla	1/2 tsp.	2 mL

MIDDLE LAYER

Semi-sweet chocolate chips	1 1/3 cups	325 mL

TOP LAYER

Large eggs	2	2
Granulated sugar	1/2 cup	125 mL
Butter (or hard margarine), melted	1/4 cup	60 mL
Vanilla	2 tsp.	10 mL
Finely chopped walnuts	3/4 cup	175 mL

Bottom Layer: Mix first 4 ingredients in medium bowl until crumbly.

Beat egg and vanilla in cup with fork. Add to flour mixture. Stir until just moistened. Spread evenly in greased 9 × 9 inch (22 × 22 cm) pan. Bake in 350°F (175°C) oven for about 10 minutes until firm.

Middle Layer: Sprinkle chocolate chips over bottom layer. Let stand for about 10 minutes until chips are softened. Gently spread in even layer.

Top Layer: Beat first 4 ingredients in medium bowl until smooth.

Add walnuts. Stir. Pour evenly over chocolate. Bake for 25 to 30 minutes until browned. Let stand in pan on wire rack until cooled completely. Cuts into 36 squares.

1 square: 114 Calories; 7.3 g Total Fat (2.1 g Mono, 1.3 g Poly, 3.5 g Sat); 27 mg Cholesterol; 11 g Carbohydrate; 1 g Fibre; 2 g Protein; 45 mg Sodium

Pictured on this page.

Muffins & Other Quick Breads

Baked fresh for an easy snack or left for midnight munchies,
these delicious recipes are sure to satisfy.
And you can even be prepared for a rainy day
—these recipes freeze well until they're needed.

Red Pepper Jalapeño Muffins

A spicy, moist cornmeal muffin that's perfect to serve warm with soup or salad, or bring cold to the next potluck!

Large red pepper, quartered (see Note)	1	1
All-purpose flour	1 1/2 cups	375 mL
Grated cheese mix (or equal amounts of Cheddar and Monterey Jack cheeses)	2/3 cup	150 mL
Yellow cornmeal	1/2 cup	125 mL
Granulated sugar	2 tbsp.	30 mL
Baking powder	1 tbsp.	15 mL
Ground cumin	1/4 tsp.	1 mL
Salt	1/4 tsp.	1 mL
Milk	1/2 cup	125 mL
Sour cream	1/4 cup	60 mL
Can of sliced pickled jalapeño peppers, drained and chopped	4 oz.	114 mL
Large egg, fork-beaten	1	1

Arrange red pepper pieces, skin-side up, on ungreased baking sheet. Broil 5 inches (12.5 cm) from heat for about 10 minutes, rearranging as necessary, until skins are blistered and blackened. Remove to small bowl. Cover with plastic wrap. Let sweat for about 15 minutes until cool enough to handle. Peel and discard skins. Chop finely. Set aside.

Combine next 7 ingredients in large bowl. Make a well in centre.

Beat remaining 4 ingredients in separate small bowl. Add to well. Add red pepper. Stir until just moistened. Grease 12 muffin cups with cooking spray. Fill cups 3/4 full. Bake in 375°F (190°C) oven for 20 to 25 minutes until wooden pick inserted in centre of muffin comes out clean. Let stand in pan for 5 minutes before removing to wire rack to cool. Serve warm or cold. Makes 12 muffins.

1 muffin: 140 Calories; 3.7 g Total Fat (1 g Mono, 0.3 g Poly, 2 g Sat); 27 mg Cholesterol; 22 g Carbohydrate; 1 g Fibre; 5 g Protein; 194 mg Sodium

Pictured on front and back cover.

Note: To speed preparation, purchase a jar of roasted red peppers. Use 2/3 cup (150 mL) drained, blotted dry and finely chopped; and omit first paragraph in method.

Cranberry Brie Muffins

Cheese, nuts and bits of cranberry give this muffin a tart flavour.

All-purpose flour	2 cups	500 mL
Granulated sugar	1 1/2 tbsp.	25 mL
Baking powder	1 tbsp.	15 mL
Salt	1/4 tsp.	1 mL
Brie cheese round, finely chopped (see Tip, below)	4 oz.	125 g
Sour cream	1/2 cup	125 mL
Whole cranberry sauce	1/2 cup	125 mL
Butter (or hard margarine), melted	1/3 cup	75 mL
Milk	1/4 cup	60 mL
Pecan pieces	1/3 cup	75 mL

Combine first 4 ingredients in large bowl.

Add Brie cheese. Stir. Make a well in centre.

Combine next 4 ingredients in medium bowl. Add to well. Stir until just moistened. Grease 12 muffin cups with cooking spray. Fill cups 3/4 full.

Divide and sprinkle pecans on each muffin. Bake in 375°F (190°C) oven for 20 to 25 minutes until wooden pick inserted in centre of muffin comes out clean but sticky from melted Brie. Let stand in pan for 5 minutes before removing to wire rack to cool. Makes 12 muffins.

1 muffin: 226 Calories; 12.1 g Total Fat (4.2 g Mono, 1 g Poly, 6.3 g Sat); 29 mg Cholesterol; 25 g Carbohydrate; 1 g Fibre; 5 g Protein; 274 mg Sodium

Pictured on front and back cover.

■ ■ ■

To cut a soft cheese such as Brie, chill for at least 1 hour and coat knife and cheese with flour before cutting.

Piña Colada Muffins

Scrumptious pineapple and coconut muffin that's moist and sweet! A tempting treat anytime.

Granulated sugar	1/2 cup	125 mL
Cooking oil	1/4 cup	60 mL
Large egg	1	1
Coconut flavouring	1 tsp.	5 mL
Reserved pineapple juice plus milk, to equal	3/4 cup	175 mL
Can of crushed pineapple, drained and juice reserved	8 oz.	227 mL
All-purpose flour	2 cups	500 mL
Medium unsweetened coconut	1/2 cup	125 mL
Baking powder	1 tbsp.	15 mL
Baking soda	1/2 tsp.	2 mL
Salt	1/2 tsp.	2 mL

Beat sugar, cooking oil and egg in large bowl for about 2 minutes until well combined.

Add coconut flavouring to pineapple juice mixture. Stir. Add to sugar mixture. Stir well.

Add pineapple. Stir.

Combine remaining 5 ingredients in medium bowl. Add to pineapple mixture. Stir until just moistened. Grease 12 muffin cups with cooking spray. Fill cups 3/4 full. Bake in 400°F (205°C) oven for about 15 minutes until wooden pick inserted in centre of muffin comes out clean. Let stand in pan for 5 minutes before removing to wire rack to cool. Makes 12 muffins.

1 muffin: 208 Calories; 8.2 g Total Fat (3.2 g Mono, 1.6 g Poly, 2.9 g Sat); 19 mg Cholesterol; 31 g Carbohydrate; 1 g Fibre; 4 g Protein; 260 mg Sodium

Pictured on page 95.

Drunken Apricot Muffins

Delicious almond-flavoured muffins sweetened with dried apricots.

Chopped dried apricots	3/4 cup	175 mL
Almond-flavoured liqueur (such as Amaretto)	1/3 cup	75 mL
Butter (or hard margarine), softened	1/3 cup	75 mL
Brown sugar, packed	3/4 cup	175 mL
Large eggs	2	2
Orange juice	3/4 cup	175 mL
Almond flavouring	1/2 tsp.	2 mL
All-purpose flour	2 cups	500 mL
Baking powder	1 tbsp.	15 mL
Salt	1/2 tsp.	2 mL

Heat and stir apricots and liqueur in small saucepan on medium until boiling. Remove from heat. Cover. Let stand for about 30 minutes until cool and liquid is almost absorbed.

Beat butter and brown sugar in large bowl until light and creamy. Add eggs, 1 at a time, beating well after each addition.

Add orange juice, almond flavouring and apricot mixture. Stir.

Combine flour, baking powder and salt in medium bowl. Add to apricot mixture. Stir until just moistened. Grease 12 muffin cups with cooking spray. Fill cups 3/4 full. Bake in 400°F (205°C) oven for 15 to 18 minutes until golden brown and wooden pick inserted in centre of muffin comes out clean. Let stand in pan for 5 minutes before removing to wire rack to cool. Makes 12 muffins.

1 muffin: 239 Calories; 6.5 g Total Fat (1.9 g Mono, 0.4 g Poly, 3.7 g Sat); 50 mg Cholesterol; 39 g Carbohydrate; 1 g Fibre; 4 g Protein; 264 mg Sodium

Pictured on page 94.

Raspberry Pear Muffins

Tart raspberries in a streusel-topped pear muffin. Delicious!

All-purpose flour	2 cups	500 mL
Brown sugar, packed	3/4 cup	175 mL
Baking powder	1 tbsp.	15 mL
Salt	1/4 tsp.	1 mL
Frozen whole raspberries	1 1/3 cups	325 mL
Coarsely grated fresh pear	2/3 cup	150 mL
Buttermilk (or reconstituted from powder)	1/3 cup	75 mL
Cooking oil	1/3 cup	75 mL
Large eggs	3	3
Finely grated lemon zest	1 tsp.	5 mL
CINNAMON STREUSEL TOPPING		
All-purpose flour	1/3 cup	75 mL
Brown sugar, packed	3 tbsp.	50 mL
Ground cinnamon	1/2 tsp.	2 mL
Cold butter (or hard margarine), cut up	3 tbsp.	50 mL

Combine first 4 ingredients in large bowl.

Add raspberries and pear. Stir until coated. Make a well in centre.

Beat next 4 ingredients in small bowl. Add to well. Stir until just moistened. Grease 12 muffin cups with cooking spray. Fill cups 3/4 full.

Cinnamon Streusel Topping: Combine first 3 ingredients in separate small bowl. Cut in butter until mixture resembles coarse crumbs. Makes about 3/4 cup (175 ml) topping. Divide and sprinkle over each muffin. Bake in 375°F (190°C) oven for about 20 minutes until wooden pick inserted in centre of muffin comes out clean but sticky from raspberries. Let stand in pan for 5 minutes before removing to wire rack to cool. Makes 12 muffins.

1 muffin: 279 Calories; 11 g Total Fat (5.1 g Mono, 2.3 g Poly, 2.7 g Sat); 62 mg Cholesterol; 41 g Carbohydrate; 2 g Fibre; 5 g Protein; 203 mg Sodium

Pictured on page 95.

Strawberry Muffins

Biscuit-textured muffins with bits of strawberry that explode in your mouth with every bite!

Butter (or hard margarine), softened	1/4 cup	60 mL
Granulated sugar	1/2 cup	125 mL
Large egg	1	1
Chopped fresh (or whole frozen, thawed and chopped) strawberries	1 1/4 cups	300 mL
Strawberry yogurt (not fat-free)	1 cup	250 mL
Vanilla	1/2 tsp.	2 mL
All-purpose flour	2 cups	500 mL
Baking powder	1 tbsp.	15 mL
Salt	1/2 tsp.	2 mL

Beat butter and sugar in large bowl until light and creamy. Add egg. Beat until well combined.

Add strawberries, yogurt and vanilla. Stir.

Combine flour, baking powder and salt in small bowl. Add to strawberry mixture. Stir until just moistened. Grease 12 muffin cups with cooking spray. Fill cups 3/4 full. Bake in 400°F (205°C) oven for about 20 minutes until wooden pick inserted in centre of muffin comes out clean. Let stand in pan for 5 minutes before removing to wire rack to cool. Makes 12 muffins.

1 muffin: 188 Calories; 5.4 g Total Fat (1.5 g Mono, 0.4 g Poly, 3.1 g Sat); 31 mg Cholesterol; 31 g Carbohydrate; 1 g Fibre; 4 g Protein; 252 mg Sodium

Pictured on page 94.

Photo Legend next page:
Top Left: Drunken Apricot Muffins, page 92
Top Right: Piña Colada Muffins, page 92
Centre Left: Strawberry Muffins, above
Bottom Right: Raspberry Pear Muffins, this page

Smoked Cheese Apple Muffins

Golden muffins with cheese and nuts on top,
and a hint of sweetness inside.

All-purpose flour	1 1/2 cups	375 mL
Yellow cornmeal	1/2 cup	125 mL
Granulated sugar	1 tbsp.	15 mL
Baking powder	1 tbsp.	15 mL
Salt	1/4 tsp.	1 mL
Grated smoked cheese (such as Applewood Smoked Cheddar)	1 cup	250 mL
Finely chopped, peeled apple	1 cup	250 mL
Large eggs	2	2
Buttermilk (or reconstituted from powder)	1 cup	250 mL
Cooking oil	1/3 cup	75 mL
Grated smoked cheese (such as Applewood Smoked Cheddar)	1/2 cup	125 mL
Pecan pieces	1/2 cup	125 mL
Brown sugar, packed	2 tbsp.	30 mL

Combine first 5 ingredients in large bowl.

Add first amount of smoked cheese and apple. Stir. Make a well in centre.

Beat eggs with fork in small bowl. Add buttermilk and cooking oil. Stir. Add to well. Stir until just moistened. Grease 12 muffin cups with cooking spray. Fill cups until full.

Combine second amount of smoked cheese, pecans and brown sugar in separate small bowl. Divide and sprinkle over each muffin. Bake in 375°F (190°C) oven for 20 to 25 minutes until wooden pick inserted in centre of muffin comes out clean. Let stand in pan for 5 minutes before removing to wire rack to cool. Makes 12 muffins.

1 muffin: 270 Calories; 15.9 g Total Fat (7.6 g Mono, 3.1 g Poly, 4.3 g Sat);
    52 mg Cholesterol; 25 g Carbohydrate; 1 g Fibre; 8 g Protein; 269 mg Sodium

Pictured on front cover.

Mango Macadamia Muffins

An appetizing muffin with pieces of mango and toasted macadamia nuts. They will make you say "Mmmm!"

Finely diced dried mango	2/3 cup	150 mL
Boiling water	1 cup	250 mL
All-purpose flour	2 cups	500 mL
Granulated sugar	1 cup	250 mL
Chopped macadamia nuts, toasted (see Tip, page 80)	1/2 cup	125 mL
Baking powder	1 1/2 tsp.	7 mL
Baking soda	1 tsp.	5 mL
Salt	1/2 tsp.	2 mL
Buttermilk (or reconstituted from powder)	2/3 cup	150 mL
Butter (or hard margarine), melted	1/2 cup	125 mL
Large eggs, fork-beaten	2	2
Vanilla	1 tsp.	5 mL
Sweetened flaked coconut	1/4 cup	60 mL

Stir mango and boiling water in small bowl. Let stand for 10 minutes until mango is softened. Drain. Set aside.

Combine next 6 ingredients in large bowl. Make a well in centre.

Add next 4 ingredients and mango to well. Stir until just moistened. Grease 12 muffin cups with cooking spray. Fill cups until full.

Sprinkle 1 tsp. (5 mL) coconut over each muffin. Bake in 400°F (205°C) oven for about 15 minutes until wooden pick inserted in centre of muffin comes out clean. Let stand in pan for 5 minutes before removing to wire rack to cool. Makes 12 muffins.

1 muffin: 312 Calories; 14.3 g Total Fat (6.2 g Mono, 0.6 g Poly, 6.6 g Sat);
    58 mg Cholesterol; 43 g Carbohydrate; 2 g Fibre; 5 g Protein; 366 mg Sodium

Pictured on page 97.

White Chocolate Muffins

A tempting treat flavoured with white chocolate and honey.

All-purpose flour	2 cups	500 mL
White chocolate chips	1 1/4 cups	300 mL
Granulated sugar	1/3 cup	75 mL
Baking powder	4 tsp.	20 mL
Chocolate-covered sponge toffee candy bars (such as Crunchie), 1 1/2 oz. (44 g) each, chopped	2	2
Buttermilk (or reconstituted from powder)	1 cup	250 mL
Large egg	1	1
Cooking oil	1/4 cup	60 mL
Liquid honey	3 tbsp.	50 mL

Combine first 5 ingredients in large bowl. Make a well in centre.

Beat remaining 4 ingredients in small bowl. Add to well. Stir until just moistened. Grease 12 muffin cups with cooking spray. Fill cups 3/4 full. Bake in 375°F (190°C) oven for about 20 minutes until wooden pick inserted in centre of muffin comes out clean. Let stand in pan for 5 minutes before removing to wire rack to cool. Makes 12 muffins.

1 muffin: 316 Calories; 13.9 g Total Fat (4.9 g Mono, 1.8 g Poly, 4 g Sat); 27 mg Cholesterol; 44 g Carbohydrate; 1 g Fibre; 5 g Protein; 186 mg Sodium

Pictured below.

Top Left and Bottom Right: White Chocolate Muffins, this page
Top Right: Mango Macadamia Muffins, page 96

Tomato Cheese Biscuits

A savoury, cheesy biscuit—delicious
served with the flavoured butter.

All-purpose flour	2 cups	500 mL
Baking powder	1 tbsp.	15 mL
Cold butter (or hard margarine)	2 tbsp.	30 mL
Grated medium white (or regular) Cheddar cheese	1 cup	250 mL
Buttermilk (or reconstituted from powder)	1 cup	250 mL
Sun-dried tomato pesto	1/4 cup	60 mL
Egg yolk (large), fork-beaten	1	1
SPICED BUTTER		
Butter (not margarine), softened	1/2 cup	125 mL
Chopped fresh chives	2 tbsp.	30 mL
Chili powder	1 tsp.	5 mL

Combine flour and baking powder in large bowl. Cut in butter until mixture resembles coarse crumbs.

Add Cheddar cheese, buttermilk and pesto. Stir until soft dough forms. Press (do not roll out) mixture onto lightly floured surface to 3/4 inch (2 cm) thickness. Cut 2 1/4 inch (5.7 cm) rounds from dough. Arrange, just touching, in greased 9 × 9 inch (22 × 22 cm) pan.

Brush tops with egg yolk. Bake in 450°F (230°C) oven for about 15 minutes until tops and bottoms are golden. Let stand in pan for 5 minutes before removing to wire rack to cool.

Spiced Butter: Combine butter, chives and chili powder in small bowl. Makes 1/2 cup (125 mL) spiced butter. Serve with biscuits. Makes 10 biscuits.

1 biscuit (with 2 1/2 tsp., 12 mL, Spiced Butter): 275 Calories; 17.5 g Total Fat (5.1 g Mono, 0.8 g Poly, 10.4 g Sat); 68 mg Cholesterol; 23 g Carbohydrate; 1 g Fibre; 7 g Protein; 347 mg Sodium

Pictured on page 99.

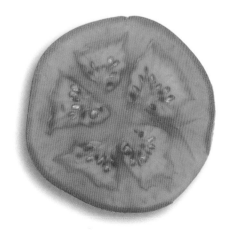

Savoury Sweet Onion Muffins

Soft, golden muffins packed with a flavourful filling.
Truly sensational!

Cooking oil	1 tbsp.	15 mL
Thinly sliced onion	2 cups	500 mL
Granulated sugar	1 tsp.	5 mL
Balsamic vinegar	1 tsp.	5 mL
Dried crushed chilies	1 tsp.	5 mL
All-purpose flour	2 1/2 cups	625 mL
Chopped salami (about 2 oz., 57 g)	1/2 cup	125 mL
Goat (chèvre) cheese, cut up (about 1/2 cup, 125 mL)	3 oz.	85 g
Baking powder	4 tsp.	20 mL
Chopped fresh rosemary leaves (or 1/2 tsp., 2 mL, dried)	2 tsp.	10 mL
Salt	1/4 tsp.	1 mL
Buttermilk (or reconstituted from powder)	1 cup	250 mL
Cooking oil	3 tbsp.	50 mL
Large eggs	2	2

Heat first amount of cooking oil in large frying pan on medium. Add onion. Cook for about 15 minutes, stirring often, until soft and golden.

Add sugar, vinegar and chilies. Stir. Transfer to large bowl. Cool.

Add next 6 ingredients to onion mixture. Toss until onion is coated with flour. Make a well in centre.

Beat buttermilk, second amount of cooking oil and eggs with fork in small bowl. Add to well. Stir until just moistened. Grease 12 muffin cups with cooking spray. Fill cups until full. Bake in 375°F (190°C) oven for about 25 minutes until wooden pick inserted in centre of muffin comes out clean but sticky from melted cheese. Let stand in pan for 5 minutes before removing to wire rack to cool. Best served warm. Makes 12 muffins.

1 muffin: 206 Calories; 8.3 g Total Fat (3.9 g Mono, 1.7 g Poly, 2.1 g Sat); 43 mg Cholesterol; 26 g Carbohydrate; 1 g Fibre; 7 g Protein; 284 mg Sodium

Pictured on page 99.

Top: Tomato Cheese Biscuits, this page
Bottom Left: Spiced Butter, this page
Bottom Right: Savoury Sweet Onion Muffins, above

Jalapeño Cheese Swirls

Spicy salsa and cheese swirled throughout a deliciously tender biscuit.

All-purpose flour	3 cups	750 mL
Baking powder	2 tbsp.	30 mL
Salt	1/2 tsp.	2 mL
Cold butter (or hard margarine), cut up	1/3 cup	75 mL
Chopped fresh cilantro or parsley (or 1 1/2 tsp., 7 mL, dried)	2 tbsp.	30 mL
Milk, approximately	1 cup	250 mL
SPICY CHEESE FILLING		
Ricotta cheese	1/2 cup	125 mL
Grated sharp Cheddar cheese	1/2 cup	125 mL
Thick and chunky salsa	1/2 cup	125 mL
Sliced pickled jalapeño peppers, drained and finely chopped	1 – 2 tbsp.	15 – 30 mL
Garlic cloves, minced (or 1/2 tsp., 2 mL, powder)	2	2
Pepper, sprinkle		

Combine flour, baking powder and salt in large bowl. Cut in butter until mixture resembles coarse crumbs.

Add cilantro. Stir, adding enough milk to form soft dough. Turn out onto lightly floured surface. Knead gently 4 or 5 times until dough just comes together. Gently roll out on waxed paper on dampened work surface to 10 x 15 inch (25 x 38 cm) rectangle.

Spicy Cheese Filling: Combine all 6 ingredients in medium bowl. Makes 1 1/4 cups (300 mL) filling. Spread over dough, leaving 1 inch (2.5 cm) edge on long side farthest from you. Roll up, jelly roll-style, from long side using waxed paper as guide. Pinch seam against roll to seal. Cut dough into 16 slices using floured knife. Arrange slices cut-side down, about 1 1/2 inches (3.8 cm) apart, on 2 greased baking sheets. Bake in 375°F (190°C) oven for 15 to 20 minutes, switching baking sheet positions at halftime, until golden. Let stand on baking sheets for 5 minutes before removing to wire racks to cool. Makes 16 swirls.

1 swirl: 166 Calories; 6.8 g Total Fat (1.9 g Mono, 0.3 g Poly, 4.1 g Sat); 20 mg Cholesterol; 21 g Carbohydrate; 1 g Fibre; 5 g Protein; 315 mg Sodium

Pictured on page 101.

Top Left: Irish Soda Bread, page 102
Top Right: Onion Walnut Biscuits, page 102
Bottom Right: Jalapeño Cheese Swirls, above

Irish Soda Bread

*A buttery, light, moist bread with a muffin-like texture.
Perfect served with a rich beef stew.*

All-purpose flour	2 1/4 cups	550 mL
Granulated sugar	1 tbsp.	15 mL
Baking powder	1 tbsp.	15 mL
Baking soda	1 tsp.	5 mL
Salt	1 tsp.	5 mL
Cold butter (or hard margarine), cut up	1/3 cup	75 mL
Buttermilk (or reconstituted from powder)	1 1/2 cups	375 mL
Large egg	1	1
All-purpose flour, approximately	1/4 cup	60 mL

Combine first 5 ingredients in large bowl. Cut in butter until mixture resembles coarse crumbs. Make a well in centre.

Beat buttermilk and egg with fork in small bowl. Add to well. Stir until soft, sticky dough forms. Turn out onto lightly floured surface.

Dust dough with second amount of flour. Gently shape into ball. Place in greased 8 inch (20 cm) springform pan. Gently press dough out to edge. Cut '+' on top of dough, about 1/2 inch (12 mm) deep and 5 inches (12.5 cm) across, using sharp knife. Bake in 400°F (205°C) oven for 30 to 35 minutes until golden and wooden pick inserted in centre comes out clean. Let stand in pan for 5 minutes before removing to wire rack to cool. Cuts into 8 wedges.

1 wedge: 258 Calories; 9.5 g Total Fat (2.7 g Mono, 0.6 g Poly, 5.6 g Sat);
    50 mg Cholesterol; 36 g Carbohydrate; 1 g Fibre; 7 g Protein; 738 mg Sodium

Pictured on pages 100/101.

Onion Walnut Biscuits

*Golden drop biscuits with the sweetness of
caramelized onions, the fragrance of fresh rosemary
and the crunch of walnuts.*

Butter (or hard margarine)	2 tbsp.	30 mL
Thinly sliced onion	2 cups	500 mL
Brown sugar, packed	2 tbsp.	30 mL
Salt	1/4 tsp.	1 mL
All-purpose flour	2 cups	500 mL
Baking powder	1 tbsp.	15 mL
Salt	1/4 tsp.	1 mL
Walnut pieces, toasted (see Tip, page 80)	3/4 cup	175 mL
Finely chopped fresh rosemary leaves	1 tsp.	5 mL
Pepper	1/4 tsp.	1 mL
Milk	2/3 cup	150 mL
Sour cream	1/2 cup	125 mL
Large egg	1	1

Melt butter in large frying pan on medium-low. Add onion. Cook for about 20 minutes, stirring often, until soft and golden.

Add brown sugar and first amount of salt. Stir until brown sugar is dissolved. Set aside.

Combine next 6 ingredients in large bowl. Stir until walnuts are coated. Make a well in centre.

Beat milk, sour cream and egg with fork in small bowl. Add to well. Add onion mixture. Stir until very soft, sticky dough forms. Drop by 1/4 cup (60 mL) amounts, about 1 1/2 inches (3.8 cm) apart, onto greased 11 x 17 inch (28 x 43 cm) baking sheet. Bake on top rack in 450°F (230°C) oven for about 15 minutes until bottoms are golden. Let stand on baking sheet for 5 minutes before removing to wire rack to cool. Serve warm. Makes 12 biscuits.

1 biscuit: 168 Calories; 6.3 g Total Fat (1.7 g Mono, 1.7 g Poly, 2.5 g Sat);
    28 mg Cholesterol; 23 g Carbohydrate; 1 g Fibre; 5 g Protein; 230 mg Sodium

Pictured on page 101.

Sesame Beer Bread

A hearty bread coated in sesame seeds, with a subtle beer flavour. Good alongside soup. Because there's no fat, should be eaten the same day.

All-purpose flour	3 1/4 cups	800 mL
Baking powder	1 tbsp.	15 mL
Granulated sugar	1 tbsp.	15 mL
Salt	2 tsp.	10 mL
Baking soda	1/2 tsp.	2 mL
Can of light beer	12 1/2 oz.	355 mL
Milk	1 1/4 tsp.	6 mL
Sesame seeds	1 tbsp.	15 mL

Combine first 5 ingredients in large bowl. Make a well in centre.

Add beer to well. Stir until soft, sticky dough forms. Turn out onto lightly floured surface. Gently shape to fit greased 9 x 5 x 3 inch (22 x 12.5 x 7.5 cm) loaf pan. Place dough in pan. Press into corners if necessary.

Brush top of loaf with milk. Sprinkle with sesame seeds. Bake in 375°F (190°C) oven for about 40 minutes until golden brown and hollow sounding when tapped. Cuts into 16 slices.

1 slice: 111 Calories; 0.6 g Total Fat (0.1 g Mono, 0.2 g Poly, 0.1 g Sat); 0 mg Cholesterol; 22 g Carbohydrate; 1 g Fibre; 3 g Protein; 408 mg Sodium

Pictured below.

Apple Streusel Coffee Cake

Tart, apple-flavoured coffee cake with the fragrance of a sugar and cinnamon topping to stir memories and taste buds.

| White vinegar | 2 tbsp. | 30 mL |
| Milk, approximately | 1 3/4 cups | 425 mL |

SPICY STREUSEL TOPPING		
Granulated sugar	2/3 cup	150 mL
All-purpose flour	1/2 cup	125 mL
Ground cinnamon	2 tsp.	10 mL
Ground nutmeg	1/4 tsp.	1 mL
Cold butter (or hard margarine)	1/4 cup	60 mL

CAKE		
Butter (or hard margarine), softened	3/4 cup	175 mL
Granulated sugar	1 3/4 cups	425 mL
Large eggs	2	2
Vanilla	1 tsp.	5 mL
All-purpose flour	3 cups	750 mL
Baking powder	2 tsp.	10 mL
Baking soda	1 tsp.	5 mL
Salt	1/4 tsp.	1 mL
Medium cooking apples (such as McIntosh), peeled, cored and thinly sliced	2	2

Measure vinegar into 2 cup (500 mL) liquid measure. Add milk to equal 1 3/4 cups (425 mL). Let stand for 10 minutes to sour.

Spicy Streusel Topping: Combine first 4 ingredients in small bowl. Cut in butter until mixture resembles coarse crumbs. Makes 1 3/4 cups (425 mL) topping.

Cake: Beat butter and sugar in large bowl until light and creamy. Add eggs, 1 at a time, beating well after each addition. Add vanilla. Stir.

Combine next 4 ingredients in medium bowl. Add flour mixture to butter mixture in 4 additions, alternating with milk mixture in 3 additions, beginning and ending with flour mixture. Spoon 1/2 of batter into greased 9 × 13 inch (22 × 33 cm) pan. Spread evenly.

Arrange apple slices close together in single layer over batter. Sprinkle about 1/2 cup (125 mL) topping over apples. Spoon remaining 1/2 of batter over top. Spread evenly. Sprinkle with remaining streusel topping. Bake in 350°F (175°C) oven for about 55 minutes until wooden pick inserted in centre comes out clean. Cuts into 15 pieces.

1 piece: 394 Calories; 14 g Total Fat (4.1 g Mono, 0.7 g Poly, 8.6 g Sat);
   65 mg Cholesterol; 62 g Carbohydrate; 1 g Fibre; 5 g Protein; 332 mg Sodium

Pictured on page 105.

Apricot Almond Loaf

Sweet apricot and crunchy almonds combine in this moist, dense loaf. The loaf needs to season for two to six weeks.

Orange juice	3/4 cup	175 mL
Chopped dried apricots	1 1/2 cups	375 mL
All-purpose flour	1 2/3 cups	400 mL
Slivered almonds, chopped and toasted (see Tip, page 80)	3/4 cup	175 mL
Baking powder	2 tsp.	10 mL
Ground cinnamon	1/8 tsp.	0.5 mL
Ground nutmeg	1/8 tsp.	0.5 mL
Ground cloves	1/16 tsp.	0.5 mL
Butter (or hard margarine), softened	1/3 cup	75 mL
Granulated sugar	1/3 cup	75 mL
Brown sugar, packed	1/4 cup	60 mL
Large eggs	2	2
Vanilla	1/2 tsp.	2 mL
Almond flavouring	3/4 tsp.	4 mL
Cheesecloth, enough to wrap loaf in double thickness		
Almond-flavoured liqueur (such as Amaretto)	1/4 cup	60 mL

Pour orange juice over apricots in medium saucepan. Bring to a boil. Remove from heat. Let stand for 5 minutes.

Combine next 6 ingredients in medium bowl. Set aside.

Beat butter and both sugars in large bowl until light and creamy. Add eggs, 1 at a time, beating well after each addition. Add vanilla and almond flavouring. Stir. Add flour mixture to butter mixture in 3 additions, alternating with apricot mixture in 2 additions, beginning and ending with flour mixture. Do not overmix. Turn into greased 9 × 5 × 3 inch (22 × 12.5 × 7.5 cm) loaf pan. Bake in 350°F (175°C) oven for 50 to 60 minutes until wooden pick inserted in centre comes out clean. Cover loaf with foil if starting to get dark. Let stand in pan for 10 minutes before removing to wire rack to cool.

Moisten cheesecloth with liqueur. Wrap loaf in cheesecloth. Wrap in waxed paper or foil. Store in cool place for 2 to 6 weeks. Check weekly and remoisten cheesecloth if necessary. Cuts into 16 slices.

1 slice: 211 Calories; 8.3 g Total Fat (3.6 g Mono, 1 g Poly, 3.1 g Sat);
   38 mg Cholesterol; 29 g Carbohydrate; 2 g Fibre; 4 g Protein; 99 mg Sodium

Pictured on page 105.

Top: Apricot Almond Loaf, above
Bottom: Apple Streusel Coffee Cake, this page

Cream Cheese Tea Ring

*Light and fluffy biscuit dough with a soft
cream cheese and fruit filling. Fabulous!*

Block of cream cheese, softened	8 oz.	250 g
Granulated sugar	1/4 cup	60 mL
Vanilla	1/2 tsp.	2 mL
FRUIT BREAD		
All-purpose flour	2 cups	500 mL
Granulated sugar	2 tbsp.	30 mL
Baking powder	4 tsp.	20 mL
Salt	3/4 tsp.	4 mL
Cold butter (or hard margarine), cut up	1/4 cup	60 mL
Milk, approximately	3/4 cup	175 mL
Chopped pecans (or walnuts or almonds)	1/3 cup	75 mL
Chopped raisins	1/3 cup	75 mL
Chopped red glazed cherries	1/3 cup	75 mL
ALMOND GLAZE		
Icing (confectioner's) sugar	1/2 cup	125 mL
Almond flavouring	1/4 tsp.	1 mL
Milk, approximately	1 tbsp.	15 mL
Chopped pecans (or walnuts or almonds), toasted (see Tip, page 80), optional	1 tbsp.	15 mL

Beat cream cheese, sugar and vanilla in small bowl until
smooth. Set aside.

Fruit Bread: Combine first 4 ingredients in large bowl. Cut in
butter until mixture resembles coarse crumbs.

Stir, adding enough milk until soft dough forms. Turn out onto
lightly floured surface. Roll out to 10 x 14 inch (25 x 35 cm)
rectangle. Spread with cream cheese mixture, leaving 3/4 inch
(2 cm) edge.

Sprinkle pecans, raisins and cherries over cream cheese
mixture. Roll up, jelly roll-style, from long side. Press seam
against roll to seal. Shape into ring. Place, seam-side down, on
greased baking sheet. Pinch ends together to seal.

Cut ring 14 times from outside
edge to within 1 inch (2.5 cm)
of centre using scissors.

Turn each cut wedge on its
side, all in the same direction,
allowing them to overlap.

Bake in 425°F (220°C) oven for 15 to 20 minutes until golden
brown. Let stand on baking sheet on wire rack for about
30 minutes until cool.

Almond Glaze: Combine icing sugar and almond flavouring in
small bowl. Stir, adding enough milk until smooth, barely
pourable consistency. Makes about 1/4 cup (60 mL) glaze.
Drizzle or pipe over tea ring.

Sprinkle with pecans. Cuts into 14 pieces.

1 piece: 254 Calories; 12.1 g Total Fat (4.1 g Mono, 0.9 g Poly, 6.4 g Sat);
   30 mg Cholesterol; 33 g Carbohydrate; 1 g Fibre; 4 g Protein; 330 mg Sodium

Pictured on pages 108/109.

Maple Pumpkin Loaf

You'll love this slightly sweet, maple-flavoured loaf filled with chewy pieces of cranberry.

Orange juice	2/3 cup	150 mL
Dried cranberries	2/3 cup	150 mL
All-purpose flour	2 1/2 cups	625 mL
Baking powder	2 1/2 tsp.	12 mL
Baking soda	1 tsp.	5 mL
Salt	1/4 tsp.	1 mL
Butter (or hard margarine), softened	1/3 cup	75 mL
Brown sugar, packed	1/3 cup	75 mL
Large eggs	2	2
Can of pure pumpkin (no spices)	14 oz.	398 mL
Maple (or maple-flavoured) syrup	1 cup	250 mL
Maple (or maple-flavoured) syrup	1/2 cup	125 mL
Chopped pecans, toasted (see Tip, page 80)	3 tbsp.	50 mL

Heat and stir orange juice and cranberries in small saucepan on medium until just boiling. Remove from heat. Let stand for about 30 minutes until cooled to room temperature.

Combine next 4 ingredients in large bowl. Make a well in centre.

Beat butter and brown sugar in medium bowl until light and creamy. Add eggs, 1 at a time, beating well after each addition.

Add pumpkin and first amount of maple syrup. Beat until smooth. Add to well. Add orange juice mixture. Stir until just moistened. Line bottom and sides of lightly greased 9 x 5 x 3 inch (22 x 12.5 x 7.5 cm) loaf pan with parchment (not waxed) paper, leaving 1 1/2 inch (3.8 cm) overhang on each side. Spoon batter into pan. Spread evenly. Bake in 350°F (175°C) oven for 70 to 75 minutes until wooden pick inserted in centre comes out clean. Remove pan to wire rack. Run knife around loaf to loosen. Do not remove from pan.

Boil second amount of maple syrup in small heavy saucepan on medium for 3 to 5 minutes until slightly reduced and thickened. Carefully pour hot syrup evenly over loaf. Immediately sprinkle with pecans. Let stand in pan on wire rack for 30 minutes. Lift loaf from pan using parchment paper edges as handles. Set on wire rack to cool completely, discarding parchment paper. Cuts into 16 slices.

1 slice: 253 Calories; 6 g Total Fat (2 g Mono, 0.6 g Poly, 2.9 g Sat);
38 mg Cholesterol; 48 g Carbohydrate; 2 g Fibre; 4 g Protein; 231 mg Sodium

Pictured on page 108.

Orange Loaf

Sensational, delicate loaf with wonderful orange flavour. Lovely and yummy!

Granulated sugar	1 cup	250 mL
Cooking oil	1/4 cup	60 mL
Large egg	1	1
Vanilla	1 tsp.	5 mL
Orange juice	1 cup	250 mL
Finely grated orange zest	3 tbsp.	50 mL
All-purpose flour	2 1/2 cups	625 mL
Baking powder	1 tbsp.	15 mL
Salt	1/2 tsp.	2 mL

Beat first 4 ingredients in large bowl. Add orange juice and zest. Stir until well combined.

Combine flour, baking powder and salt in medium bowl. Add to orange mixture. Stir until just moistened. Turn into greased 9 x 5 x 3 inch (22 x 12.5 x 7.5 cm) loaf pan. Bake in 350°F (175°C) oven for about 45 minutes until wooden pick inserted in centre comes out clean. Let stand in pan for 10 minutes before removing to wire rack to cool. Cuts into 16 slices.

1 slice: 172 Calories; 4.2 g Total Fat (2.3 g Mono, 1.2 g Poly, 0.4 g Sat);
13 mg Cholesterol; 31 g Carbohydrate; 1 g Fibre; 3 g Protein; 82 mg Sodium

Pictured on page 109.

Photo Legend next page:
Top Right: Cream Cheese Tea Ring, page 106
Left: Maple Pumpkin Loaf, this page
Bottom Right: Orange Loaf, above

Sugar-Capped Rhubarb Loaf

A moist, tart rhubarb and orange loaf crusted with sparkling sugar. Great to make when fresh rhubarb is in season.

Milk	3/4 cup	175 mL
White vinegar	2 tsp.	10 mL
Brown sugar, packed	1 1/3 cups	325 mL
Cooking oil	1/2 cup	125 mL
Large egg	1	1
Finely grated orange zest	1 tbsp.	15 mL
Vanilla	1 tsp.	5 mL
All-purpose flour	2 1/2 cups	625 mL
Baking powder	1 1/2 tsp.	7 mL
Baking soda	1/2 tsp.	2 mL
Salt	1/2 tsp.	2 mL
Finely diced fresh rhubarb	2 cups	500 mL
Butter (not margarine), melted	2 tsp.	10 mL
Granulated sugar	1/3 cup	75 mL

Combine milk and vinegar in 1 cup (250 mL) liquid measure. Let stand for 10 minutes to sour.

Beat next 5 ingredients in large bowl until well combined. Add milk mixture. Stir.

Combine next 4 ingredients in medium bowl. Add to brown sugar mixture. Stir.

Add rhubarb. Stir until just moistened. Line bottom of greased 9 x 5 x 3 inch (22 x 12.5 x 7.5 cm) loaf pan with waxed paper. Turn batter into pan. Spread evenly.

Combine butter and sugar in small bowl until crumbly. Sprinkle over top of batter in thick layer. Bake in 350°F (175°C) oven for 1 1/4 to 1 1/2 hours until top has domed and wooden pick inserted in centre comes out clean. Let stand in pan for 10 minutes before removing to wire rack to cool. Cuts into 16 slices.

1 slice: 247 Calories; 8.4 g Total Fat (4.6 g Mono, 2.3 g Poly, 1 g Sat); 15 mg Cholesterol; 41 g Carbohydrate; 1 g Fibre; 3 g Protein; 173 mg Sodium

Pictured on front and back cover.

Lemon Coffee Cake

Light coffee cake with crumb topping and a slightly sweet lemon taste. Serve with whipped cream and lemon curd.

Milk	1 cup	250 mL
Lemon juice	1 tbsp.	15 mL
Butter (or hard margarine), softened	1/2 cup	125 mL
Granulated sugar	1/2 cup	125 mL
Large eggs	2	2
Finely grated lemon peel	1 tbsp.	15 mL
Vanilla	1 tsp.	5 mL
All-purpose flour	2 cups	500 mL
Baking powder	1 1/2 tsp.	7 mL
Baking soda	1/2 tsp.	2 mL
Salt	1/4 tsp.	1 mL
LEMON STREUSEL TOPPING		
All-purpose flour	1/2 cup	125 mL
Brown sugar, packed	1/4 cup	60 mL
Cold butter (or hard margarine), cut up	1/4 cup	60 mL
Finely grated lemon peel	1 tbsp.	15 mL

Combine milk and lemon juice in 1 cup (250 mL) liquid measure. Let stand for 10 minutes to sour.

Beat butter and granulated sugar in large bowl for about 4 minutes until light and creamy. Add eggs, 1 at a time, beating well after each addition. Add lemon peel and vanilla. Stir well.

Combine next 4 ingredients in small bowl. Add flour mixture to butter mixture in 3 additions, alternating with milk mixture in 2 additions, beginning and ending with flour mixture. Spread in greased 9 x 9 inch (22 x 22 cm) pan.

Lemon Streusel Topping: Combine flour and brown sugar in medium bowl. Cut in butter until mixture resembles coarse crumbs.

Add lemon peel. Stir. Makes 3/4 cup (175 mL) topping. Sprinkle evenly over batter. Bake in 350°F (175°C) oven for about 30 to 35 minutes until golden brown and wooden pick inserted in centre comes out clean. Let stand in pan on wire rack for 15 minutes. Serve warm. Cuts into 9 pieces.

1 piece: 379 Calories; 18 g Total Fat (5.2 g Mono, 0.9 g Poly, 10.7 g Sat); 93 mg Cholesterol; 48 g Carbohydrate; 1 g Fibre; 6 g Protein; 397 mg Sodium

Pictured on page 111.

Bottom Left: Lemon Coffee Cake, page 110

Top: Biscuit Fruit Roll, this page

Biscuit Fruit Roll

You'll enjoy this rich loaf. Sweet, creamy fruit filling drizzled with a coffee glaze.

All-purpose flour	2 cups	500 mL
Granulated sugar	1/3 cup	75 mL
Baking powder	4 tsp.	20 mL
Salt	1/2 tsp.	2 mL
Cold butter (or hard margarine), cut up	6 tbsp.	100 mL
Large egg	1	1
Milk	1/2 cup	125 mL
MIXED FRUIT FILLING		
Block of cream cheese, softened	4 oz.	125 g
Vanilla	1/2 tsp.	2 mL
Chopped mixed glazed fruit	1/2 cup	125 mL
Chopped walnuts	3 tbsp.	50 mL
COFFEE GLAZE		
Icing (confectioner's) sugar	1/2 cup	125 mL
Cold prepared strong coffee, approximately	1 tbsp.	15 mL

Combine first 4 ingredients in large bowl. Cut in butter until mixture resembles coarse crumbs.

Beat egg and milk with fork in small cup. Add to flour mixture. Stir until soft dough forms. Turn out onto lightly floured surface. Knead 4 or 5 times until dough comes together. Press or roll out dough into 8 × 8 inch (20 × 20 cm) square, 5/8 inch (15 mm) thick.

Mixed Fruit Filling: Mash cream cheese and vanilla with fork in small bowl until well combined. Spread over dough.

Sprinkle with glazed fruit and walnuts. Roll up, jelly roll-style. Press seam against roll to seal. Place, seam-side down, on greased baking sheet. Cut 10 slits crosswise, 1/2 inch (12 mm) deep, along length of roll using floured knife. Bake in 425°F (220°C) oven for about 20 minutes until lightly browned. Remove to wire rack to cool.

Coffee Glaze: Beat icing sugar and enough coffee together in small bowl until thick, drizzling consistency. Makes about 1/4 cup (60 mL) glaze. Drizzle over warm roll. Cuts into 10 slices.

1 slice: 282 Calories; 12.4 g Total Fat (3.5 g Mono, 1.4 g Poly, 6.8 g Sat); 50 mg Cholesterol; 38 g Carbohydrate; 1 g Fibre; 5 g Protein; 360 mg Sodium

Pictured above.

Caramel Peach Pull-Aparts

Discover a sweet caramel peach flavour in this moist, sticky pull-apart. All you need is a cup of tea or coffee.

All-purpose flour	2 cups	500 mL
Baking powder	1 tbsp.	15 mL
Ground cinnamon	1/4 tsp.	1 mL
Ground ginger	1/4 tsp.	1 mL
Salt	1/4 tsp.	1 mL
Ground nutmeg	1/8 tsp.	0.5 mL
Cold butter (or hard margarine), cut up	1/3 cup	75 mL
Milk, approximately	1/2 cup	125 mL
Brown sugar, packed	1/3 cup	75 mL
Ground cinnamon	1/4 tsp.	1 mL
Can of sliced peaches, drained and chopped	14 oz.	398 mL
CARAMEL SAUCE		
Brown sugar, packed	1/2 cup	125 mL
Butter (or hard margarine)	1/4 cup	60 mL
Whipping cream	1/4 cup	60 mL
Coarsely chopped pistachios (or almonds), toasted (see Tip, page 80)	3 tbsp.	50 mL

Combine first 6 ingredients in large bowl. Cut in butter until mixture resembles coarse crumbs.

Stir, adding enough milk until soft dough forms. Turn out onto lightly floured surface. Knead gently 4 or 5 times until dough comes together. Roll out on waxed paper on dampened work surface to 7 1/2 x 15 inch (19 x 38 cm) rectangle.

Combine brown sugar and cinnamon in small dish. Sprinkle over dough, leaving 1 inch (2.5 cm) edge at long side farthest from you.

Scatter peach slices over brown sugar mixture. Roll up, jelly roll-style, from long side closest to you using waxed paper as guide. Press seam against roll to seal. Cut into 12 slices using floured knife.

Place 9 slices, cut-side down, around edge of greased 9 inch (22 cm) springform pan, crowding together to fit. Fit remaining 3 slices in centre of pan.

Bake in 375°F (190°C) oven for 25 to 30 minutes until golden. Let stand in pan on wire rack for 5 minutes before removing side of pan. Transfer to serving plate. Keep warm.

Caramel Sauce: Combine brown sugar, butter and whipping cream in small heavy saucepan. Heat and stir on medium until brown sugar is dissolved. Boil gently for about 3 minutes, without stirring, until mixture is slightly thickened. Makes 2/3 cup (150 mL) sauce. Drizzle over warm pull-aparts.

Sprinkle with pistachios. Serve warm. Makes 12 pull-aparts.

1 pull-apart: 267 Calories; 12.6 g Total Fat (4 g Mono, 0.7 g Poly, 7.2 g Sat); 32 mg Cholesterol; 36 g Carbohydrate; 1 g Fibre; 3 g Protein; 254 mg Sodium

Pictured on page 113.

Pies & Other Pastries

Pastry-making is one baking style that's both fun and rewarding to try.
Show off your skills with a tangy fruit-filled pie or sweet, cream-filled pastry.
These culinary jewels are unmatched by their store-bought counterparts!

Banana Streusel Pie

Sweet ginger and banana-flavoured pie with a nutty streusel top. Serve with ice cream.

Sliced banana (about 5 medium)	4 cups	1 L
Pineapple juice	3/4 cup	175 mL
Cornstarch	2 tsp.	10 mL
Brown sugar, packed	1/3 cup	75 mL
Finely grated lime zest	1 tsp.	5 mL
Ground ginger	1/2 tsp.	2 mL
Ground cardamom	1/8 tsp.	0.5 mL
Pastry for 9 inch (22 cm) pie shell	1	1
MACADAMIA STREUSEL TOPPING		
All-purpose flour	1/2 cup	125 mL
Brown sugar, packed	1/2 cup	125 mL
Cold butter (or hard margarine), cut up	1/4 cup	60 mL
Coarsely chopped macadamia nuts, toasted (see Tip, page 80)	1/3 cup	75 mL

Combine banana and pineapple juice in medium bowl. Toss until well coated. Drain juice into small saucepan.

Add cornstarch and brown sugar to juice. Heat and stir on medium for 7 to 8 minutes until boiling and thickened. Let stand for 5 minutes.

Add lime zest, ginger, cardamom and thickened juice mixture to banana mixture. Stir.

Roll out pastry on lightly floured surface to about 1/8 inch (3 mm) thickness. Line pie plate. Trim, leaving 1/2 inch (12 mm) overhang. Roll under and crimp decorative edge. Spoon banana mixture into pie shell.

Macadamia Streusel Topping: Combine flour and brown sugar in separate medium bowl. Cut in butter until mixture resembles coarse crumbs. Add macadamia nuts. Stir. Sprinkle over banana filling. Bake on bottom rack in 375°F (190°C) oven for about 35 minutes until top is golden and filling is bubbling. Cuts into 8 wedges.

1 wedge: 381 Calories; 16.1 g Total Fat (7.7 g Mono, 1.1 g Poly, 6.3 g Sat); 17 mg Cholesterol; 59 g Carbohydrate; 2 g Fibre; 3 g Protein; 176 mg Sodium

Pictured on page 117.

Peachy Plum Pie

Lovely glazed crust with a pretty peach and plum filling.

Granulated sugar	1 cup	250 mL
Minute tapioca	3 tbsp.	50 mL
Lemon juice	2 tsp.	10 mL
Ground nutmeg	1/4 tsp.	1 mL
Peeled and sliced fresh peaches (about 1 lb., 454 g)	2 1/2 cups	625 mL
Sliced red plums (about 1 lb., 454 g)	2 1/2 cups	625 mL
Pastry for 2 crust 9 inch (22 cm) pie	1	1
Egg yolk (large), fork-beaten	1	1
Granulated sugar	1/2 tsp.	2 mL

Combine first 4 ingredients in large bowl.

Add peaches and plums. Stir.

Divide pastry into 2 portions, 1 slightly larger than the other. Roll out larger portion on lightly floured surface to about 1/8 inch (3 mm) thickness. Line pie plate. Trim, leaving 1/2 inch (12 mm) overhang. Cover. Chill for 1 hour. Roll out smaller portion on lightly floured surface to about 1/8 inch (3 mm) thickness. Set aside. Spoon fruit mixture into pie shell. Dampen pastry edge with water. Cover with remaining pastry. Trim and crimp decorative edge to seal.

Brush top and edge of pastry with egg yolk. Sprinkle with second amount of sugar. Cut slits in top. Bake on bottom rack in 350°F (175°C) oven for 50 to 60 minutes until golden brown and filling is bubbling. Cuts into 8 wedges.

1 wedge: 253 Calories; 6.2 g Total Fat (3 g Mono, 0.8 g Poly, 1.9 g Sat); 27 mg Cholesterol; 50 g Carbohydrate; 2 g Fibre; 2 g Protein; 103 mg Sodium

Pictured on pages 116/117.

Two-Layer Pecan Pie

A cream cheese layer on top of a sweet, nutty bottom layer. Cream cheese cuts the sweetness of this traditionally very sweet pie.

Pastry for 9 inch (22 cm) pie shell	1	1
Dried beans (or uncooked rice)	2 cups	500 mL
Block of cream cheese, softened	8 oz.	250 g
Large egg	1	1
Granulated sugar	1/3 cup	75 mL
Vanilla	1 tsp.	5 mL
Large eggs	2	2
Corn syrup	2/3 cup	150 mL
Granulated sugar	1/3 cup	75 mL
Vanilla	1 tsp.	5 mL
All-purpose flour	1 tbsp.	15 mL
Chopped pecans	1 cup	250 mL

Roll out pastry on lightly floured surface to about 1/8 inch (3 mm) thickness. Line pie plate. Trim, leaving 1/2 inch (12 mm) overhang. Roll under and crimp decorative edge. Cover pastry with parchment paper, bringing paper up over crimped edge. Fill halfway up side with dried beans. Bake on bottom rack in 375°F (190°C) oven for 15 minutes. Carefully remove beans and paper. (These can be kept for the next time you bake pastry.) Let pie shell stand on wire rack until cool.

Beat next 4 ingredients in medium bowl until smooth. Spread evenly in bottom of partially baked pie shell.

Beat remaining eggs in separate medium bowl with clean beaters until frothy. Add corn syrup, second amounts of sugar and vanilla and flour. Beat until combined.

Stir in pecans. Pour over cream cheese layer. Bake on bottom rack in 350°F (175°C) oven for about 50 minutes until golden brown and evenly risen across top. Filling may still wobble in centre but will set upon cooling. Cuts into 8 wedges.

1 wedge: 470 Calories; 27.6 g Total Fat (12.3 g Mono, 3.7 g Poly, 9.9 g Sat); 115 mg Cholesterol; 52 g Carbohydrate; 1 g Fibre; 7 g Protein; 254 mg Sodium

Pictured on pages 116 and 117.

Top Left: Peachy Plum Pie, page 115
Top Right and Bottom Left: Two-Layer Pecan Pie, above
Centre Right: Banana Streusel Pie, page 115

Cran-Berry Pie

An absolutely gorgeous pie! Beautiful crust with sugared lattice on top. Subtle cranberry taste in a glossy pink filling—delicious!

CRUST

All-purpose flour	1 3/4 cups	425 mL
Icing (confectioner's) sugar	3 tbsp.	50 mL
Baking powder	1/2 tsp.	2 mL
Cold butter (or hard margarine), cut up	1/2 cup	125 mL
Large egg, fork-beaten	1	1
Egg yolk (large), fork-beaten	1	1
Lemon juice, approximately	2 tbsp.	30 mL

FILLING

Sliced fresh strawberries	4 cups	1 L
Chopped fresh cranberries (or frozen, thawed)	1 cup	250 mL
Granulated sugar	1 cup	250 mL
Cornstarch	1/4 cup	60 mL
Ground cinnamon	1/2 tsp.	2 mL
Salt	1/4 tsp.	1 mL
Egg white (large), fork-beaten	1	1
Sanding (decorating) sugar (see Glossary, page 9)	2 tsp.	10 mL

Crust: Combine first 3 ingredients in large bowl. Cut in butter until mixture resembles coarse crumbs.

Add egg and egg yolk. Stir, adding just enough lemon juice until soft dough forms. Divide dough into 2 portions, 1 slightly larger than the other. Roll out larger portion on lightly floured surface to about 1/8 inch (3 mm) thickness. Line 9 inch (22 cm) pie plate. Trim, leaving 1/2 inch (12 mm) overhang. Cover. Chill for 1 hour. Roll out smaller portion on lightly floured surface to 9 x 11 inch (22 x 28 cm) rectangle. Cut into 11 strips, 3/4 inch (2 cm) wide, using fluted pastry cutter. Place on baking sheet. Cover. Chill until ready to use.

Filling: Combine first 6 ingredients in separate large bowl. Pour into pie shell. Spread evenly.

Dampen edge of shell and both ends of pastry strips with water. Place 6 strips, side-by-side, equally spaced apart, on top of filling. Fold back 3 alternate strips to centre.

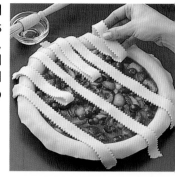

Lay 7th strip across 3 flat strips at centre. Return folded strips to flat position. Repeat, folding back 3 alternate strips and laying 8th strip across flat strips evenly spaced from centre strip. Repeat process, working from centre outward, until all strips are woven into lattice.

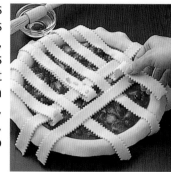

Trim strips at crust edge, leaving 1 inch (2.5 cm) overhang. Moisten and tuck strip ends under crust. Crimp decorative edge to seal.

Brush lattice and edge with egg white. Sprinkle with sanding sugar. Bake on bottom rack in 375°F (190°C) oven for 50 to 55 minutes until pastry is golden brown and filling is bubbling. Cuts into 8 wedges.

1 wedge: 400 Calories; 14.1 g Total Fat (4.1 g Mono, 0.9 g Poly, 8 g Sat); 87 mg Cholesterol; 65 g Carbohydrate; 4 g Fibre; 5 g Protein; 239 mg Sodium

Pictured on front cover.

Variation: If you prefer a more tart pie, add 1/4 cup (60 mL) more cranberries.

Apple And Pear Strudel

Flaky pastry with a moist pear, apple and raisin filling. Serve warm with ice cream.

Peeled and sliced fresh pears (about 2 medium)	2 cups	500 mL
Peeled and sliced tart cooking apples (such as Granny Smith), about 2 medium	2 cups	500 mL
Dark raisins	3 tbsp.	50 mL
Port (or water)	2 tbsp.	30 mL
Fine dry bread crumbs	1/2 cup	125 mL
Brown sugar, packed	1/4 cup	60 mL
Ground cinnamon	3/4 tsp.	4 mL
Ground ginger	1/2 – 3/4 tsp.	2 – 4 mL
Finely grated orange zest	1/2 tsp.	2 mL
Frozen phyllo pastry sheets, thawed according to package directions	8	8
Butter (or hard margarine), melted	1/3 cup	75 mL
Sanding (decorating) sugar (see Glossary, page 9)	1 tbsp.	15 mL

Combine first 4 ingredients in large saucepan. Cook on medium for about 10 minutes, stirring occasionally, until apples and pears are tender and liquid is evaporated. Cool.

Add next 5 ingredients. Stir.

Lay tea towel on work surface, short end closest to you. Work with phyllo sheets 1 at a time. Keep remaining sheets covered with damp tea towel to prevent drying. Place 1 pastry sheet on towel, lining up short end of sheet with closest end of towel. Place second pastry sheet at far end of first sheet with 6 inches (15 cm) overlapping in middle. Working quickly, brush pastry (now 1 long sheet) with melted butter. Place 2 more pastry sheets on top in same manner. Brush with melted butter. Repeat, layering with remaining pastry sheets and melted butter. Mound apple mixture onto pastry, 6 inches (15 cm) from closest edge. Fold closest edge up and over filling. Roll up tightly to enclose filling, using tea towel as a guide. Pack any loose filling back into roll. Leave ends open. Place, seam-side down, on greased baking sheet.

Brush with remaining melted butter. Sprinkle with sanding sugar. Bake in 375°F (190°C) oven for about 45 minutes until golden brown and crisp. Cut into eight 1 1/2 inch (3.8 cm) slices.

1 slice: 233 Calories; 9.7 g Total Fat (2.7 g Mono, 1.1 g Poly, 5.3 g Sat); 22 mg Cholesterol; 35 g Carbohydrate; 2 g Fibre; 3 g Protein; 240 mg Sodium

Pictured above.

Chocolate-Crusted Walnut Pie

Buttery, nutty and gooey with lots of walnuts and coconut.
A rich delight!

CHOCOLATE CRUST

Package of pie crust mix (1/2 of 19 oz., 540 g, box)	1	1
Cocoa, sifted if lumpy	3 tbsp.	50 mL
Granulated sugar	3 tbsp.	50 mL
Cold water, approximately	1/4 cup	60 mL

FILLING

Butter (or hard margarine)	2/3 cup	150 mL
Golden corn syrup	1 cup	250 mL
Brown sugar, packed	3/4 cup	175 mL
Large eggs, fork-beaten	3	3
Salt	1/8 tsp.	0.5 mL
Chopped walnuts, toasted (see Tip, page 80)	2 cups	500 mL
Medium unsweetened coconut, toasted (see Tip, page 80)	1 cup	250 mL
White vinegar	1 tbsp.	15 mL
Vanilla	1 1/2 tsp.	7 mL

Whipped cream (or frozen whipped topping, thawed), for garnish
Chocolate shavings, for garnish
Walnut pieces, for garnish

Chocolate Crust: Combine pie crust mix, cocoa and sugar in medium bowl.

Add water, 1 tbsp. (15 mL) at a time, stirring well with fork after each addition, until dough holds together and comes away from side of bowl. Shape dough into flattened round. Cover with plastic wrap. Chill for 1 hour. To prevent flour from discolouring dough, roll out dough between 2 sheets of waxed paper on dampened work surface to 12 inch (30 cm) circle. Line ungreased 9 inch (22 cm) deep dish pie plate. Trim, leaving 1/2 inch (12 mm) overhang. Roll under and crimp decorative edge. Cover. Chill for 15 minutes.

Filling: Melt butter in medium saucepan on medium. Add corn syrup and brown sugar. Heat and stir for 7 to 8 minutes until sugar is dissolved. Remove from heat. Let stand, stirring occasionally, until cooled to room temperature.

Beat eggs and salt in large bowl on high for about 5 minutes until thick and pale. Add corn syrup mixture. Beat well.

Add next 4 ingredients. Stir until combined. Spoon into pie shell. Spread evenly. Bake on bottom rack in 350°F (175°C) oven for about 50 minutes until filling is just set. Filling may still wobble in centre but will set upon cooling.

Garnish individual servings with dollop of whipped cream, chocolate shavings and walnut piece. Cuts into 12 wedges.

1 wedge: 570 Calories; 36.9 g Total Fat (10.7 g Mono, 9.8 g Poly, 14.4 g Sat); 83 mg Cholesterol; 57 g Carbohydrate; 2 g Fibre; 9 g Protein; 365 mg Sodium

Pictured on page 121.

Chocolate Almond Tart

Something to satisfy a chocolate craving.
Loads of chocolate with lots of almonds in a
fudgy filling. Serve warm with whipped cream.
It's also great cold as a picnic dessert.

ALMOND CRUST

Sliced almonds	1 cup	250 mL
All-purpose flour	3/4 cup	175 mL
Icing (confectioner's) sugar	1/4 cup	60 mL
Cocoa, sifted if lumpy	3 tbsp.	50 mL
Cold butter (or hard margarine), cut up	1/2 cup	125 mL

FILLING

Butter (or hard margarine)	1/2 cup	125 mL
Unsweetened chocolate baking squares (1 oz., 28 g, each), chopped	2	2
Sliced almonds, toasted (see Tip, page 80)	1 1/2 cups	375 mL
Brown sugar, packed	3/4 cup	175 mL
Dark corn syrup	1/2 cup	125 mL
Large eggs, fork-beaten	3	3
Almond-flavoured liqueur (such as Amaretto), see Note	2 tbsp.	30 mL
Vanilla	1 tsp.	5 mL
Almond flavouring	1/2 tsp.	2 mL
Whipped cream (or 1/2 envelope of dessert topping, prepared), optional	1 cup	250 mL

Almond Crust: Hand Method: Combine first 4 ingredients in medium bowl. Cut in butter until mixture resembles fine crumbs.

Food Processor Method: Process first 4 ingredients in food processor for 5 seconds. Add butter. Pulse with on/off motion until mixture resembles fine crumbs.

Press crumb mixture into bottom and up side of lightly greased 9 inch (22 cm) tart pan with fluted side and removable bottom. Place pan on baking sheet (to make it easier to remove hot pan from oven).

Filling: Heat and stir butter and chocolate in small heavy saucepan on lowest heat until almost melted. Do not overheat. Remove from heat. Stir until smooth. Transfer to separate medium bowl.

Add next 7 ingredients. Stir. Spoon into crust. Spread evenly. Bake on centre rack in 350°F (175°C) oven for about 45 minutes until wooden pick inserted in centre comes out clean. Let stand in pan on wire rack until cool. Remove to serving plate.

Pipe whipped cream in small rosettes around edge of tart. Cuts into 12 wedges.

1 wedge: 467 Calories; 32.5 g Total Fat (14 g Mono, 3.4 g Poly, 13.3 g Sat); 98 mg Cholesterol; 41 g Carbohydrate; 4 g Fibre; 8 g Protein; 212 mg Sodium

Pictured on page 125.

Note: If you prefer not to use liqueur, substitute with 1/2 tsp. (2 mL) almond extract combined with 5 1/2 tsp. (27 mL) water to make 2 tbsp. (30 mL).

Cherry Apricot Tart

An attractive, rustic-looking pie with a subtle nut flavour
in the pastry and sweet cherries in the filling.

PECAN CRUST

All-purpose flour	1 cup	250 mL
Ground ginger	1/2 tsp.	2 mL
Salt	1/4 tsp.	1 mL
Cold butter (or hard margarine), cut up	1/3 cup	75 mL
Icing (confectioner's) sugar	1/3 cup	75 mL
Ground pecans	1/4 cup	60 mL
Egg yolks (large)	2	2
Ice water, approximately	1 tbsp.	15 mL

FILLING

Ground pecans, toasted (see Tip, page 80)	1/2 cup	125 mL
Dried cherries	2/3 cup	150 mL
Can of apricot halves in light syrup, drained and sliced	14 oz.	398 mL
Brown sugar, packed	1/3 cup	75 mL
Ground ginger	1/2 tsp.	2 mL

Icing (confectioner's) sugar, for dusting

Pecan Crust: Combine flour, ginger and salt in large bowl. Cut in butter until mixture resembles coarse crumbs.

Add icing sugar and ground pecans. Stir.

Add egg yolks. Stir, adding enough water until soft dough forms. Do not overmix. Wrap dough in plastic wrap. Chill for 1 hour. Roll out dough on lightly floured surface to 12 inch (30 cm) circle. Carefully transfer to lightly greased 12 inch (30 cm) pizza pan.

Filling: Sprinkle ground pecans over pastry, leaving 2 inch (5 cm) edge. Sprinkle cherries over top of pecans. Arrange apricot slices over cherries in single layer.

Combine brown sugar and ginger in small bowl. Sprinkle over apricot slices. Fold over 2 inch (5 cm) pastry edge towards centre to partially cover filling. Bake on bottom rack in 375°F (190°C) oven for about 30 minutes until pastry is lightly browned. Let stand on wire rack until cool.

Dust with icing sugar. Cuts into 8 wedges.

1 wedge: 308 Calories; 16.4 g Total Fat (7 g Mono, 2.3 g Poly, 6.1 g Sat); 76 mg Cholesterol; 39 g Carbohydrate; 2 g Fibre; 4 g Protein; 164 mg Sodium

Pictured on pages 124/125.

Pear Tart

This rich, smooth custard with tender, sweet pears in a buttery nut pastry will delight your taste buds.

BUTTER NUT CRUST		
All-purpose flour	1 cup	250 mL
Finely chopped pecans (or walnuts)	6 tbsp.	100 mL
Icing (confectioner's) sugar	1 tbsp.	15 mL
Salt, pinch		
Cold butter (or hard margarine), cut up	1/2 cup	125 mL
Ice water, approximately	2 tbsp.	30 mL
Dried beans (or uncooked rice)	2 cups	500 mL
Egg yolk (large), fork-beaten	1	1
FILLING		
Fresh medium pears, peeled and cored	2	2
Butter (or hard margarine)	2 tbsp.	30 mL
Granulated sugar	3 tbsp.	50 mL
Egg yolks (large)	3	3
Whipping cream	3/4 cup	175 mL
Sanding (decorating) sugar (see Glossary, page 9)	3 tbsp.	50 mL
Apple (or other light-coloured) jelly, warmed (optional)	1/4 cup	60 mL

Butter Nut Crust: Combine first 4 ingredients in large bowl. Cut in butter until mixture resembles coarse crumbs.

Add ice water, 1 tbsp. (15 mL) at a time while stirring, until dough forms soft ball. Shape into flattened round. Cover with plastic wrap. Chill for 30 minutes. Roll out pastry on lightly floured surface to about 1/8 inch (3 mm) thickness. Press into bottom and up side of lightly greased 9 inch (22 cm) tart pan with fluted side and removable bottom. Trim edge.

Cover pastry with parchment paper, bringing paper up over edge. Fill halfway up side with dried beans. Place pan on baking sheet (to make it easier to remove hot pan from oven). Bake on bottom rack in 375°F (190°C) oven for 15 minutes. Carefully remove beans and paper. (These can be kept for the next time you bake pastry.)

Brush egg yolk over bottom of tart shell. Let stand in pan on wire rack until cool.

Filling: Cut pears into 1/2 inch (12 mm) slices. Heat large frying pan on medium-high for 1 minute until hot. Add butter. Heat until melted and sizzling. Add pear slices. Cook, stirring once or twice, for 3 to 4 minutes until starting to brown. Sprinkle with sugar. Stir until slices are softened. Remove from heat. Reserve any juice and caramelized sugar remaining in frying pan. Arrange slices in concentric circles in bottom of tart shell.

Beat egg yolks and whipping cream in medium bowl. Add reserved juice and caramelized sugar. Pour cream mixture over pears in tart shell.

Sprinkle with sanding sugar. Place pan on baking sheet (to make it easier to remove hot pan from oven). Bake on bottom rack in 350°F (175°C) oven for 40 to 45 minutes until filling is set and browned. Let stand in pan on wire rack until cool.

Brush with warm jelly. Cuts into 8 wedges.

1 wedge: 384 Calories; 29.2 g Total Fat (9.9 g Mono, 2.1 g Poly, 15.3 g Sat); 176 mg Cholesterol; 28 g Carbohydrate; 2 g Fibre; 4 g Protein; 167 mg Sodium

Pictured on pages 124/125.

Portuguese Custard Tarts

Delicious, crisp pastries with sweet custard filling.
Wonderful served warm with fresh fruit and
a dollop of whipped cream.

Package of frozen puff pastry, thawed according to package directions	14 oz.	397 g
Granulated sugar	1 cup	250 mL
Water	1/3 cup	75 mL
Salt	1/8 tsp.	0.5 mL
Large eggs	2	2
Egg yolks (large)	2	2
Half-and-half cream	1/2 cup	125 mL
Vanilla	2 tsp.	10 mL
Cornstarch	2 tbsp.	30 mL

Roll out 1/2 (1 square) of pastry to 9 x 13 1/2 inch (22 x 34 cm) rectangle. Cut into six 4 1/2 inch (11 cm) squares. Line greased muffin cups with pastry squares. Pinch or ruffle top edge extending over cup. Repeat with second 1/2 of pastry, for a total of 12 muffin cups. Cover. Chill.

Combine sugar, water and salt in small saucepan. Heat and stir on medium for 4 minutes until boiling. Brush inside edge of saucepan with damp pastry brush to dissolve any sugar crystals. Boil for 1 minute. Remove from heat. Let stand until cooled completely.

Beat eggs and egg yolks in medium bowl until frothy.

Stir cream and vanilla into cornstarch in cup until smooth. Add to eggs. Beat. Add cooled sugar mixture. Beat until well combined. Pour into 2 cup (500 mL) liquid measure. Makes 1 3/4 cups (425 mL) custard. Pour about 2 tbsp. (30 mL) into each pastry shell. Bake on bottom rack in 425°F (220°C) oven for 20 to 25 minutes until filling is domed and golden. Let stand in pan for 5 minutes before removing to wire rack to cool. Custard will settle. Makes 12 tarts.

1 tart: 293 Calories; 15.4 g Total Fat (3.8 g Mono, 7.5 g Poly, 3 g Sat); 75 mg Cholesterol; 34 g Carbohydrate; trace Fibre; 4 g Protein; 125 mg Sodium

Pictured on page 125.

Top Left: Cherry Apricot Tart, page 122
Top Right: Chocolate Almond Tart, page 122
Bottom Left: Pear Tart, page 123
Bottom Right: Portuguese Custard Tarts, above

Plum And Almond Tart

Moist, dark plums nestled in a marzipan-like filling.
You'll enjoy the sweet and delicate flavours.

SWEET BUTTER CRUST

All-purpose flour	1 1/2 cups	375 mL
Granulated sugar	1/4 cup	60 mL
Baking powder	1/2 tsp.	2 mL
Salt	1/4 tsp.	1 mL
Cold butter (not margarine), cut up	1/2 cup	125 mL
Egg yolks (large)	2	2
Milk	2 tbsp.	30 mL
Dried beans (or uncooked rice)	2 cups	500 mL

FILLING

Ground almonds (or whole almonds for Food Processor Method)	1 cup	250 mL
Granulated sugar	1/2 cup	125 mL
Butter (not margarine), cut up	1/2 cup	125 mL
All-purpose flour	1/4 cup	60 mL
Egg whites (large)	2	2
Almond flavouring	1/2 tsp.	2 mL
Cans of plums in heavy syrup (14 oz., 398 mL, each), drained (or fresh prune plums, enough to cover)	3	3
Sliced almonds, toasted (see Tip, page 80)	1/3 cup	75 mL
Sanding (decorating) sugar (see Glossary, page 9)	1 tbsp.	15 mL

Sweet Butter Crust: Hand Method: Combine first 4 ingredients in medium bowl. Cut in butter until mixture resembles fine crumbs.

Beat egg yolks and milk with fork in 1 cup (250 mL) liquid measure. Slowly add to flour mixture, stirring constantly with fork, until dough starts to come together.

Food Processor Method: Process first 4 ingredients in food processor for 5 seconds. Add butter. Pulse with on/off motion for about 15 seconds until mixture resembles fine crumbs.

Beat egg yolks and milk with fork in 1 cup (250 mL) liquid measure. With food processor motor running, add egg yolk mixture through feed chute until well combined and dough can be formed into ball.

Shape dough into flattened round. Cover with plastic wrap. Chill for 1 hour. Roll out pastry on lightly floured surface to about 1/8 inch (3 mm) thickness. Press into bottom and up side of lightly greased 10 inch (25 cm) tart pan with fluted side and removable bottom. Trim edge. Chill for 1 hour. Place pan on baking sheet (to make it easier to remove hot pan from oven). Cover pastry with parchment paper, bringing paper up over edge. Fill halfway up side with dried beans. Bake on bottom rack in 375°F (190°C) oven for 15 minutes. Carefully remove beans and paper. (These can be kept for the next time you bake pastry.) Let stand on wire rack until cool.

Filling: Hand Method: Combine ground almonds and next 5 ingredients. Beat until mixture is fine paste.

Food Processor Method: Put first 6 ingredients in same food processor bowl. Pulse with on/off motion until almonds are finely ground and paste forms.

Spoon almond mixture into tart pan. Spread evenly.

Cut plums in half lengthwise and remove pits. Blot dry. Arrange nicest plums, cut side up and overlapping, in a single layer in concentric circles over almond mixture until filling is covered.

Sprinkle with sliced almonds and sanding sugar. Bake on bottom rack in 350°F (175°C) oven for about 45 minutes until crust is golden and filling is evenly raised across top. Filling may still wobble in centre but will set upon cooling. Cuts into 8 wedges.

1 wedge: 626 Calories; 38.2 g Total Fat (15.5 g Mono, 3.8 g Poly, 16.8 g Sat); 120 mg Cholesterol; 66 g Carbohydrate; 4 g Fibre; 10 g Protein; 367 mg Sodium

Pictured on page 127.

Spiced Nut Cockscombs

A tender, flaky treat. Sugary, golden pastry filled with spiced almonds.

FILLING

Ground almonds (or whole almonds for Food Processor Method)	1 cup	250 mL
Granulated sugar	1/2 cup	125 mL
Ground cinnamon	1/2 tsp.	2 mL
Ground nutmeg	1/4 tsp.	1 mL
Butter (not margarine), softened	1/4 cup	60 mL
Large egg	1	1
Package of frozen puff pastry, thawed according to package directions	14 oz.	397 g
Large egg	1	1
Milk	1 tbsp.	15 mL
Sanding (decorating) sugar (see Glossary, page 9)	3 tbsp.	50 mL

Filling: Hand Method: Combine ground almonds and next 3 ingredients in medium bowl. Add butter and egg. Beat until mixture is fine paste.

Food Processor Method: Put first 4 ingredients in food processor. Pulse with an on/off motion for about 1 minute until almonds are finely chopped. Add butter and egg to processor. Process for about 1 minute until almonds are finely ground and paste forms.

Chill for 30 minutes. Makes 1 1/3 cups (325 mL) filling.

Roll out 1/2 (1 square) of pastry on lightly floured surface to very thin 12 × 16 inch (30 × 40 cm) rectangle. Cut twelve 4 inch (10 cm) squares.

Place about 1 1/2 tsp. (7 mL) filling just off centre on 1 square.

Beat egg and milk with fork in small cup. Brush 1 edge of pastry with egg mixture. Fold up over filling and seal to other edge, leaving short ends open. Brush top of pastry with egg mixture. Cut 5 or 6 deep slits into sealed edge with sharp knife. Repeat with remaining 11 squares.

Repeat with remaining 1/2 (1 square) of pastry and remaining filling, for a total of 24. Sprinkle each pastry with sanding sugar.

Arrange pastries, about 1 1/2 inches (3.8 cm) apart, on ungreased baking sheets, curving them so slits open slightly to resemble a rooster's comb. Place on centre rack in 400°F (205°C) oven. Immediately reduce heat to 350°F (175°C). Bake for about 15 minutes until golden brown and puffed. Makes 24 pastries.

1 pastry: 175 Calories; 11.9 g Total Fat (4.2 g Mono, 4.4 g Poly, 2.6 g Sat); 24 mg Cholesterol; 15 g Carbohydrate; 1 g Fibre; 3 g Protein; 68 mg Sodium

Pictured on this page.

Lemon Cream Profiteroles

These profiteroles (pruh-FIHT-uh-rohls) are dainty, golden pastry puffs filled with lemon cream and drizzled with a crunchy toffee.

Butter (or hard margarine)	3 tbsp.	50 mL
Water	1/2 cup	125 mL
Salt	1/8 tsp.	0.5 mL
All-purpose flour	1/2 cup	125 mL
Large eggs	2	2
LEMON CREAM FILLING		
Whipping cream	1/2 cup	125 mL
Crumbled mascarpone cheese	1/2 cup	125 mL
Lemon curd	1/3 cup	75 mL
TOFFEE GLAZE		
Granulated sugar	3/4 cup	175 mL
Water	1/4 cup	60 mL

Heat and stir butter, water and salt in heavy medium saucepan on medium-high until boiling and butter is melted. Reduce heat to medium.

Add flour all at once. Stir vigorously for about 1 minute until mixture pulls away from side of saucepan to form soft dough. Immediately remove from heat.

Add eggs, 1 at a time, beating well after each addition, until dough is smooth and glossy. Drop by rounded teaspoonfuls (about 2 tsp., 10 mL, each), about 1 inch (2.5 cm) apart, on greased baking sheets. Bake in 425°F (220°C) oven for about 15 minutes until golden and dry. Remove to wire racks to cool. Makes 24 profiteroles.

Lemon Cream Filling: Beat whipping cream in small bowl until soft peaks form. Add cheese and lemon curd. Beat well. Chill. Makes 1 1/2 cups (375 mL) filling. Cut off tops of profiteroles. Fill each bottom with 1 tbsp. (15 mL) filling. Replace tops. Place on wire rack set on waxed paper-lined baking sheet.

Toffee Glaze: Heat and stir sugar and water in small saucepan on medium until sugar is dissolved. Increase heat to medium-high. Brush inside edge of saucepan with damp pastry brush to dissolve any sugar crystals. Boil, without stirring, for about 5 minutes until sugar mixture becomes a deep, golden brown. Drizzle toffee over each profiterole. Makes 24 filled profiteroles.

1 filled profiterole: 105 Calories; 6.2 g Total Fat (1.9 g Mono, 0.5 g Poly, 3.4 g Sat); 40 mg Cholesterol; 11 g Carbohydrate; trace Fibre; 2 g Protein; 88 mg Sodium

Pictured below.

Baklava

This popular Greek dessert is made with multiple layers of phyllo pastry and a rich ground nut mixture. After baking, a sweet syrup is poured over and allowed to soak all the layers.

Finely chopped pistachios, toasted (see Tip, page 80)	1 1/2 cups	375 mL
Finely chopped pecans, toasted (see Tip, page 80)	1 1/2 cups	375 mL
Granulated sugar	1/3 cup	75 mL
Brown sugar, packed	1/4 cup	60 mL
Ground nutmeg	1/2 tsp.	2 mL
Ground cinnamon	1/2 tsp.	2 mL
Frozen phyllo pastry sheets, thawed according to package directions	16	16
Butter (not margarine), melted	3/4 cup	175 mL
ORANGE SYRUP		
Granulated sugar	3 cups	750 mL
Water	2 cups	500 mL
Ground cardamom	1/4 tsp.	1 mL
Small navel orange, cut into 1/4 inch (6 mm) thick slices (end slices discarded)	1	1

Combine first 6 ingredients in medium bowl. Set aside.

Work with phyllo sheets 1 at a time. Keep remaining sheets covered with damp tea towel to prevent drying. Lay 1 pastry sheet on work surface. Brush with melted butter. Fold in half crosswise. Place in 9 x 13 inch (22 x 33 cm) pan. Brush with melted butter. Repeat with 4 more pastry sheets and melted butter, finishing with melted butter. Sprinkle 1/3 of nut mixture over top. Repeat layering with another 3 folded sheets of pastry over nut mixture, brushing with melted butter after each layer. Sprinkle with another 1/3 of nut mixture. Repeat layering with another 3 sheets of pastry over nut mixture, brushing with melted butter after each layer. Sprinkle with remaining 1/3 of nut mixture. Repeat layering with remaining pastry sheets, brushing with remaining melted butter. Score diamond pattern across pastry using a sharp knife. Insert knife down into pastry, almost, but not quite through, to bottom of pan. Make 5 cuts lengthwise, about 1 1/2 inches (3.8 cm) apart. Cut at an angle across lengthwise cuts to make diamond shapes (see diagram). Bake in 350°F (175°C) oven for about 40 minutes until deep golden brown and crisp. Keep hot.

Orange Syrup: Combine sugar, water and cardamom in medium saucepan. Add orange slices. Heat and stir on medium for about 2 minutes until sugar is dissolved. Increase heat to medium-high. Brush side of saucepan with damp pastry brush to dissolve any sugar crystals. Boil for 12 minutes without stirring. Remove from heat. Discard orange slices. Makes 2 3/4 cups (675 mL) syrup. Slowly pour hot syrup over hot pastry, allowing it to fill in spaces and score marks. Let stand, uncovered, at room temperature overnight. Cut through to bottom, following scored diamond pattern. Baklava can be covered with sheet of waxed paper and stored at room temperature for 3 to 4 days or wrapped and frozen for longer storage. Makes about 30 diamond-shaped pieces.

1 piece: 251 Calories; 12.9 g Total Fat (6.4 g Mono, 2 g Poly, 3.9 g Sat); 13 mg Cholesterol; 34 g Carbohydrate; 1 g Fibre; 2 g Protein; 100 mg Sodium

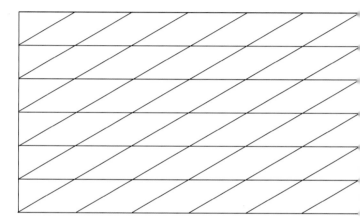

Pictured on page 131.

Lemon Poppy Seed Spirals

A striped twist of pastry and poppy seeds with a tart lemon glaze. Can be made ahead and frozen.

Package of frozen puff pastry, thawed according to package directions	14 oz.	397 g
Cream cheese, softened	1/4 cup	60 mL
Finely grated lemon zest	4 tsp.	20 mL
Lemon flavouring (optional)	1 tsp.	5 mL
Sanding (decorating) sugar (see Glossary, page 9)	2 tbsp.	30 mL
Poppy seeds	2 tsp.	10 mL
Large egg, fork-beaten	1	1
LEMON GLAZE		
Icing (confectioner's) sugar	1/2 cup	125 mL
Lemon juice	1 tbsp.	15 mL

Roll out 1/2 (1 square) of puff pastry on lightly floured surface to 8 x 12 inch (20 x 30 cm) rectangle. Keep remaining pastry chilled.

Beat cream cheese, lemon zest and flavouring in small bowl until smooth. Thinly spread pastry with 1/2 of cream cheese mixture. Sprinkle 1 tbsp. (15 mL) sanding sugar and 1 tsp. (5 mL) poppy seeds over cream cheese mixture. Fold pastry in half crosswise, to 6 x 8 inch (15 x 20 cm) rectangle. Lightly press edges together. Transfer to flat plate. Cover with plastic wrap. Chill for 1 1/2 hours. Repeat with second 1/2 of pastry, cream cheese mixture, sanding sugar and poppy seeds.

Place each pastry on work surface. Using a ruler and pizza cutter or very sharp knife, cut twelve 1/2 x 8 inch (12 mm x 20 cm) strips from each. Twist each strip several times.

Form twisted strip into loose coil, tucking outside end underneath coiled strip. Arrange coils, about 2 inches (5 cm) apart, on parchment paper-lined baking sheets. Cover with plastic wrap. Chill for 15 minutes. Lightly brush coils with egg. Bake in 400°F (205°C) oven for about 15 minutes until golden brown and crisp. Remove to wire racks to cool completely.

Lemon Glaze: Combine icing sugar and lemon juice in separate small bowl until smooth, drizzling consistency. Makes 2 tbsp. (30 mL) glaze. Drizzle from spoon in zigzag pattern over cooled pastries. Makes 24 spirals.

1 spiral: 119 Calories; 7.5 g Total Fat (1.8 g Mono, 3.8 g Poly, 1.5 g Sat); 12 mg Cholesterol; 11 g Carbohydrate; trace Fibre; 2 g Protein; 52 mg Sodium

Pictured on page 133.

Rhubarb Cream Tarts

Sweet, tangy filling in cheesecake-topped tart.

RHUBARB FILLING		
Chopped fresh (or frozen, thawed) rhubarb	2 cups	500 mL
Granulated sugar	1/2 cup	125 mL
Water	1/4 cup	60 mL
Cornstarch	2 tbsp.	30 mL
Ground cinnamon	1/4 tsp.	1 mL
Salt	1/8 tsp.	0.5 mL
Unbaked frozen 3 inch (7.5 cm) tart shells (in foil cups), thawed	12	12
CREAM CHEESE TOPPING		
Block of cream cheese, softened	4 oz.	125 g
Granulated sugar	1/4 cup	60 mL
Large egg	1	1

Rhubarb Filling: Combine first 6 ingredients in medium saucepan. Heat and stir on medium for about 10 minutes until boiling and thickened. Remove from heat. Let stand until cooled to room temperature.

Place tart shells (in foil cups) on ungreased baking sheet. Divide and fill each shell 3/4 full with rhubarb filling. Smooth gently with teaspoon.

Cream Cheese Topping: Beat cream cheese and sugar in medium bowl. Add egg. Beat until smooth. Makes about 1 cup (250 mL) topping. Transfer to 2 cup (500 mL) liquid measure. Pour about 1 tbsp. (15 mL) over rhubarb layer in each shell until even with top of shell. Bake in 350°F (175°C) oven for about 30 minutes until set and edges are golden. Let stand in foil cups on wire rack to cool. Remove from foil cups before serving. Makes 12 tarts.

1 tart: 168 Calories; 8.2 g Total Fat (3.1 g Mono, 0.7 g Poly, 3.7 g Sat); 29 mg Cholesterol; 22 g Carbohydrate; trace Fibre; 2 g Protein; 144 mg Sodium

Pictured on page 133.

Top and Bottom: Rhubarb Cream Tarts, above
Centre Left: Lemon Poppy Seed Spirals, this page

Cheese Sticks

Serve these crisp, buttery chive and cheese-flavoured sticks as a snack or with soup or salad.

All-purpose flour	1 1/2 cups	375 mL
Cold butter (or hard margarine), cut up	1/2 cup	125 mL
Grated sharp Cheddar cheese	3/4 cup	75 mL
Chopped fresh chives	2 tbsp.	30 mL
Pepper	1/4 tsp.	1 mL
Egg yolks (large), fork-beaten	2	2
Ice water, approximately	2 tbsp.	30 mL

Food Processor Method: Process flour and butter until mixture resembles coarse crumbs.

Add cheese, chives and pepper. Pulse with on/off motion until well combined. With motor running, add egg yolks and just enough ice water through feed chute until soft dough starts to come together.

Hand Method: Cut butter into flour in large bowl until mixture resembles coarse crumbs.

Add cheese, chives and pepper. Stir until combined. Add egg yolks. Stir, adding just enough ice water until soft ball forms.

Shape dough into balls, using 2 tsp. (10 mL) per ball. Roll each ball into 5 inch (12.5 cm) rope. (Sticks will shrink when baked.) Arrange on lightly greased baking sheets about 1/2 inch (12 mm) apart. Cover with plastic wrap. Chill for 30 minutes. Bake in 400°F (205°C) oven for 10 to 15 minutes until golden brown and crisp. Makes 40 cheese sticks.

1 cheese stick: 47 Calories; 3.1 g Total Fat (0.9 g Mono, 0.2 g Poly, 1.8 g Sat); 18 mg Cholesterol; 4 g Carbohydrate; trace Fibre; 1 g Protein; 31 mg Sodium

Pictured on back cover.

Tomato Goat Cheese Tartlets

A rich red tomato filling in golden pastry cups topped with lightly browned goat cheese. Tartlets may be frozen after baking and reheated later for a perfect make-ahead appetizer.

TOMATO FILLING

Olive (or cooking) oil	2 tsp.	10 mL
Chopped onion	1 cup	250 mL
Can of diced tomatoes, drained	14 oz.	398 mL
Granulated sugar	1/2 tsp.	2 mL
Pepper	1/8 tsp.	0.5 mL
Chopped fresh parsley (or 1 1/4 tsp., 6 mL, flakes)	1 1/2 tbsp.	25 mL
Chopped fresh basil (or 3/4 tsp., 4 mL, dried)	1 tbsp.	15 mL
Large eggs, fork-beaten	2	2
Frozen unbaked mini-tart shells, thawed	24	24
Goat (chèvre) cheese (about 1/3 cup, 75 mL), cut up	2 oz.	57 g

Tomato Filling: Heat olive oil in medium frying pan on medium. Add onion. Cook for 8 to 10 minutes, stirring often, until soft and golden.

Increase heat to medium-high. Add tomatoes, sugar and pepper. Cook, stirring occasionally, for 3 to 4 minutes until liquid is evaporated. Remove from heat.

Add parsley and basil. Stir. Let stand for 15 minutes.

Add eggs. Stir until well combined. Makes 1 1/2 cups (375 mL) filling.

Place mini-tart shells on large ungreased baking sheet. Spoon 1 tbsp. (15 mL) filling into each shell.

Place about 1/2 tsp. (2 mL) goat cheese on top of each filled shell. Bake on bottom rack in 375°F (190°C) oven for 20 to 25 minutes until filling is set and lightly browned. Remove to wire rack. Let stand for 10 minutes before serving. Serve warm. Makes 24 tartlets.

1 tartlet: 73 Calories; 4.6 g Total Fat (2.1 g Mono, 0.5 g Poly, 1.7 g Sat); 20 mg Cholesterol; 6 g Carbohydrate; trace Fibre; 2 g Protein; 106 mg Sodium

Pictured on page 137.

Onion Pepper Phyllo Squares

A delicious blend of flavours in these squares—sweet onion and peppers in a crisp, flaky crust.

Cooking oil	1 tbsp.	15 mL
Thinly sliced onion	2 cups	500 mL
Garlic cloves, minced (or 1/2 tsp., 2 mL, powder)	2	2
Liquid honey	1 1/2 tsp.	7 mL
Dried crushed chilies	1 tsp.	5 mL
Frozen phyllo pastry sheets, thawed according to package directions	12	12
Butter (or hard margarine), melted	1/2 cup	125 mL
Thinly sliced roasted red peppers (or 1/2 of 13 oz., 370 mL, jar, drained and thinly sliced)	1/2 cup	125 mL
Part-skim mozzarella cheese, thinly sliced	8 oz.	225 g
Torn fresh basil	2 tbsp.	30 mL
Finely grated fresh Parmesan cheese	1/2 cup	125 mL

Heat cooking oil in large frying pan on medium. Add onion. Cook for 12 to 15 minutes, stirring often, until soft and golden.

Add garlic, honey and chilies. Cook, stirring constantly, for about 2 minutes until fragrant. Let stand until slightly cooled.

Work with phyllo sheets 1 at a time. Keep remaining sheets covered with damp tea towel to prevent drying. Lay 1 pastry sheet on work surface. Brush with melted butter. Lay second pastry sheet on top. Brush with melted butter. Repeat with remaining pastry sheets and melted butter. Carefully lift pastry layers into greased 10 x 15 inch (25 x 38 cm) jelly roll pan. Press into corners and up sides of pan.

Scatter onion mixture, red peppers and mozzarella cheese slices over pastry. Sprinkle with basil and Parmesan cheese. Bake in 375°F (190°C) oven for 15 to 20 minutes until pastry is golden and crisp. Pastry may puff during baking but will deflate once removed from oven. Cuts into 8 squares.

1 square: 336 Calories; 22.4 g Total Fat (6.8 g Mono, 2.2 g Poly, 12.2 g Sat); 55 mg Cholesterol; 22 g Carbohydrate; 1 g Fibre; 13 g Protein; 651 mg Sodium

Pictured above.

Spinach Triangles

Buttery, rich and delicious! Will remind you of spanikopita.

SPINACH FILLING

Olive (or cooking) oil	1 tbsp.	15 mL
Finely chopped onion	1 cup	250 mL
Garlic cloves, minced (or 1/2 tsp., 2 mL, powder)	2	2
Brown sugar, packed	1 tsp.	5 mL
Packages of frozen spinach (10 oz., 300 g, each), thawed, squeezed dry and chopped	2	2
Ricotta cheese	1/2 cup	125 mL
Finely grated fresh Parmesan cheese	1/2 cup	125 mL
Crumbled feta cheese (about 2 1/2 oz., 71 g)	1/2 cup	125 mL
Large eggs, fork-beaten	3	3
Chopped fresh dill (or 3/4 tsp., 4 mL, dill weed)	1 tbsp.	15 mL
Lemon juice	2 tsp.	10 mL
Salt	1/2 tsp.	2 mL
Ground nutmeg	1/8 tsp.	0.5 mL
Frozen phyllo pastry sheets, thawed according to package directions	12	12
Butter (or hard margarine), melted	1/2 cup	125 mL
Sesame seeds	1 tbsp.	15 mL
Poppy seeds	1 tsp.	5 mL

Spinach Filling: Heat olive oil in medium frying pan on medium. Add onion. Cook for 5 to 10 minutes, stirring often, until softened. Add garlic. Cook for 1 to 2 minutes until fragrant. Add brown sugar. Stir until dissolved. Transfer to large bowl.

Add next 9 ingredients. Stir well. Makes 3 1/3 cups (825 mL) filling.

Work with pastry sheets 1 at a time. Keep remaining sheets covered with damp tea towel to prevent drying. Lay 1 pastry sheet on work surface. Brush with melted butter. Lay second sheet over top. Brush with melted butter. Repeat with 1 more sheet and melted butter. Cut stack in half lengthwise to make 2 long pieces. Cut each piece in half lengthwise, for a total of 4 long strips.

Place 2 tbsp. (30 mL) filling on angle at 1 end of strip. Fold pastry over to enclose filling and form triangle. Continue folding triangle over and over until end of strip. Place triangle on greased baking sheet. Cover with damp tea towel.

Repeat entire process 3 more times with remaining pastry sheets, melted butter and filling, for a total of 16 triangles. Brush tops with remaining melted butter.

Sprinkle sesame seeds and poppy seeds over each triangle. Bake in 350°F (175°C) oven for about 30 minutes until golden brown. Makes 16 appetizers.

1 appetizer: 178 Calories; 12.4 g Total Fat (3.8 g Mono, 1.2 g Poly, 6.5 g Sat); 68 mg Cholesterol; 11 g Carbohydrate; 1 g Fibre; 7 g Protein; 366 mg Sodium

Pictured on page 137.

Mango Pastry Appetizers

Pretty hors d'oeuvres with herbed goat cheese and slivers of mango.

Package of frozen puff pastry, thawed according to package directions	14 oz.	397 g
Large egg, fork-beaten	1	1
Goat (chèvre) cheese (about 3/4 cup, 175 mL), cut up	6 oz.	170 g
Finely chopped fresh chives	1 tbsp.	15 mL
Chili sauce	1 tbsp.	15 mL
Can of sliced mango (14 oz., 398 mL), drained, blotted dry and cut into thin slivers	1/2	1/2
Thinly sliced red onion	1/4 cup	60 mL
Fresh parsley, for garnish		

Roll out each half (1 square) of pastry on lightly floured surface to 7 1/2 x 10 inch (19 x 25 cm) rectangle. Cut 24 rounds using 2 1/2 inch (6.4 cm) fluted cookie cutter. Arrange rounds, about 1/2 inch (12 mm) apart, on greased baking sheets. Pierce each round all over with fork.

Brush rounds with egg. Bake in 400°F (205°C) oven for 15 to 20 minutes until puffed and lightly browned. Remove from oven. Press down centre of each puffed round with back of small spoon. Remove to wire racks to cool completely.

Combine goat cheese, chives and chili sauce in small bowl. Makes about 3/4 cup (175 mL) topping. Spread 1 1/2 tsp. (7 mL) topping on each round.

Top with mango slivers, onion and parsley. Makes 24 appetizers.

1 appetizer: 124 Calories; 8.6 g Total Fat (2 g Mono, 3.7 g Poly, 2.4 g Sat); 15 mg Cholesterol; 9 g Carbohydrate; trace Fibre; 3 g Protein; 90 mg Sodium

Pictured on page 137.

Top Right: Tomato Goat Cheese Tartlets, page 134
Centre Left: Spinach Triangles, this page
Bottom Right: Mango Pastry Appetizers, above

Gift Baking

These recipes have been hand-picked for this special gift section
because of their tempting appearance and simple-to-wrap convenience.
Remember, your reward comes from knowing that both the gift
and the effort were genuinely appreciated!

Panettone

Pronounced pan-uh-TOH-nee.
Attractive Italian yeast bread, just sweet enough to satisfy.

Dark raisins, coarsely chopped	1/2 cup	125 mL
Golden raisins	1/2 cup	125 mL
Diced mixed peel	1/3 cup	75 mL
Dry sherry (or Marsala)	1/3 cup	75 mL
Milk	1/2 cup	125 mL
Granulated sugar	1 tbsp.	15 mL
Active dry yeast	2 1/2 tbsp.	37 mL
All-purpose flour	5 cups	1.25 L
Granulated sugar	1/3 cup	75 mL
Salt	1 tsp.	5 mL
Milk	3/4 cup	175 mL
Butter (or hard margarine)	1/2 cup	125 mL
Large eggs	3	3
Egg yolks (large)	3	3
Finely grated lemon zest	2 tsp.	10 mL
Vanilla	1 tsp.	5 mL
Large egg, fork-beaten	1	1

Measure first 4 ingredients into small bowl. Stir. Let stand for 30 minutes.

Heat and stir first amounts of milk and sugar in small heavy saucepan on medium until warm and sugar is dissolved. Pour into separate small bowl. Let stand for 5 minutes.

Sprinkle yeast over top. Let stand for 10 minutes. Stir until yeast is dissolved.

Combine flour, second amount of sugar and salt in extra-large bowl. Make a well in centre. Add fruit mixture to well. Stir. Add yeast mixture. Stir well.

Heat and stir second amount of milk and butter in same small heavy saucepan on medium until butter is almost melted. Pour into separate small bowl. Stir until butter is melted. Let stand for 5 minutes.

Add warm milk mixture and next 4 ingredients to flour mixture. Mix until dough starts to pull away from side of bowl. Cover with greased waxed paper and tea towel. Let stand in oven with light on and door closed for about 30 minutes until doubled in bulk. Punch dough down. Turn out onto lightly floured surface. Knead for 3 to 5 minutes until smooth. Divide into 2 equal portions. Roll 1 portion into ball. Press into bottom of greased 8 inch (20 cm) springform pan. Repeat with remaining portion and separate greased springform pan. Cover each with greased waxed paper and tea towel. Let stand in oven with light on and door closed for 30 minutes until doubled in size.

Brush top of each loaf with beaten egg. Bake in 350°F (175°C) oven for 40 to 50 minutes until golden brown and hollow sounding when tapped. Let stand in pans for 10 minutes before removing to wire racks to cool. Makes 2 loaves. Each loaf cuts into 12 slices, for a total of 24 slices.

1 slice: 209 Calories; 6 g Total Fat (1.8 g Mono, 0.5 g Poly, 3.1 g Sat);
74 mg Cholesterol; 33 g Carbohydrate; 2 g Fibre; 5 g Protein; 160 mg Sodium

Pictured above.

Piped Shortbread Cookies

Always a favourite at Christmas time.
Easy enough to make any time of year.

Butter (not margarine), softened	1 cup	250 mL
Granulated sugar	1/3 cup	75 mL
Vanilla	1 tsp.	5 mL
All-purpose flour	1 1/2 cups	375 mL
Cornstarch	1/4 cup	60 mL
Salt	1/4 tsp.	1 mL
Milk chocolate chips (optional)	1 cup	250 mL

Beat butter, sugar and vanilla in large bowl until light and creamy.

Add next 3 ingredients. Stir until just moistened. Spoon mixture into piping bag fitted with large open star tip. Pipe 3 inch (7.5 cm) long strips, about 1 1/2 inches (3.8 cm) apart, onto greased cookie sheets. Bake in 350°F (175°C) oven for about 15 minutes until edges start to turn golden. Let stand on cookie sheets for 5 minutes before removing to wire racks to cool completely. Cool cookie sheets between batches if using more than once.

Heat and stir chocolate chips in small heavy saucepan on lowest heat until almost melted. Do not overheat. Remove from heat. Stir until smooth. Transfer to small deep bowl. Dip 1 end of each cooled cookie into chocolate. Set on wire rack or waxed paper until chocolate is set. Makes about 2 1/2 dozen (30) cookies.

1 cookie: 94 Calories; 6.5 g Total Fat (1.9 g Mono, 0.3 g Poly, 4 g Sat);
    17 mg Cholesterol; 8 g Carbohydrate; trace Fibre; 1 g Protein; 86 mg Sodium

Pictured on page 141.

Pecan Crescents

This delicate, nutty cookie covered in icing sugar
will surely melt in your mouth.

All-purpose flour	1 cup	250 mL
Granulated sugar	2 tbsp.	30 mL
Cold butter (or hard margarine), cut up	1/2 cup	125 mL
Ground pecans	6 tbsp.	100 mL
Egg yolk (large)	1	1
Vanilla	1/2 tsp.	2 mL
Icing (confectioner's) sugar, for dusting	1/4 cup	60 mL

Combine flour and sugar in large bowl. Cut in butter until mixture resembles coarse crumbs.

Add next 3 ingredients. Stir well. Turn out onto lightly floured surface. Press dough together. Roll 1 1/2 tsp. (7 mL) of dough into 2 inch (5 cm) rope. Shape into crescent by gently curving rope and making ends slightly pointed. Repeat with remaining dough. Arrange, about 1 inch (2.5 cm) apart, on greased cookie sheets. Bake in 325°F (160°C) oven for about 15 minutes until lightly browned. Let stand on cookie sheets for 5 minutes before removing to wire racks.

Sift icing sugar liberally over warm crescents. Cool completely before storing. May be frozen. Makes 3 dozen (36) cookies.

1 cookie: 53 Calories; 3.7 g Total Fat (1.3 g Mono, 0.3 g Poly, 1.8 g Sat);
    13 mg Cholesterol; 5 g Carbohydrate; trace Fibre; 1 g Protein; 28 mg Sodium

Pictured on page 141.

Amaretti

A tasty gift for any time—golden, round cookie with a
chewy centre, crisp edges and sweet almond flavour.

Icing (confectioner's) sugar	1 cup	250 mL
Ground almonds	1 cup	250 mL
Salt	1/8 tsp.	0.5 mL
Egg whites (large), room temperature	2	2
Almond flavouring	3/4 tsp.	4 mL
Whole almonds	20 – 25	20 – 25

Measure icing sugar, ground almonds and salt into small bowl.

Beat egg whites in separate small bowl until stiff peaks form.

Fold sugar mixture and almond flavouring into egg white. Drop, using 2 tbsp. (30 mL), for each, about 3 inches (7.5 cm) apart, onto greased and floured cookie sheets. Spread each to about 2 inch (5 cm) round (see Note). Cookies should be about 1 inch (2.5 cm) apart.

Place 1 almond in centre of each cookie. Let stand, uncovered, at room temperature for 2 hours. Bake in 350°F (175°C) oven for about 15 minutes until golden brown. Let stand on cookie sheets for 5 minutes before removing to wire racks to cool. Makes 1 1/2 dozen (18) cookies.

1 cookie: 59 Calories; 2.6 g Total Fat (1.7 g Mono, 0.6 g Poly, 0.2 g Sat);
    0 mg Cholesterol; 8 g Carbohydrate; trace Fibre; 1 g Protein; 23 mg Sodium

Pictured on page 141.

Note: To make a guide for spreading dough, lightly press 2 inch (5 cm) cookie cutter into flour on cookie sheet to leave impression.

Top Right: Piped Shortbread Cookies, this page
Centre Left: Amaretti, above
Bottom: Pecan Crescents, this page

Pecan Mini-Loaves

Pretty little loaves—pretty little gifts!
Soft apricot colour with bits of pecan peeking through.

All-purpose flour	1 cup	250 mL
Granulated sugar	1 cup	250 mL
Baking powder	1 tbsp.	15 mL
Baking soda	1/2 tsp.	2 mL
Salt	1/4 tsp.	1 mL
Ground cardamom	1/8 tsp.	0.5 mL
Large eggs	2	2
Milk	1 cup	250 mL
Mashed cooked yam (or sweet potato), see Note	1 cup	250 mL
Butter (or hard margarine), softened	1/3 cup	75 mL
Finely grated orange zest	1 tbsp.	15 mL
All-purpose flour	2 cups	500 mL
Chopped pecans, toasted (see Tip, page 80)	1 cup	250 mL

ORANGE CARDAMOM ICING

Icing (confectioner's) sugar	1/2 cup	125 mL
Orange juice	2 1/2 – 3 tsp.	12 – 15 mL
Ground cardamom	1/16 tsp.	0.5 mL

Combine first 6 ingredients in large bowl.

Add next 5 ingredients. Beat well.

Stir in second amount of flour and pecans until just moistened. Do not overmix. Divide and fill 10 greased 4 x 2 1/4 x 1 1/4 inch (10 × 5.75 × 3.5 cm) foil or metal mini-loaf pans about 2/3 full. Bake in 350°F (175°C) oven for about 30 minutes until wooden pick inserted in centre of loaf comes out clean. Let stand in pans for 5 minutes before removing to wire racks to cool completely.

Orange Cardamom Icing: Stir all 3 ingredients in small bowl until smooth. Add more orange juice if necessary until barely pourable consistency. Makes about 1/4 cup (60 mL) icing. Drizzle about 1 tsp. (5 mL) over each loaf. Let stand until icing is set. Makes 10 mini-loaves.

1 mini-loaf: 448 Calories; 16 g Total Fat (7.2 g Mono, 2.5 g Poly, 5.2 g Sat);
    62 mg Cholesterol; 70 g Carbohydrate; 3 g Fibre; 8 g Protein; 303 mg Sodium

Pictured on page 143.

Note: Cook about 1 1/2 cups (375 mL) yam to yield 1 cup (250 mL) mashed cooked yam.

Variation: For slightly larger loaves, divide and spoon batter into four 5 3/4 x 3 1/4 x 2 inch (14 × 8 × 5 cm) loaf pans. Bake in 350°F (175°C) oven for about 35 minutes until wooden pick inserted in centre of loaf comes out clean. Let stand in pans for 5 minutes before removing to wire racks to cool completely. Drizzle each loaf with icing. Let stand until icing is set. Makes 4 small loaves.

Pistachio Almond Fingers

These bars have a chewy, sticky, nutty topping on a buttery base.

Butter (or hard margarine), softened	1/3 cup	75 mL
Ground almonds (about 3 1/4 oz., 92 g)	1 cup	250 mL
Granulated sugar	1/2 cup	125 mL
Large eggs	2	2
All-purpose flour	1/2 cup	125 mL
Salt	1/4 tsp.	1 mL

NUT TOPPING

Butter (or hard margarine)	1/3 cup	75 mL
Granulated sugar	1/3 cup	75 mL
Golden corn syrup	1/3 cup	75 mL
Sliced almonds, toasted	3/4 cup	175 mL
Coarsely chopped pistachios, toasted (see Tip, page 80)	3/4 cup	175 mL

Beat butter, almonds and sugar in medium bowl until well combined. Add eggs, 1 at a time, beating well after each addition.

Add flour and salt. Stir. Spread mixture in bottom of greased, waxed paper-lined 9 x 13 inch (22 × 33 cm) pan. Bake in 375°F (190°C) oven for about 12 minutes until golden brown. Let stand in pan on wire rack for 10 minutes.

Nut Topping: Heat and stir butter, sugar and syrup in medium saucepan on medium until sugar is dissolved.

Add almonds and pistachios. Increase heat to medium-high. Bring to a boil. Brush side of saucepan with damp pastry brush to dissolve any sugar crystals. Boil for about 3 minutes, without stirring, until slightly thickened. Quickly spread over base. Bake for about 10 minutes until golden brown. Let stand on wire rack to cool slightly. Cut while still warm. Cuts into 24 pieces.

1 piece: 169 Calories; 11.4 g Total Fat (5.4 g Mono, 1.3 g Poly, 4.1 g Sat);
    32 mg Cholesterol; 16 g Carbohydrate; 1 g Fibre; 3 g Protein; 92 mg Sodium

Pictured on page 143.

Top: Pecan Mini-Loaves, this page
Bottom: Pistachio Almond Fingers, above

Chocolate Mini-Fruitcakes

People will love receiving these moist, fruity cakes. Make them at least 2 days in advance. You will need extra-large (jumbo) muffin cups for these.

Currants	1 1/3 cups	325 mL
Golden raisins	1 1/4 cups	300 mL
Dark raisins	1 cup	250 mL
Chopped dried pitted prunes	3/4 cup	175 mL
Orange-flavoured liqueur (such as Grand Marnier)	2/3 cup	150 mL
Red glazed cherries, halved	1/2 cup	125 mL
Diced mixed peel	1/3 cup	75 mL
Golden corn syrup	3 tbsp.	50 mL
Butter (or hard margarine), softened	1/2 cup	125 mL
Brown sugar, packed	3/4 cup	175 mL
Finely grated orange zest	1 1/2 tsp.	7 mL
Large eggs	3	3
Semi-sweet chocolate baking squares (1 oz., 28 g, each), grated	2	2
Chopped walnuts, toasted (see Tip, page 80)	3/4 cup	175 mL
All-purpose flour	1/2 cup	125 mL
Cocoa, sifted if lumpy	2 tbsp.	30 mL
Baking powder	1/2 tsp.	2 mL
Salt	1/4 tsp.	1 mL
Red glazed cherries, halved	5	5
Walnut halves	30	30
Orange-flavoured liqueur (such as Grand Marnier)	3 tbsp.	50 mL

Combine first 8 ingredients in extra-large bowl. Stir well. Cover. Let stand overnight.

Beat butter, brown sugar and orange zest in medium bowl until light and creamy. Add eggs, 1 at a time, beating well after each addition. Add to fruit mixture. Stir.

Add grated chocolate and chopped walnuts. Stir.

Measure next 4 ingredients into small bowl. Stir. Add to fruit mixture. Stir well.

Grease 10 extra-large muffin cups with cooking spray. Fill each 3/4 full. Place 1 cherry half in centre of each cake. Arrange 3 walnut halves around edge. Bake in 275°F (140°C) oven for about 1 1/4 hours until wooden pick inserted in centre of cake comes out sticky but not wet.

Set pan on wire rack. Brush hot cakes with second amount of liqueur. Cover pan with foil. Let stand until cool. Chill, covered, in pan for 24 hours before removing from cups. Makes 10 mini-fruitcakes.

1 mini-fruitcake: 609 Calories; 22.5 g Total Fat (6.1 g Mono, 6.7 g Poly, 8.3 g Sat); 91 mg Cholesterol; 93 g Carbohydrate; 6 g Fibre; 9 g Protein; 216 mg Sodium

Pictured on page 147.

Hazelnut Shortbread

No one will be able to resist these sweet, nutty cookies. Delicious!

Butter (or hard margarine), softened	1 cup	250 mL
Granulated sugar	1 cup	250 mL
Hazelnuts, toasted (see Tip, page 80), skins removed (see Tip, page 145), and finely chopped	1 cup	250 mL
All-purpose flour	2 cups	500 mL
Baking powder	1/4 tsp.	1 mL
Salt	1/4 tsp.	1 mL
Egg white (large), fork-beaten	1	1
Sanding (decorating) sugar (see Glossary, page 9)	2 tbsp.	30 mL

Beat butter and sugar in large bowl until light and creamy.

Add hazelnuts. Stir.

Combine flour, baking powder and salt in medium bowl. Add to butter mixture. Stir until soft crumbly dough forms. Shape into flattened disc. Roll out to 1/3 inch (8 mm) thickness between 2 sheets of lightly floured waxed paper. Remove top sheet of waxed paper. Cut out dough using lightly floured 2 inch (5 cm) round fluted cookie cutter. Roll out scraps to cut more rounds. Arrange, about 1 inch (2.5 cm) apart, on ungreased cookie sheets.

Brush each cookie with egg white. Sprinkle with sanding sugar. Bake in 375°F (190°C) oven for about 7 minutes until edges start to turn golden. Let stand on cookie sheets for 5 minutes before removing to wire racks to cool. Cool cookie sheets between batches if using more than once. Makes about 3 1/2 dozen (42) cookies.

1 cookie: 104 Calories; 6.4 g Total Fat (2.7 g Mono, 0.4 g Poly, 3 g Sat); 12 mg Cholesterol; 10 g Carbohydrate; trace Fibre; 1 g Protein; 64 mg Sodium

Pictured on pages 146 and 147.

Cherry Mini-Loaves

Eye-catching, pale pink loaf speckled with deep red cherries and nuts. Makes a nice afternoon tea loaf. Tie some herbal tea bags to each loaf when giving!

All-purpose flour	2 1/2 cups	625 mL
Baking powder	2 tsp.	10 mL
Salt	1/2 tsp.	2 mL
Granulated sugar	1 cup	250 mL
Reserved juice from cherries plus water, to equal	1 cup	250 mL
Cooking oil	1/4 cup	60 mL
Large egg	1	1
Almond flavouring	1 tsp.	5 mL
Red maraschino cherries, halved and juice reserved	3/4 cup	175 mL
Chopped walnuts (or pecans)	1/2 cup	125 mL

Measure flour, baking powder and salt into large bowl. Stir. Make a well in centre.

Beat next 5 ingredients in medium bowl until well combined. Pour into well.

Add cherries and walnuts. Stir until just moistened. Divide and fill 4 greased 5 3/4 × 3 1/4 × 2 inch (14 × 8 × 5 cm) loaf pans about 2/3 full. Bake in 350°F (175°C) oven for about 30 minutes until wooden pick inserted in centre of loaf comes out clean. Let stand in pans for 10 minutes before removing to wire racks to cool. Makes 4 small loaves.

1 loaf: 816 Calories; 26 g Total Fat (11.2 g Mono, 11 g Poly, 2.2 g Sat); 54 mg Cholesterol; 134 g Carbohydrate; 4 g Fibre; 14 g Protein; 501 mg Sodium

Pictured on pages 146 and 147.

Variation: Use 1/2 red and 1/2 green cherries.

■ ■ ■

To peel hazelnuts, spread toasted nuts on half of tea towel. Fold other half over to cover nuts. Rub vigorously back and forth for 1 to 2 minutes, pressing down until skins are removed. You may not be able to remove all skins of nuts, but outer paper skins should come off.

Hazelnut Chocolate Cupcakes

Delightful little domed cakes studded with pieces of hazelnuts.

Hazelnuts, toasted (see Tip, page 80) and skins removed (see Tip, this page)	1 cup	250 mL
Egg whites (large)	6	6
All-purpose flour	1 1/3 cups	325 mL
Icing (confectioner's) sugar	2 cups	500 mL
Cocoa, sifted if lumpy	1/3 cup	75 mL
Butter (not margarine), melted	3/4 cup	175 mL
Icing (confectioner's) sugar, for dusting (optional)		

Process hazelnuts in blender or food processor until finely ground.

Beat egg whites in medium bowl until frothy. Do not overbeat.

Combine next 3 ingredients in large bowl. Stir in hazelnuts. Make a well in centre.

Add egg white and butter to well. Stir well. Fill 12 greased muffin cups 3/4 full. Bake in 400°F (205°C) oven for 20 to 25 minutes until wooden pick inserted in centre of cupcake comes out clean. Let stand in pan for 5 minutes before removing to wire rack to cool completely.

Dust with icing sugar. Makes 12 cupcakes.

1 cupcake: 333 Calories; 20.2 g Total Fat (9.5 g Mono, 1.2 g Poly, 8.4 g Sat); 33 mg Cholesterol; 36 g Carbohydrate; 2 g Fibre; 5 g Protein; 153 mg Sodium

Pictured on page 146.

Photo Legend next page:

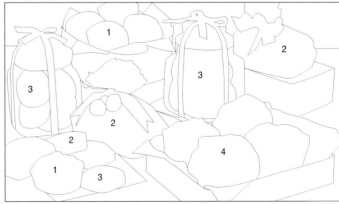

1. Hazelnut Chocolate Cupcakes, above
2. Cherry Mini-Loaves, this page
3. Hazelnut Shortbread, page 144
4. Chocolate Mini-Fruitcakes, page 144

Cranberry Cashew Biscotti

Crunchy biscotti that are perfect for dunking. Lively flavours of cranberry and lemon delight the taste buds.

All-purpose flour	2 cups	500 mL
Granulated sugar	1 cup	250 mL
Baking powder	1/4 tsp.	1 mL
Large eggs, fork-beaten	3	3
Finely grated lemon zest	1 tsp.	5 mL
Coarsely chopped cashews, toasted (see Tip, page 80)	2/3 cup	150 mL
Dried cranberries	1/2 cup	125 mL

Combine flour, sugar and baking powder in large bowl. Add eggs. Mix until stiff dough forms.

Add remaining 3 ingredients. Mix well. Turn out onto lightly floured surface. Divide dough in half. Shape each half into 8 inch (20 cm) roll, about 2 1/4 inches (6 cm) in diameter. Flatten slightly. Arrange crosswise, about 3 1/2 inches (9 cm) apart, on greased baking sheet. Bake in 350°F (175°C) oven for about 30 minutes until golden brown and crusty. Remove from oven. Let stand on baking sheet for about 1 1/2 hours until cool. Remove to cutting board. Cut on diagonal with serrated knife into 1/2 inch (12 mm) thick slices. Arrange in single layer, cut-side up, on same baking sheet. Bake for about 20 minutes until dry and browned on bottom. Makes about 2 dozen (24) biscotti.

1 biscotti: 107 Calories; 2.3 g Total Fat (1.1 g Mono, 0.4 g Poly, 0.5 g Sat); 22 mg Cholesterol; 20 g Carbohydrate; 1 g Fibre; 2 g Protein; 12 mg Sodium

Pictured on page 149.

Apricot Pistachio Biscotti

Pretty with orange apricots and light green pistachios. The apricots add chewiness to an otherwise crisp biscotti.

All-purpose flour	2 cups	500 mL
Baking powder	1/4 tsp.	1 mL
Salt	1/4 tsp.	1 mL
Pistachios, shelled and toasted (see Tip, page 80)	2/3 cup	150 mL
Granulated sugar	1/2 cup	125 mL
Brown sugar, packed	1/2 cup	125 mL
Finely chopped dried apricots	1/2 cup	125 mL
Large eggs	3	3
Finely grated lemon zest	1 tsp.	5 mL
Vanilla	1 tsp.	5 mL

Combine flour, baking powder and salt in large bowl.

Add next 4 ingredients. Stir.

Beat eggs, lemon zest and vanilla with fork in small bowl. Add to flour mixture. Mix until stiff dough forms. Turn out onto lightly floured surface. Divide dough in half. Shape each half into 8 inch (20 cm) roll, about 2 1/4 inches (6 cm) in diameter. Flatten slightly. Arrange crosswise, about 3 1/2 inches (9 cm) apart, on greased baking sheet. Bake in 350°F (175°F) oven for about 30 minutes until golden brown and crusty. Remove from oven. Let stand on baking sheet for about 1 1/2 hours until cool. Remove to cutting board. Cut on diagonal with serrated knife into 1/2 inch (12 mm) thick slices. Arrange in single layer, cut-side up, on same baking sheet. Bake for about 20 minutes until dry and browned on bottom. Makes about 2 dozen (24) biscotti.

1 biscotti: 114 Calories; 2.7 g Total Fat (1.6 g Mono, 0.4 g Poly, 0.5 g Sat); 27 mg Cholesterol; 21 g Carbohydrate; 1 g Fibre; 3 g Protein; 40 mg Sodium

Pictured on page 149.

Top : Apricot Pistachio Biscotti, above
Bottom: Cranberry Cashew Biscotti, this page

Gingerbread Stars

Star light, star bright—these cookies are sure to delight!
Simple and delicious.

Butter (or hard margarine), softened	1/2 cup	125 mL
Brown sugar, packed	1/2 cup	125 mL
Ground ginger	1 1/4 tsp.	6 mL
Baking powder	1 tsp.	5 mL
Ground cinnamon	3/4 tsp.	4 mL
Baking soda	1/2 tsp.	2 mL
Salt	1/4 tsp.	1 mL
Ground cloves	1/8 tsp.	0.5 mL
Fancy (mild) molasses	1/2 cup	125 mL
Large egg	1	1
White vinegar	1 tbsp.	15 mL
All-purpose flour	2 1/2 cups	625 mL
HONEY LEMON ICING		
Liquid honey	2 tbsp.	30 mL
Lemon juice	2 tbsp.	30 mL
Icing (confectioner's) sugar	2 – 2 1/2 cups	500 – 625 mL
Gold or silver dragées (see Glossary, page 9), optional		

Beat butter in large bowl for 1 minute. Add next 7 ingredients. Beat well.

Add molasses, egg and vinegar. Beat until smooth. Mixture will look slightly curdled.

Add 1/2 of flour. Beat well. Mix in remaining flour well. Divide dough in half. Wrap each half in plastic wrap. Chill for at least 3 hours. Roll out 1 portion of dough on lightly floured surface to 1/4 inch (6 mm) thickness. Cut out, using lightly floured 2 1/2 inch (6.4 cm) star cookie cutter. Roll out scraps to cut more stars. Repeat with remaining portion of dough. Arrange cookies, about 1 inch (2.5 cm) apart, on greased cookie sheets. Bake in 375°F (190ºC) oven for about 8 minutes until edges start to brown. Let stand on cookie sheets for 5 minutes before removing to wire racks to cool completely.

Honey Lemon Icing: Combine honey and lemon juice in medium heatproof bowl or top of double boiler. Place over small saucepan of simmering water. Heat and stir for about 4 minutes, adding icing sugar, 1 tbsp. (15 mL) at a time, until barely pourable consistency. Makes about 2/3 cup (150 mL) icing. Spoon into piping bag fitted with small plain writing tip or small resealable freezer bag with tiny piece snipped off corner. Outline cookie edge with icing.

Press dragée into icing at each point on star. Work quickly, as icing sets almost immediately. Makes about 3 1/2 dozen (42) cookies.

1 cookie: 109 Calories; 2.8 g Total Fat (0.8 g Mono, 0.1 g Poly, 1.7 g Sat); 13 mg Cholesterol; 21 g Carbohydrate; trace Fibre; 1 g Protein; 73 mg Sodium

Pictured on front and back cover and on page 151.

Chocolate Panforte

Pronounced pan-FOR-tay. A rich, chewy,
dark chocolate, fruit-laden slice.

Whole cashews, toasted (see Tip, page 80)	1 2/3 cups	400 mL
Whole almonds, toasted (see Tip, page 80)	1 1/2 cups	375 mL
All-purpose flour	1 1/2 cups	375 mL
Chopped dried apricots	1/2 cup	125 mL
Rings of glazed pineapple, chopped	4	4
Diced mixed peel	1/4 cup	60 mL
Chopped red glazed cherries	1/4 cup	60 mL
Cocoa, sifted if lumpy	1/4 cup	60 mL
Ground cinnamon	2 tsp.	10 mL
Liquid honey	1 cup	250 mL
Granulated sugar	1 cup	250 mL
Semi-sweet chocolate baking squares (1 oz., 28 g, each), chopped	4	4

Measure first 9 ingredients into extra-large bowl. Mix well.

Heat and stir honey and sugar in small saucepan on medium until sugar is dissolved. Bring to a boil on medium-high. Boil for 5 minutes without stirring. Remove from heat. Immediately add to nut mixture. Stir well.

Heat and stir chocolate in small heavy saucepan on lowest heat until almost melted. Do not overheat. Remove from heat. Stir until smooth. Add to nut mixture. Stir. Line greased 9 x 13 inch (22 x 33 cm) pan with parchment (not waxed) paper, extending slightly over both long sides of pan (to use for lifting). Press mixture evenly in bottom of pan. Bake in 375°F (190°C) oven for 20 minutes. Let stand in pan on wire rack until cooled completely. Invert onto work surface. Remove paper. Cut in half lengthwise. Cut each half crosswise into 1/2 inch (12 mm) slices. Makes 48 bars.

1 bar: 138 Calories; 4.9 g Total Fat (3 g Mono, 0.9 g Poly, 0.7 g Sat); 0 mg Cholesterol; 23 g Carbohydrate; 1 g Fibre; 2 g Protein; 2 mg Sodium

Pictured on page 151.

Top: Chocolate Panforte, above
Bottom: Gingerbread Stars, this page

Holiday Baking

Spread your indulgences throughout the year. Have something warm and sticky for Easter, something tantalizing for Thanksgiving, then round out the season with something creamy for Christmas. There are large batch recipes—perfect for serving to a crowd or packaging for a baking exchange with friends.

Hot Cross Buns

*Traditional, shiny-topped buns full of spices
and fruit with a vanilla glaze.*

All-purpose flour	2 cups	500 mL
Granulated sugar	1/2 cup	125 mL
Instant yeast	2 tbsp.	30 mL
Ground cinnamon	1 1/2 tsp.	7 mL
Salt	3/4 tsp.	4 mL
Ground allspice	1/4 tsp.	1 mL
Ground nutmeg	1/4 tsp.	1 mL
Can of evaporated milk	13 1/2 oz.	385 mL
Water	1/4 cup	60 mL
Butter (or hard margarine), cut up	1/3 cup	75 mL
Large eggs	2	2
Egg yolk (large)	1	1
All-purpose flour, approximately	3 1/4 cups	800 mL
Finely chopped mixed glazed fruit	1/2 cup	125 mL
Chopped raisins	1/2 cup	125 mL
Egg white (large), fork-beaten	1	1
WHITE ICING		
Icing (confectioner's) sugar	1 cup	250 mL
Half-and-half cream	1 1/2 tbsp.	25 mL
Clear vanilla (or almond flavouring)	1/4 tsp.	1 mL

Combine first 7 ingredients in large bowl. Make a well in centre.

Heat and stir evaporated milk, water and butter in small heavy saucepan on medium until butter is almost melted. Remove from heat. Stir until butter is melted. Let stand for 5 minutes. Add to well. Stir until smooth batter forms.

Beat eggs and egg yolk with fork in small bowl. Add to batter. Stir well.

Work in enough of second amount of flour, 1/2 cup (125 mL) at a time, until soft dough forms. Turn out onto lightly floured surface. Knead dough for 5 to 10 minutes, adding flour 1 tbsp. (15 mL) at a time if necessary to prevent sticking, until smooth and elastic. Place in greased large bowl, turning once to grease top. Cover with greased waxed paper and tea towel. Let stand for 15 minutes.

Add glazed fruit and raisins. Work into dough until well distributed. Turn out onto lightly floured surface. Divide dough in half. Divide each half into 12 equal portions. Roll each into ball. Arrange on greased baking sheets. Cover with greased waxed paper and tea towel. Let stand in oven with light on and door closed for about 60 minutes until doubled in size.

Brush egg white over each bun. Bake in 375°F (190°C) oven for about 20 minutes until golden brown. Let stand on baking sheets for 5 minutes before removing to wire racks to cool completely.

White Icing: Stir icing sugar into cream and vanilla in small bowl until barely pourable consistency. Spoon into piping bag fitted with small plain writing tip or small resealable freezer bag with tiny piece snipped off corner. Pipe crosses onto buns. Makes 24 buns.

1 bun: 227 Calories; 5.1 g Total Fat (1.5 g Mono, 0.4 g Poly, 2.8 g Sat);
    40 mg Cholesterol; 40 g Carbohydrate; 1 g Fibre; 6 g Protein; 132 mg Sodium

Pictured on page 155.

Photo Legend next page:
Top Left: Ukrainian Easter Paska, page 156
Centre Right: Hot Cross Buns, this page
Bottom Left: Easter Babka, page 157

Ukrainian Easter Paska

Paska is a round-shaped bread, traditionally served at Easter. Enjoy this pretty loaf with its braided top.

Warm water	1/2 cup	125 mL
Granulated sugar	1 tsp.	5 mL
Envelope of active dry yeast (about 2 1/4 tsp., 11 mL)	1/4 oz.	8 g
Milk	1 1/2 cups	375 mL
Granulated sugar	1/3 cup	75 mL
Butter (or hard margarine)	1/4 cup	60 mL
Salt	2 tsp.	10 mL
All-purpose flour	2 cups	500 mL
Large eggs, fork-beaten	2	2
All-purpose flour, approximately	4 1/2 cups	1.1 L
Large egg	1	1
Water	2 tsp.	10 mL

Stir water and first amount of sugar in small bowl until sugar is dissolved. Sprinkle yeast over top. Let stand for 10 minutes. Stir until yeast is dissolved.

Heat and stir next 4 ingredients in small heavy saucepan on medium until butter is almost melted. Pour into extra-large bowl. Stir until butter is melted. Let stand for 5 minutes.

Add first amounts of flour, eggs and yeast mixture. Stir until smooth batter forms.

Work in enough of second amount of flour, 1/2 cup (125 mL) at a time, until soft sticky dough forms. Turn out onto well-floured surface. Knead for 5 to 10 minutes, adding flour 1 tbsp. (15 mL) at a time if necessary to prevent sticking, until smooth and elastic. Place in greased extra-large bowl, turning once to grease top. Cover with greased waxed paper and tea towel. Let stand in oven with light on and door closed for about 1 hour until doubled in bulk. Punch dough down. Turn out onto lightly floured surface. Knead for 1 minute. Press about 3/4 of dough firmly into bottom of greased round 3 quart (3 L) casserole. Divide remaining dough into 4 equal portions.

Roll 2 portions into 36 inch (90 cm) ropes. Twist together. Place on top of loaf, circling against side of casserole and tucking ends under. Remove 1/3 of dough from both remaining portions. Set aside. Roll each 2/3 portion into 36 inch (90 cm) rope, a bit thinner than the first ones. Twist together. Place along inside of first braid, tucking ends under.

Roll both remaining 1/3 portions into 18 inch (45 cm) ropes. Twist middle of ropes together 3 or 4 times. Place in centre of loaf, curling 4 loose ends inward.

Cover with greased waxed paper and tea towel. Let stand in oven with light on and door closed for 10 to 15 minutes until slightly risen. If paska rises too much, some of the decoration will be lost. It will continue to rise while baking.

Beat remaining egg and water with fork in small bowl until frothy. Brush top of paska with egg wash. Bake in 350°F (175°C) oven for 15 minutes. Reduce heat to 325°F (160°C). Bake for about 40 minutes, covering loosely with foil if necessary to prevent over-browning, until golden brown and hollow sounding when tapped. Cuts into 30 slices.

1 slice: 142 Calories; 2.6 g Total Fat (0.7 g Mono, 0.3 g Poly, 1.3 g Sat); 26 mg Cholesterol; 25 g Carbohydrate; 1 g Fibre; 4 g Protein; 188 mg Sodium

Pictured on page 154.

Easter Babka

A delightful, sweet seasonal egg bread. A good workout too—a little extra kneading time, but results are worth the effort! To make babka, you will need 3 empty 48 oz. (1.4 L) juice cans and 1 empty 2 lb. (900 g) coffee can. Leave bottom end on each can. Grease insides well.

Butter (or hard margarine), softened	1/2 cup	125 mL
Granulated sugar	1 cup	250 mL
Egg yolks (large)	10	10
Salt	1 tsp.	5 mL
Milk	1 1/2 cups	375 mL
Envelope of active dry yeast (about 2 1/4 tsp., 11 mL)	1/4 oz.	8 g
All-purpose flour	2 1/2 cups	625 mL
Orange juice	1/3 cup	75 mL
Finely grated orange zest	2 tsp.	10 mL
Vanilla	1 tsp.	5 mL
All-purpose flour, approximately	5 1/3 cups	1.35 L
Golden raisins	2/3 cup	150 mL

Beat butter and sugar in large bowl until light and creamy. Add egg yolks and salt. Beat well.

Heat milk in small saucepan on medium until just warm. Remove from heat. Sprinkle yeast over top. Let stand for 10 minutes. Stir until yeast is dissolved. Beat into egg yolk mixture.

Add first amount of flour, 1/2 cup (125 mL) at a time.

Add orange juice, orange zest and vanilla. Mix well. Transfer to extra-large bowl. Work in enough of second amount of flour, 1/2 cup (125 mL) at a time, until soft sticky dough forms. Turn out onto lightly floured surface. Knead for about 15 minutes, adding more flour if necessary to prevent sticking, until smooth and elastic but still a bit tacky. Place in greased extra-large bowl, turning once to grease top. Cover with greased waxed paper and tea towel. Let stand in oven with light on and door closed for about 1 1/2 hours until doubled in bulk. Punch dough down.

Add raisins. Work into dough until well distributed. Divide dough into 4 equal portions. Shape each portion into smooth ball. Drop into prepared cans. Cans should be about 1/3 full. Punch dough down evenly in cans. Cover with greased waxed paper and tea towel. Let stand in oven with light on and door closed for about 1 1/2 hours until dough almost reaches tops of cans. Bake in 350°F (175°C) oven for about 30 minutes for large cans and about 25 minutes for smaller can, covering top of babkas loosely with foil if necessary to prevent over-browning, until tops are domed above edge and golden brown. Remove cans from oven. Immediately slide out each loaf onto its side onto folded hand towels covered with tea towels. Rotate loaves occasionally, 1/4 turn, to prevent delicate bread from settling unevenly while cooling. Do not stand loaves upright until completely cooled. Makes 4 loaves. Each loaf cuts into about 12 slices, for a total of 48 slices.

1 slice: 137 Calories; 3.4 g Total Fat (1 g Mono, 0.3 g Poly, 1.7 g Sat); 51 mg Cholesterol; 23 g Carbohydrate; 1 g Fibre; 3 g Protein; 76 mg Sodium

Pictured on page 154.

Sweet Potato Pie

Looks just like pumpkin pie—and almost tastes like it too!
Serve with a dollop of whipped cream.

Fresh sweet potatoes (with peel), 1 1/2 lbs. blemishes removed		680 g
Boiling water		
Salt	1/2 tsp.	2 mL
Cans of evaporated milk (not skim), 5 1/2 oz. (160 mL) each	2	2
Granulated sugar	1/2 cup	125 mL
Brown sugar, packed	1/3 cup	75 mL
All-purpose flour	1 1/2 tbsp.	25 mL
Ground cinnamon	1/2 tsp.	2 mL
Ground nutmeg	1/4 tsp.	1 mL
Large eggs	2	2
Vanilla	1/4 tsp.	1 mL
Pastry for 9 inch (22 cm) deep dish pie shell	1	1

Cook sweet potato in boiling water and salt in large pot or Dutch oven on medium-high until soft but not mushy. Drain. Run under cold water to cool. Drain well. Peel and discard skin. Chop coarsely.

Process sweet potato and evaporated milk in blender or food processor until smooth.

Combine next 5 ingredients in large bowl.

Add eggs, vanilla and sweet potato mixture. Beat until smooth.

Roll out pastry on lightly floured surface to about 1/8 inch (3 mm) thickness. Line pie plate. Trim, leaving 1/2 inch (12 mm) overhang. Roll under and crimp decorative edge. Pour filling into pie shell. Bake on bottom rack in 425°F (220°C) oven for 15 minutes. Reduce heat to 350°F (175°C). Bake for about 45 minutes until knife inserted in centre comes out clean. Pie might puff up but will settle when cooling. Let stand on wire rack for at least 30 minutes before serving. Cuts into 8 wedges.

1 wedge: 337 Calories; 10.1 g Total Fat (4 g Mono, 1 g Poly, 4.2 g Sat);
66 mg Cholesterol; 56 g Carbohydrate; 3 g Fibre; 7 g Protein; 178 mg Sodium

Pictured on pages 158 and 159.

Top Left and Bottom Right: Sweet Potato Pie, above
Top Right and Bottom Left: Pumpkin Nut Cake, page 160

Pumpkin Nut Cake

Sparkly sugar glaze on a moist, spicy cake.

Butter (or hard margarine), softened	1/2 cup	125 mL
Granulated sugar	1 cup	250 mL
Brown sugar, packed	1/2 cup	125 mL
Large eggs	2	2
Cooked mashed pumpkin (or canned pure pumpkin, no spices)	1 cup	250 mL
All-purpose flour	2 cups	500 mL
Chopped pecans, toasted (see Tip, page 80)	1 cup	250 mL
Baking powder	2 tsp.	10 mL
Baking soda	1 tsp.	5 mL
Ground cinnamon	1 tsp.	5 mL
Ground nutmeg	1/2 tsp.	2 mL
Ground ginger	1/2 tsp.	2 mL
Salt	1/4 tsp.	1 mL
Milk	1/2 cup	125 mL
CINNAMON TOPPING		
Granulated sugar	2 tbsp.	30 mL
Ground cinnamon	1/2 tsp.	2 mL
Butter (or hard margarine), melted	2 tbsp.	30 mL

Beat butter and both sugars in large bowl until light and creamy. Add eggs, 1 at a time, beating well after each addition.

Add pumpkin. Beat well. Mixture may look slightly curdled.

Combine next 8 ingredients in medium bowl.

Add flour mixture to pumpkin mixture in 3 additions, alternating with milk in 2 additions, beginning and ending with flour mixture. Stir well. Spread evenly in greased 12 cup (2.7 L) bundt pan. Bake in 350°F (175°C) oven for about 45 minutes until wooden pick inserted in centre of cake comes out clean. Let stand in pan for 10 minutes before inverting onto wire rack to cool slightly.

Cinnamon Topping: Combine sugar and cinnamon in small bowl. Brush top of warm cake with melted butter. Sprinkle with sugar mixture. Cuts into 16 pieces.

1 piece: 276 Calories; 13.3 g Total Fat (5.5 g Mono, 1.6 g Poly, 5.4 g Sat); 48 mg Cholesterol; 37 g Carbohydrate; 1 g Fibre; 4 g Protein; 256 mg Sodium

Pictured on pages 158 and 159.

Pecan Tart

Sweet filling that's loaded with pecans. A delight to serve anytime.

Pastry for 9 inch (22 cm) pie shell	1	1
Large eggs	4	4
Brown sugar, packed	1 cup	250 mL
Golden corn syrup	2/3 cup	150 mL
Butter (or hard margarine), melted	1/4 cup	60 mL
Vanilla	1 tsp.	5 mL
Finely grated orange zest	1 tsp.	5 mL
Salt	1/4 tsp.	1 mL
Chopped pecans, toasted (see Tip, page 80)	2 cups	500 mL
Pecan halves	16	16

Roll out pastry on lightly floured surface to about 1/8 inch (3 mm) thickness. Press in bottom and up side of 9 inch (22 cm) tart pan with fluted side and removable bottom. Trim edge. Cover. Chill for 30 minutes.

Beat eggs in large bowl until frothy. Add next 6 ingredients. Beat well.

Place tart pan on baking sheet (to make it easier to remove hot pan from oven). Sprinkle chopped pecans over pastry. Pour egg mixture over pecans.

Arrange pecan halves around edge of filling. Bake on bottom rack in 400°F (205°C) oven for 10 minutes. Reduce heat to 350°F (175°C). Bake for about 35 minutes until filling is set and pastry is golden brown. Let stand in pan on wire rack to cool completely. Cuts into 8 wedges.

1 wedge: 597 Calories; 37.3 g Total Fat (19.9 g Mono, 7 g Poly, 8.2 g Sat); 124 mg Cholesterol; 65 g Carbohydrate; 2 g Fibre; 7 g Protein; 317 mg Sodium

Pictured on page 161.

Streusel-Topped Pumpkin Pie

Sweet, crunchy streusel makes an old favourite into something new.

Pastry for 9 inch (22 cm) deep dish pie shell	1	1
Brown sugar, packed	1 cup	250 mL
Ground cinnamon	3/4 tsp.	4 mL
Ground ginger	1/2 tsp.	2 mL
Ground nutmeg	1/2 tsp.	2 mL
Ground cloves	1/8 tsp.	0.5 mL
Salt	1/4 tsp.	1 mL
Large eggs	2	2
Can of pure pumpkin (no spices)	14 oz.	398 mL
Can of evaporated milk	13 1/2 oz.	385 mL

GRAHAM STREUSEL TOPPING

Butter (or hard margarine)	3 tbsp.	50 mL
All-purpose flour	1/3 cup	75 mL
Graham cracker crumbs	1/3 cup	75 mL
Brown sugar, packed	1/3 cup	75 mL
Ground cinnamon	1/4 tsp.	1 mL
Salt	1/4 tsp.	1 mL

Roll out pastry on lightly floured surface to about 1/8 inch (3 mm) thickness. Line pie plate. Trim, leaving 1/2 inch (12 mm) overhang. Roll under and crimp decorative edge.

Combine next 6 ingredients in large bowl.

Add eggs and pumpkin. Beat until smooth.

Add evaporated milk. Stir until no white streaks remain. Pour into pie shell.

Graham Streusel Topping: Melt butter in small saucepan on medium. Add remaining 5 ingredients. Stir well. Makes 1 cup (250 mL) topping. Sprinkle over pumpkin filling. Bake on bottom rack in 425°F (220°C) oven for 10 minutes. Reduce heat to 350°F (175°C). Bake for about 45 minutes until knife inserted in centre comes out clean. Knife may have some crumbs on it from the streusel topping. Top will be puffed on sides and lower in centre. Let stand on wire rack until cooled completely. Cuts into 8 wedges.

1 wedge: 409 Calories; 15.5 g Total Fat (5.7 g Mono, 1.2 g Poly, 7.4 g Sat);
    81 mg Cholesterol; 62 g Carbohydrate; 1 g Fibre; 7 g Protein; 405 mg Sodium

Pictured on page 163.

Pear And Maple Crumble

Serve this warm, sweet dessert with a small scoop of ice cream or a dollop of whipped cream.

Maple (or maple-flavoured) syrup	1/3 cup	75 mL
Brown sugar, packed	1/4 cup	60 mL
Cornstarch	1 1/2 tbsp.	25 mL
Ground cardamom (optional)	1/8 tsp.	0.5 mL
Salt, sprinkle		
Fresh medium pears, peeled and sliced 1/4 inch (6 mm) thick (see Note)	5	5

NUT TOPPING

All-purpose flour	1 cup	250 mL
Granulated sugar	1/2 cup	125 mL
Brown sugar, packed	1/2 cup	125 mL
Baking powder	1/4 tsp.	1 mL
Cold butter (or hard margarine), cut up	1/2 cup	125 mL
Medium unsweetened coconut	1/4 cup	60 mL
Chopped Brazil nuts, toasted (see Tip, page 80)	1/4 cup	60 mL

Combine first 5 ingredients in large bowl.

Add pear slices. Stir until coated. Turn into greased 2 to 2 1/2 quart (2 to 2.5 L) casserole.

Nut Topping: Combine first 4 ingredients in medium bowl. Cut in butter until mixture resembles coarse crumbs.

Add coconut and Brazil nuts. Stir well. Sprinkle over pear mixture. Bake in 375°F (190°C) oven for 45 to 60 minutes until topping is crisp and golden brown and pears are tender. Let stand on wire rack for 15 minutes before serving. Serves 8.

1 serving: 451 Calories; 20.4 g Total Fat (5.7 g Mono, 2.8 g Poly, 10.8 g Sat);
    33 mg Cholesterol; 67 g Carbohydrate; 3 g Fibre; 4 g Protein; 149 mg Sodium

Pictured on page 163.

Note: Pears should be ripe but still firm for best results.

Top Right: Streusel-Topped Pumpkin Pie, this page
Bottom: Pear And Maple Crumble, above

Striped Corners

Enjoy the Irish cream flavour in this attractive cookie. Almost too pretty to eat! Recipe is easy to double to make about 128 cookies—perfect for a baking exchange.

Butter (or hard margarine), softened	1 cup	250 mL
Icing (confectioner's) sugar	1 1/2 cups	375 mL
Large egg	1	1
All-purpose flour	3 cups	750 mL
Salt	1/4 tsp.	1 mL
Powdered Irish cream-flavoured coffee whitener	1/3 cup	75 mL
Cocoa, sifted if lumpy	1 tbsp.	15 mL
Milk chocolate chips	1 cup	250 mL
Flake coconut, toasted (see Tip, page 80)	2/3 cup	175 mL
Chopped sliced almonds, toasted (see Tip, page 80)	2/3 cup	175 mL

Beat butter and icing sugar in large bowl until light and creamy. Add egg. Beat well.

Add 1/2 of flour, 1/4 cup (60 mL) at a time while beating, until well combined. Add remaining flour and salt. Mix well. Divide dough into 2 equal portions.

Add coffee whitener and cocoa to 1 portion. Mix until evenly coloured. Shape into flattened disc. Shape remaining portion into flattened disc. Cover each with plastic wrap. Chill for 2 hours. Roll out each disc between 2 sheets of waxed paper on dampened work surface to 4 x 24 inch (10 x 60 cm) rectangle, about 1/8 inch (3 mm) thick. Remove and discard top sheet of waxed paper from both rectangles. Flip 1 rectangle onto the other, aligning edges of dough as best as possible. Press together. Remove and discard waxed paper. Roll up tightly, jelly roll-style, from short side, using bottom sheet of waxed paper as guide. Discard waxed paper. Roll should be about 4 inches (10 cm) long and 3 1/2 inches (9 cm) in diameter. Cover tightly with plastic wrap. Chill for at least 6 hours. Slice chilled dough into 1/4 inch (6 mm) slices. Cut each slice into 4 wedges. Arrange about 1 inch (2.5 cm) apart on ungreased cookie sheets. Bake in 400°F (205°C) oven for about 7 minutes until golden brown. Let stand on cookie sheets for 5 minutes before removing to wire racks to cool completely. Cool cookie sheets between batches if using more than once.

Heat and stir chocolate chips in small heavy saucepan on lowest heat until almost melted. Do not overheat. Remove from heat. Stir until smooth. Keep warm over hot water. Dip round edge of cooled cookies in chocolate, then immediately into coconut and/or almonds. Makes 5 1/2 dozen (66) cookies.

1 cookie: 93 Calories; 5.5 g Total Fat (1.6 g Mono, 0.3 g Poly, 3.2 g Sat); 12 mg Cholesterol; 10 g Carbohydrate; trace Fibre; 1 g Protein; 45 mg Sodium

Pictured on page 166.

Spiced Heart Cookies

Gingerbread hearts will warm yours. Serve with tea or eggnog while decorating the Christmas tree. Makes a large batch.

Granulated sugar	1 cup	250 mL
Fancy (mild) molasses	1 cup	250 mL
Butter (or hard margarine)	1/2 cup	125 mL
All-purpose flour	5 cups	1.25 L
Ground cinnamon	2 tsp.	10 mL
Ground nutmeg	3/4 tsp.	4 mL
Ground allspice	1/2 tsp	2 mL
Baking soda	1/2 tsp.	2 mL
Salt	1/4 tsp.	1 mL
Large eggs, fork-beaten	2	2
Egg white (large), fork-beaten	1	1
Finely chopped walnuts, toasted (see Tip, page 80)	1/2 cup	125 mL

Heat and stir sugar, molasses and butter in small saucepan on medium until sugar is dissolved. Pour into medium bowl. Cool.

Combine next 6 ingredients in extra-large bowl. Make a well in centre.

Add eggs and sugar mixture to well. Stir until soft dough forms. Divide dough into 2 equal portions. Cover each with plastic wrap. Chill for 3 hours.

Roll out 1 portion of dough on lightly floured surface to 1/8 inch (3 mm) thickness. Cut out dough using lightly floured heart-shaped cookie cutters. Roll out scraps to cut more hearts. Arrange about 1 inch (2.5 cm) apart on greased cookie sheets. Brush cookies with egg white. Sprinkle with walnuts. Bake in 375°F (190°C) oven for 5 to 7 minutes until edges are golden brown. Let stand on cookie sheets for 5 minutes before removing to wire racks to cool. Repeat with remaining dough, egg white and walnuts. Cool cookie sheets between batches if using more than once. Makes about 12 dozen (144) cookies.

1 cookie: 41 Calories; 1.1 g Total Fat (0.3 g Mono, 0.2 g Poly, 0.5 g Sat); 5 mg Cholesterol; 7 g Carbohydrate; trace Fibre; 1 g Protein; 19 mg Sodium

Pictured on page 166.

Orange Sour Cream Cookies

*A delicate cookie with lots of orange flavour.
These freeze well, layered between sheets of
waxed paper, whether iced or not.*

Butter (or hard margarine), softened	1 1/3 cups	325 mL
Granulated sugar	1 cup	250 mL
Sour cream	1/2 cup	125 mL
Egg yolks (large)	3	3
Finely grated orange zest	2 tbsp.	30 mL
Vanilla	1 tsp.	5 mL
All-purpose flour	3 cups	750 mL
Baking powder	1 tbsp.	15 mL
Baking soda	1 tsp.	5 mL
Salt	1/4 tsp.	1 mL
ORANGE ICING		
Icing (confectioner's) sugar	3 cups	750 mL
Orange juice	1/4 cup	60 mL
Finely grated orange zest	1 tsp.	5 mL

Beat first 6 ingredients in large bowl until well combined.

Measure next 4 ingredients into medium bowl. Stir. Add to butter mixture. Mix well. Chill for 3 hours. Roll into balls, using 2 tbsp. (30 mL) for each (or use 1 1/4 inch, 3 cm, scoop to drop mounds). Arrange about 1 1/2 inches (3.8 cm) apart on greased cookie sheets. Flatten slightly with fork dipped in flour or granulated sugar. Bake on centre rack in 350°F (175°F) oven for about 15 minutes until just golden. Let stand on cookie sheets for 5 minutes before removing to wire racks to cool completely. Cool cookie sheets between batches if using more than once.

Orange Icing: Combine icing sugar, orange juice and zest in medium heatproof bowl until stiff paste forms. Place bowl over small saucepan of simmering water. Heat and stir for about 2 minutes until icing is barely pourable consistency. Makes about 1 1/4 cups (300 mL) icing. Pipe or drizzle over each cookie. Let stand for about 1 hour until icing is set. Makes about 6 dozen (72) cookies.

1 cookie: 90 Calories; 4.1 g Total Fat (1.2 g Mono, 0.2 g Poly, 2.5 g Sat); 19 mg Cholesterol; 13 g Carbohydrate; trace Fibre; 1 g Protein; 79 mg Sodium

Pictured on pages 166/167.

Cranberry Macadamia Mounds

*Hide these from the kids! Extra-special cookies that
are sure to impress. These are for company.*

Dried cranberries	1 1/2 cups	375 mL
Orange juice	1/2 cup	125 mL
Orange-flavoured liqueur (such as Grand Marnier)	2 tbsp.	30 mL
All-purpose flour	3 cups	750 mL
Brown sugar, packed	1 1/2 cups	375 mL
White chocolate chips	1 cup	250 mL
Coarsely chopped macadamia nuts, toasted (see Tip, page 80)	1 cup	250 mL
Baking powder	1 1/2 tbsp.	25 mL
Salt	1/2 tsp.	2 mL
Buttermilk (or reconstituted from powder)	1 cup	250 mL
Butter (or hard margarine), melted	2/3 cup	150 mL
Large egg	1	1
Finely grated orange zest	1 tbsp.	15 mL

Measure first 3 ingredients into small bowl. Stir. Let stand for 30 minutes, stirring occasionally. Drain liquid. Discard liquid or use another time as a quick dessert topping over cut up fresh fruit.

Combine next 6 ingredients in large bowl. Make a well in centre.

Beat remaining 4 ingredients with whisk in small bowl. Add to well. Add cranberry mixture. Mix. Do not overmix. Drop, using 2 tbsp. (30 mL), for each, about 1 1/2 inches (12 mm) apart on greased cookie sheets. Bake on centre rack in 375°F (190°C) oven for 10 to 15 minutes until golden and wooden pick inserted in centre comes out clean. Let stand on cookie sheets for 5 minutes before removing to wire racks to cool. Cool cookie sheets between batches if using more than once. Makes about 6 dozen (72) cookies.

1 cookie: 90 Calories; 4.2 g Total Fat (2 g Mono, 0.2 g Poly, 1.8 g Sat); 9 mg Cholesterol; 12 g Carbohydrate; 1 g Fibre; 1 g Protein; 67 mg Sodium

Pictured on front and back cover and on page 167.

Photo Legend next page:
Top Left: Spiced Heart Cookies, page 164
Top Centre and Bottom Right: Cranberry Macadamia Mounds, page 165
Top Right: Mocha Diamonds, page 168
Centre: Orange Sour Cream Cookies, this page
Bottom Left: Striped Corners, page 164

Recipe for: SPICED HEART COOKIES

from the kitchen of: JEAN

THE SLIGHT SHEEN AND SPRINKLING

OF CHO''

EAD HE

R   1

SES

ARG)

R   5

From The Kitchen Of

Ashley

Honey

Cranberry Macadamia Mounds
from the kitchen of: JEAN

FLAVOURFUL TREATS WITH A BURST
OF SWEET ORANGE, A POP OF TART
CRANBERRIES, A CRUNCH OF MACADAMIA NUTS.

RRIES   1½ CUPS – 375 mL
        ½ CUP   – 125 mL
ED   2 TBSP   – 30 mL

Serves:

Cranberry
Macadamia
Mounds

Mocha Diamonds

Makes a very large batch.

Butter (or hard margarine), softened	1 1/2 cups	375 mL
Brown sugar, packed	1 1/2 cups	375 mL
Instant coffee granules, crushed to fine powder	1 1/2 tsp.	7 mL
Almond flavouring	1 1/2 tsp.	7 mL
All-purpose flour	3 1/3 cups	825 mL
Baking powder	3/4 tsp.	4 mL
Salt	1/2 tsp.	2 mL
Chopped sliced almonds	3/4 cup	175 mL
Milk chocolate bars (3 1/2 oz., 100 g, each), finely chopped	3	3

Beat first 4 ingredients in extra-large bowl until creamy.

Combine flour, baking powder and salt in medium bowl. Slowly add to butter mixture, mixing well, until no dry flour remains.

Add almonds and chocolate. Stir until evenly distributed. Line greased 11 × 17 inch (28 × 43 cm) baking sheet with sides with parchment (not waxed) paper, extending slightly over both long sides (to use for lifting). Press mixture evenly in pan. Bake on centre rack in 325°F (160°C) oven for about 35 minutes until golden brown and firm. Let stand in pan on wire rack for 20 minutes. While still warm, make 10 evenly spaced lengthwise cuts, about 1 inch (2.5 cm) apart. Cut diagonally across lengthwise cuts to create small diamond shapes (see diagram, below). Let stand in pan on wire rack until cooled completely. Invert onto work surface. Remove parchment paper. Re-cut if necessary. There will be some irregularly shaped pieces. Makes about 11 dozen (132) cookies.

1 cookie: 57 Calories; 3.3 g Total Fat (1.1 g Mono, 0.2 g Poly, 1.8 Sat);
   6 mg Cholesterol; 7 g Carbohydrate; trace Fibre; 1 g Protein; 37 mg Sodium

Pictured on page 167.

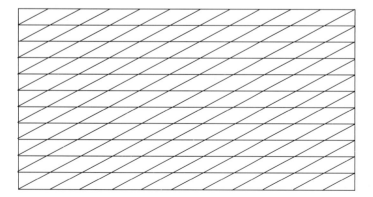

Fruit Scrolls

Palmier-style cookie with swirling spirals of dark, mincemeat filling. Very pretty for a cookie exchange.

Butter (or hard margarine), softened	1 cup	250 mL
Brown sugar, packed	2 cups	500 mL
Large eggs	3	3
All-purpose flour	4 1/2 cups	1.1 L
Ground ginger	1/2 tsp.	2 mL
Ground cinnamon	1/2 tsp.	2 mL
Ground cloves	1/4 tsp.	1 mL
Mincemeat with rum and brandy, blended or processed until slightly smooth	2 cups	500 mL

Beat butter and brown sugar in extra-large bowl until light and creamy. Add eggs, 1 at a time, beating well after each addition.

Combine next 4 ingredients in large bowl. Add to sugar mixture in 3 batches, mixing well after each addition, until no dry flour remains. Turn out onto lightly floured work surface. Shape mixture into ball. Divide into 4 equal portions. Shape each portion into flattened square. Cover each square with plastic wrap. Chill for 3 hours.

Roll out each square between 2 sheets of waxed paper on dampened work surface to 10 × 14 inch (25 × 35 cm) rectangle, about 1/4 inch (6 mm) thick. Remove and discard top sheet of waxed paper from each square. Spread 1 rectangle with 1/2 cup (125 mL) mincemeat to edges. Roll up halfway, jelly roll-style, from long side using bottom piece of waxed paper as guide. Repeat from opposite long side until rolls meet in centre. Discard waxed paper. Place scroll on ungreased cookie sheet. Repeat with remaining squares and mincemeat, for a total of 4 rolls. Cover. Freeze for about 2 hours until firm. Cut each roll into 1/2 inch (12 mm) thick slices. Arrange, cut-side down, on greased cookie sheets. Bake in 350°F (175°C) oven for 10 to 15 minutes until golden brown and firm. Let stand on cookie sheets for 5 minutes before removing to wire racks to cool. Cool cookie sheets between batches if using more than once. Makes about 9 dozen (108) cookies.

1 cookie: 65 Calories; 2.1 g Total Fat (0.6 g Mono, 0.1 g Poly, 1.2 g Sat);
   11 mg Cholesterol; 11 g Carbohydrate; trace Fibre; 1 g Protein; 32 mg Sodium

Pictured on page 171.

Maple Nut Fingers

An appealing, moist and nutty bar. A treat for any time.

All-purpose flour	1 1/2 cups	375 mL
Icing (confectioner's) sugar	1/4 cup	60 mL
Baking powder	1/2 tsp.	2 mL
Ground cinnamon	1/4 tsp.	1 mL
Ground nutmeg	1/4 tsp.	1 mL
Salt	1/4 tsp.	1 mL
Cold butter (or hard margarine), cut up	1/2 cup	125 mL
Large egg, fork-beaten	1	1
Coarsely chopped pecans	3/4 cup	175 mL
Coarsely chopped macadamia nuts	3/4 cup	175 mL
Coarsely chopped sliced almonds	1/2 cup	125 mL
Brown sugar, packed	1/2 cup	125 mL
All-purpose flour	1/4 cup	60 mL
Butter (or hard margarine), melted	1/2 cup	125 mL
Golden corn syrup, warmed	1/2 cup	125 mL
Large egg, fork-beaten	1	1
Maple flavouring	1/2 tsp.	2 mL

Combine first 6 ingredients in large bowl. Cut in butter until mixture resembles coarse crumbs.

Add egg. Stir well. Line greased 9 x 13 inch (22 x 33 cm) pan with parchment (not waxed) paper extending slightly over both long sides (to use for lifting). Press mixture evenly in bottom of pan. Bake on centre rack in 350°F (175°C) oven for about 15 minutes until golden brown.

Sprinkle pecans, macadamia nuts and almonds evenly over top.

Combine brown sugar and second amount of flour in medium bowl. Add remaining 4 ingredients. Stir. Makes about 1 cup (250 mL) topping. Pour over nuts. Bake in 350°F (175°C) oven for about 15 minutes until topping is golden brown and set. Let stand in pan on wire rack until cool. Invert onto work surface. Remove parchment paper. Cut crosswise into 16 narrow strips. Cut each strip into 3 fingers. Makes 4 dozen (48) fingers.

1 finger: 115 Calories; 8 g Total Fat (3.9 g Mono, 0.7 g Poly, 3 g Sat); 20 mg Cholesterol; 10 g Carbohydrate; 1 g Fibre; 1 g Protein; 66 mg Sodium

Pictured on this page.

Cranberry Orange Bars

*A soft but firm bar with a crunchy nut
and tart orange filling.*

Cold butter (or hard margarine), cut up	1 1/2 cups	375 mL
All-purpose flour	2 cups	500 mL
Quick-cooking rolled oats (not instant)	1 1/2 cups	375 mL
Medium unsweetened coconut	1 cup	250 mL
Brown sugar, packed	1 cup	250 mL
Finely grated orange zest	2 tsp.	10 mL
Baking soda	1 tsp.	5 mL
Ground ginger	1 tsp.	5 mL
Chopped pecans, toasted (see Tip, page 80)	1 cup	250 mL
CRANBERRY ORANGE FILLING		
Orange marmalade	1 cup	250 mL
Can of whole cranberry sauce	14 oz.	398 mL

Cut butter into flour in large bowl until mixture resembles coarse crumbs.

Add next 6 ingredients. Stir well.

Transfer 1/2 of rolled oat mixture to separate large bowl. Add pecans. Stir. Set aside. Press remaining oat mixture evenly in greased 10 x 15 inch (25 x 38 cm) jelly roll pan.

Cranberry Orange Filling: Combine marmalade and cranberry sauce in medium bowl. Makes about 2 1/2 cups (625 mL) filling. Carefully spread evenly over base. Sprinkle reserved pecan mixture over filling. Press down lightly. Bake in 350°F (175°C) oven for about 30 minutes until golden brown. Let stand in pan on wire rack for about 3 hours until completely cooled. Cut into 1 x 1 1/2 inch (2.5 x 3.8 cm) pieces. Makes about 7 1/2 dozen (90) bars.

1 bar: 88 Calories; 4.9 g Total Fat (1.5 g Mono, 0.4 g Poly, 2.7 g Sat);
    9 mg Cholesterol; 11 g Carbohydrate; trace Fibre; 1 g Protein; 52 mg Sodium

Pictured on page 171.

Cherry Almond Butter Cookies

*These are hard to resist. A pretty addition
to a plate of baked goodies.*

Butter (not margarine), softened	2 cups	500 mL
Granulated sugar	1 1/2 cups	375 mL
Large egg	1	1
Vanilla	2 tsp.	10 mL
All-purpose flour	5 cups	1.25 L
Baking powder	2 tsp.	10 mL
Salt	1/2 tsp.	2 mL
Dried cherries	1 1/3 cups	325 mL
Slivered almonds, toasted (see Tip, page 80)	1 cup	250 mL

Beat first 4 ingredients in large bowl until light and creamy.

Combine flour, baking powder and salt in medium bowl. Add to butter mixture in 2 batches, alternating with cherries, stirring well after each addition. Divide mixture into 3 equal portions. Shape each into 1 1/2 inch (3.8 cm) diameter roll. Cover with plastic wrap. Chill for at least 3 hours until firm. Cut each roll into 1/3 inch (1 cm) thick slices. Arrange about 1 inch (2.5 cm) apart on greased cookie sheets.

Gently press 2 or 3 almond slivers into each cookie. Bake in 350°F (175°C) oven for about 10 minutes until just golden. Let stand on cookie sheets for 5 minutes before removing to wire racks to cool. Cool cookie sheets between batches if using more than once. Makes about 6 dozen (72) cookies.

1 cookie: 119 Calories; 6.7 g Total Fat (2.3 g Mono, 0.5 g Poly, 3.5 g Sat);
    18 mg Cholesterol; 14 g Carbohydrate; 1 g Fibre; 2 g Protein; 83 mg Sodium

Pictured on page 171.

CHERRY PECAN BUTTER COOKIES: Substitute chopped pecans for slivered almonds.

Top: Cherry Almond Butter Cookies, above
Centre Left: Cranberry Orange Bars, this page
Bottom Right: Fruit Scrolls, page 168

Crisp Almond Pepper Bread

Spread this delicate, peppery bread with Brie or other soft cheese and serve as an appetizer. Store in airtight container at room temperature for up to 1 week. Also freezes well.

Egg whites (large)	2	2
Granulated sugar	1/3 cup	75 mL
All-purpose flour	3/4 cup	175 mL
Ground allspice	1/2 tsp.	2 mL
Whole almonds (with skins)	1 cup	250 mL
Coarse ground pepper	1 1/2 tsp.	7 mL

Beat egg whites and sugar in medium bowl for about 5 minutes until thickened.

Combine flour and allspice in small bowl. Add to egg white mixture. Stir.

Fold in almonds and pepper. Line greased 8 x 4 x 3 inch (20 x 10 x 7.5 cm) loaf pan with parchment (not waxed) paper. Transfer batter to pan. Spread evenly. Bake in 350°F (175°C) oven for about 35 minutes until golden brown. Let stand in pan on wire rack for 1 hour. Remove to wire rack to cool completely. Cut cooled bread into 1/4 inch (6 mm) thick slices using serrated knife. Arrange about 1 inch (2.5 cm) apart on ungreased baking sheet. Bake in 300°F (150°C) oven for about 20 minutes, turning once, until slices are dry and crisp. Makes about 32 slices.

1 slice: 49 Calories; 2.5 g Total Fat (1.6 g Mono, 0.5 g Poly, 0.2 g Sat);
  0 mg Cholesterol; 6 g Carbohydrate; trace Fibre; 1 g Protein; 4 mg Sodium

Pictured on page 173.

Stilton Puffs

Elegant appetizer with subtle blue cheese and bacon flavour. Make ahead, bake, cool and freeze in airtight container. Reheat frozen puffs in 350°F (175°C) oven for about 5 minutes until hot.

Water	1 cup	250 mL
Butter (or hard margarine)	1/2 cup	125 mL
Salt	1/8 tsp.	0.5 mL
All-purpose flour	1 cup	250 mL
Large eggs	4	4
Finely crumbled Stilton cheese (about 4 oz., 113 g)	3/4 cup	175 mL
Bacon slices, cooked crisp and crumbled	8	8
Finely chopped green onion	1/4 cup	60 mL
Pepper	1/2 tsp.	2 mL

Heat and stir water, butter and salt in heavy medium saucepan on medium-high until boiling and butter is melted. Reduce heat to medium.

Add flour all at once. Stir vigorously for about 1 minute until mixture pulls away from side of saucepan to form soft dough. Immediately remove from heat.

Add eggs, 1 at a time, beating well after each addition until dough is smooth and glossy.

Add remaining 4 ingredients. Mix. Drop by rounded teaspoonfuls (about 2 tsp., 10 mL, each), about 2 inches (5 cm) apart, on greased baking sheets. Bake in 425°F (220°C) oven for 15 to 17 minutes until golden brown. Let stand on baking sheets for 5 minutes before removing to wire racks to cool. Makes about 6 dozen (72) puffs.

1 puff: 33 Calories; 2.5 g Total Fat (0.8 g Mono, 0.2 g Poly, 1.4 g Sat);
  18 mg Cholesterol; 2 g Carbohydrate; trace Fibre; 1 g Protein; 57 mg Sodium

Pictured on page 173.

Top: Crisp Almond Pepper Bread, this page
Bottom: Stilton Puffs, above

Vinarterta

*A festive, Icelandic tradition, perfect for
a holiday gathering or buffet. Serve this dense,
rich dessert in small pieces. For best results,
make 2 weeks ahead to allow layers to soften.*

Butter (or hard margarine), softened	2 cups	500 mL
Granulated sugar	1 1/2 cups	375 mL
Large eggs	2	2
Half-and-half cream	1 tbsp.	15 mL
Almond flavouring	1 tsp.	5 mL
All-purpose flour	4 cups	1 L
Ground almonds	1/2 cup	125 mL
Baking powder	2 tsp.	10 mL
Ground cardamom (optional)	1 tsp.	5 mL
Salt	1/16 tsp.	0.5 mL

PRUNE FILLING

Package of pitted prunes	13 1/4 oz.	375 g
Water	2 cups	500 mL
Granulated sugar	1 cup	250 mL
Ground cinnamon	1 tsp.	5 mL
Vanilla	1 tsp.	5 mL

ALMOND BUTTERCREAM ICING

Icing (confectioner's) sugar	3 3/4 cups	925 mL
Butter (not margarine), softened	1 cup	250 mL
Milk	1/3 cup	75 mL
Almond flavouring	3/4 tsp.	4 mL

Beat butter and sugar in large bowl until light and creamy. Add eggs, 1 at a time, beating well after each addition. Add cream and almond flavouring. Beat well.

Combine next 5 ingredients in separate large bowl. Gradually add to butter mixture, stirring until just moistened. Do not overmix. Divide dough into 6 equal portions. Shape each into flattened disc. Cover each with plastic wrap. Chill for 1 hour. Draw 8 inch (20 cm) circle on 1 sheet of parchment (not waxed) paper. Turn paper over. Roll out each round to 8 inch (20 cm) circle between 2 sheets of parchment paper on dampened work surface, using sheet with drawing on top as guide. Peel off top sheet of parchment paper to re-use. Place 1 layer, paper-side down, on ungreased baking sheet. Chill remaining layers. Bake in 350°F (175°C) oven for about 20 minutes until golden brown. Remove layer with paper to wire rack to cool completely. Remove paper. Repeat with remaining layers, baking 1 at a time. Layers may break, but dessert softens over the 2 week "aging" process, so breaks will not be apparent.

Prune Filling: Simmer prunes in water in large saucepan on medium for about 20 minutes until very soft. Drain liquid into small bowl. Set liquid aside.

Add sugar, cinnamon and vanilla to prunes in saucepan. Stir until sugar is dissolved. Process in blender or food processor until smooth, adding 1/2 to 3/4 cup (125 to 175 mL) reserved liquid through hole in lid or feed chute until mixture is spreadable and slightly moist. Cool completely. Add more liquid to cooled mixture if necessary until desired spreading consistency. Makes about 4 1/2 cups (1.1 L) filling. Place 1 cake layer on separate serving plate. Spread about 1/2 cup (125 mL) filling to edge. Top with second layer. Repeat with remaining filling and cake layers, ending with cake layer on top.

Almond Buttercream Icing: Beat all 4 ingredients in large bowl until light and creamy, adding more icing sugar or milk if necessary until spreading consistency. Spread on top and sides of cake. Chill, uncovered, until buttercream is firm. Cover with plastic wrap. Store in refrigerator for 2 weeks before cutting. Cut whole cake across diameter, from top down, into 3/4 inch (2 cm) slices (see diagram). Cut each slice into serving size pieces. There will be some irregularly shaped pieces. Makes 34 pieces.

1 piece: 362 Calories; 18.3 g Total Fat (5.5 g Mono, 0.9 g Poly, 10.9 g Sat);
    59 mg Cholesterol; 49 g Carbohydrate; 1 g Fibre; 3 g Protein; 207 mg Sodium

Pictured above.

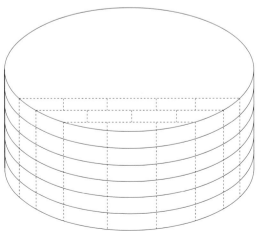

Rich Dark Fruitcake

Any special occasion is an opportunity to enjoy this dark, moist fruitcake with its rich sherry flavour. Make at least 3 days in advance.

Red glazed cherries, halved	1 1/2 cups	375 mL
Chopped pitted dates	1 1/2 cups	375 mL
Golden raisins	1 1/3 cups	325 mL
Currants	1 1/3 cups	325 mL
Chopped pitted prunes	1/2 cup	125 mL
Brandy	1/2 cup	125 mL
Sweet sherry	1/2 cup	125 mL
Butter (or hard margarine), softened	2/3 cup	150 mL
Dark brown sugar, packed	2/3 cup	150 mL
Large eggs	3	3
Apricot jam, warmed	1/3 cup	75 mL
Finely grated lemon zest	1 tbsp.	15 mL

All-purpose flour	2 cups	500 mL
Cocoa, sifted if lumpy	2 tbsp.	30 mL
Baking powder	1 tsp.	5 mL
Ground cinnamon	1 tsp.	5 mL
Ground nutmeg	1 tsp.	5 mL
Ground cloves	1/4 tsp.	1 mL
Chopped walnuts, toasted (see Tip, page 80)	1 1/2 cups	375 mL
Walnut halves	1/4 cup	60 mL
Red (or green) glazed cherries, halved	2 tbsp.	30 mL
Sweet sherry	1/4 cup	60 mL

Combine first 7 ingredients in large bowl. Cover. Let stand at room temperature for 2 days. Do not stir.

Beat butter and brown sugar in separate large bowl until light and creamy. Add eggs, 1 at a time, beating well after each addition. Do not overbeat.

Add jam and lemon zest. Stir. Mixture may look curdled.

Measure next 6 ingredients into medium bowl. Stir. Add to butter mixture. Add chopped walnuts and fruit mixture. Stir well. Line bottom of ungreased 9 inch (22 cm) springform pan with 3 layers of parchment (not waxed) paper. Line side with 3 layers, extending about 2 inches (5 cm) higher than side of pan. Pour batter into pan. Spread evenly.

Arrange walnut halves and cherry halves around edge of batter. Bake in 325°F (160°C) oven for 2 to 2 1/2 hours until cake is firm and knife inserted in centre comes out clean. Let stand in pan on wire rack set in baking sheet with sides.

Drizzle second amount of sherry over hot cake. Cover loosely with foil. Let stand in pan on wire rack until cooled completely. Remove cake from pan. Cover with plastic wrap, then foil. Place in airtight container. May be stored for up to 1 month in refrigerator. To serve, cut into very thin wedges or cut into 1 inch (2.5 cm) slices then cut each slice into 4 to 8 pieces (depending on length of slice). Cuts into about 64 wedges.

1 wedge: 129 Calories; 4.4 g Total Fat (1.1 g Mono, 1.5 g Poly, 1.5 g Sat); 16 mg Cholesterol; 20 g Carbohydrate; 1 g Fibre; 2 g Protein; 32 mg Sodium

Pictured on page 177.

Christmas Shortbread

Traditional, buttery, melt-in-your-mouth shortbread.

Butter (not margarine), softened	1 cup	250 mL
Granulated sugar	2/3 cup	150 mL
All-purpose flour	2 cups	500 mL
Cornstarch	1/2 cup	125 mL
Egg white (large), fork-beaten	1	1
Sanding (decorating) sugar (see Glossary, page 9)	2 tbsp.	30 mL

Beat butter and sugar in large bowl until light and creamy.

Add flour. Stir. Add cornstarch. Stir well. Shape mixture into ball. Do not over handle. Trace circle on parchment (not waxed) paper using 8 inch (20 cm) round pan. Turn paper over and dust with flour. Roll out dough on paper to 8 inch (20 cm) circle, 1/2 inch (12 mm) thick, using drawing as guide. Invert pan over dough. Run sharp knife around edge of pan to trim excess dough. Remove pan. Slide paper and dough onto ungreased baking sheet.

Crimp decorative edge. Score into 12 wedges using sharp knife. Chill for 15 minutes.

Brush with egg white. Sprinkle with sanding sugar. Bake in 325°F (160°C) oven for about 30 minutes until golden. Let stand on baking sheet on wire rack until cooled completely. Cuts into 12 wedges.

1 wedge: 300 Calories; 16.4 g Total Fat (4.7 g Mono, 0.7 g Poly, 10.1 g Sat); 44 mg Cholesterol; 36 g Carbohydrate; 1 g Fibre; 3 g Protein; 171 mg Sodium

Pictured on page 179.

Apple Cranberry Tart

Wonderful blend of tart and sweet. Use your imagination to create your own cutouts to decorate the top.

Pastry for 2 crust 9 inch (22 cm) pie	1	1
Tart cooking apples (such as Granny Smith), peeled, cored and thinly sliced (about 5 large)	7 cups	1.75 L
Water	1/4 cup	60 mL
Granulated sugar	2/3 cup	150 mL
Dried cranberries	1/3 cup	75 mL
Finely grated lemon zest	1 tsp.	5 mL
Egg white (large), fork-beaten	1	1
Sanding (decorating) sugar (see Glossary, page 9), optional	2 tbsp.	30 mL

Roll out 3/4 of pastry on lightly floured surface to about 1/8 inch (3 mm) thickness. Press in bottom and up side of 9 inch (22 cm) tart pan with fluted side and removable bottom. Trim edge. Cover. Chill for 1 hour.

Combine apple and water in large saucepan. Bring to a boil. Cover. Reduce heat to medium. Simmer for about 8 minutes, stirring occasionally, until apple is tender.

Add granulated sugar, cranberries and lemon zest. Stir. Remove from heat. Cool. Drain and discard liquid. Place tart pan on baking sheet (to make it easier to remove hot pan from oven). Pour filling into pastry shell. Spread evenly.

Roll out remaining pastry on lightly floured surface to 1/8 inch (3 mm) thickness. Cut out pastry shapes. Place around edge of tart. Brush top with egg white. Sprinkle with sanding sugar. Bake on bottom rack in 375°F (190°C) oven for about 45 minutes until golden brown. Cuts into 8 wedges.

1 wedge: 297 Calories; 10.7 g Total Fat (5 g Mono, 1.4 g Poly, 3.4 g Sat); 0 mg Cholesterol; 50 g Carbohydrate; 3 g Fibre; 2 g Protein; 212 mg Sodium

Pictured on page 179.

Top: Christmas Shortbread, this page
Bottom: Apple Cranberry Tart, above

Overnight Christmas Bread

A pretty braid glazed with honey. Good toasted and buttered. Make at least 1 day in advance.

Warm water	1/2 cup	125 mL
Granulated sugar	1 tsp.	5 mL
Envelope of active dry yeast (or 2 1/4 tsp., 11 mL)	1/4 oz.	8 g
Milk	1/2 cup	125 mL
Liquid honey	1/4 cup	60 mL
Butter (or hard margarine)	1/4 cup	60 mL
Salt	1 1/2 tsp.	7 mL
Large eggs, fork-beaten	2	2
All-purpose flour	2 cups	500 mL
Ground cardamom	1/2 tsp.	2 mL
Ground cinnamon	1/2 tsp.	2 mL
All-purpose flour, approximately	2 cups	500 mL
Chopped golden raisins	1/2 cup	125 mL
Chopped mixed glazed fruit	1/2 cup	125 mL
Cooking oil (for greasing hands and work surface)		
Liquid honey (or melted butter), optional	1 tbsp.	15 mL

Stir warm water and sugar in small bowl until sugar is dissolved. Sprinkle yeast over top. Let stand for 10 minutes. Stir until yeast is dissolved.

Heat and stir next 4 ingredients in small saucepan on medium until butter is almost melted. Pour into large bowl. Stir until butter is melted. Let stand for 5 minutes.

Add eggs and yeast mixture. Stir well.

Add first amount of flour, cardamom and cinnamon. Mix until smooth batter forms.

Work in enough of second amount of flour, 1/2 cup (125 mL) at a time, until soft sticky dough forms. Turn out onto lightly floured surface. Knead for 5 to 10 minutes, adding flour 1 tbsp. (15 mL) at a time if necessary to prevent sticking, until smooth and elastic. Place in greased large bowl, turning once to grease top. Cover with greased waxed paper and tea towel. Let stand in oven with light on and door closed for about 1 hour until almost doubled in bulk. Punch dough down.

Add raisins and glazed fruit. Work into dough until well distributed.

Turn out onto lightly greased surface. Lightly grease hands. Divide dough into 3 equal portions. Roll each into 18 inch (45 cm) rope.

Lay ropes side by side. Pinch together at one end. Loosely braid ropes. Pinch together at opposite end. Place on greased 11 x 17 inch (28 x 43 cm) baking sheet. Tuck ends under. Cover loosely (to allow for expansion) with greased plastic wrap. Chill for at least 24 hours.

Remove from refrigerator. If braid has not doubled, let stand at room temperature until doubled in size. Remove and discard plastic wrap. Bake braid on centre rack in 375°F (190°C) oven for about 30 minutes until golden brown and hollow sounding when tapped. Remove to wire rack.

Brush warm bread with honey. Cool completely. Cuts into 30 slices.

1 slice: 116 Calories; 2.2 g Total Fat (0.6 g Mono, 0.2 g Poly, 1.2 g Sat); 19 mg Cholesterol; 22 g Carbohydrate; 1 g Fibre; 3 g Protein; 145 mg Sodium

Pictured on page 181.

Top and Bottom Right: Overnight Christmas Bread, this page
Centre Left: Festive Fruit 'N' Nut Loaf, page 182

Festive Fruit 'N' Nut Loaf

The large pieces of fruit and nuts give the look of stained glass in this rich, tasty loaf. Make at least 1 day in advance.

Whole pitted dates (about 8 oz., 225 g)	1 1/3 cups	325 mL
Brazil nuts, toasted (see Tip, page 80)	1 1/3 cups	325 mL
Whole almonds	1 cup	250 mL
Red glazed cherries	3/4 cup	175 mL
Green glazed cherries	3/4 cup	175 mL
Dried apricots (or peaches), cut into 1 inch (2.5 cm) pieces	2/3 cup	150 mL
Glazed pineapple rings, cut into 1 inch (2.5 cm) pieces	2	2
Large eggs	2	2
Brown sugar, packed	2/3 cup	150 mL
Butter (or hard margarine), softened	1/3 cup	75 mL
Spiced rum	2 tbsp.	30 mL
All-purpose flour	1/2 cup	125 mL
Baking powder	1/4 tsp.	1 mL
Baking soda	1/4 tsp.	1 mL

Measure first 7 ingredients into extra-large bowl.

Beat eggs in small bowl until thick and creamy. Add brown sugar, butter and spiced rum. Beat well.

Combine flour, baking powder and baking soda in small bowl. Add to fruit mixture. Stir until well coated. Add egg mixture. Mix well. Line bottom and sides of greased 9 × 5 × 3 inch (22 × 12.5 × 7.5 cm) loaf pan with parchment (not waxed) paper. Spoon batter into pan, pressing into corners. Spread evenly. Bake in 300°F (150°C) oven for about 2 hours until browned and firm. Cover pan with foil. Let stand in pan on wire rack until cool. Remove loaf. Remove and discard parchment paper. Cover loaf with plastic wrap. Chill overnight. About 1 hour before serving, cut into 18 slices.

1 slice: 330 Calories; 15.9 g Total Fat (6.6 g Mono, 3.8 g Poly, 4.6 g Sat);
     34 mg Cholesterol; 45 g Carbohydrate; 3 g Fibre; 5 g Protein; 73 mg Sodium

Pictured on page 181.

Eggnog Cheesecake

A perfect dessert for a festive occasion.

VANILLA WAFER CRUST		
Crushed vanilla wafers (about 2 cups, 500 mL, wafers)	1 1/2 cups	375 mL
Butter (or hard margarine)	1/3 cup	75 mL
Granulated sugar	1 tbsp.	15 mL
EGGNOG FILLING		
Blocks of cream cheese (8 oz., 250 g, each), softened	3	3
Granulated sugar	2/3 cup	150 mL
Rum flavouring	2 1/2 tsp.	12 mL
Vanilla	1 tsp.	5 mL
Ground nutmeg	1/2 tsp.	2 mL
Large eggs	3	3
Sour cream	1 cup	250 mL
RUM SAUCE		
Brown sugar, packed	2/3 cup	150 mL
Water	1 cup	250 mL
Butter (or hard margarine)	1 tbsp.	15 mL
Salt	1/4 tsp.	1 mL
Water	1/4 cup	60 mL
Cornstarch	4 tsp.	20 mL
Vanilla	1/2 tsp.	2 mL
Rum flavouring	1/2 tsp.	2 mL

Vanilla Wafer Crust: Grease bottom and side of 9 inch (22 cm) springform pan. Process wafers in blender or food processor until fine crumbs. Melt butter in medium saucepan. Remove from heat. Add wafer crumbs and sugar. Stir well. Press mixture evenly in bottom of pan. Bake in 350°F (175°C) oven for about 10 minutes until browned and firm. Let stand in pan on wire rack until cool.

Eggnog Filling: Beat cream cheese and sugar in large bowl until smooth. Add rum flavouring, vanilla and nutmeg. Beat. Add eggs, 1 at a time, beating after each addition. Add sour cream. Beat well. Pour over crust. Bake in 325°F (160°C) oven for 55 to 60 minutes until centre is almost set. Run knife around inside edge of pan to allow cheesecake to settle evenly. Let stand in pan on wire rack until cooled completely. Cover. Chill for at least 6 hours.

Rum Sauce: Combine first 4 ingredients in medium saucepan. Bring to a boil on medium-high.

Stir second amount of water into cornstarch in small cup. Add to brown sugar mixture. Stirring until thickened. Remove from heat.

Add vanilla and rum flavouring. Stir. Cool. Makes 1 1/2 cups (375 mL) sauce. Cheesecake cuts into 12 wedges. Drizzle individual servings with sauce. Serves 12.

1 serving (1 wedge with 2 tbsp., 30 mL, sauce): 490 Calories; 34.4 g Total Fat
    (10.1 g Mono, 1.8 g Poly, 20.4 g Sat); 156 mg Cholesterol;
    39 g Carbohydrate; trace Fibre; 8 g Protein; 373 mg Sodium

Pictured above.

Mincemeat Puffs

A delicious addition to a plate of sweet treats.

Package of frozen puff pastry, thawed according to package directions	14 oz.	397 g
Large egg	1	1
Milk	1 tsp.	5 mL
Mincemeat with rum and brandy, packed	3/4 cup	175 mL
Sanding (decorating) sugar (see Glossary, page 9)	4 tsp.	20 mL

Roll out 1/2 (1 square) of pastry on lightly floured surface to 9 x 9 inch (22 x 22 cm) square. Cut into nine 3 inch (7.5 cm) squares. Repeat with remaining pastry, for a total of 18 squares.

Beat egg and milk with fork in small bowl.

Place 2 tsp. (10 mL) mincemeat in centre of each pastry square. Dampen top edge and halfway down both sides with egg wash. Bring bottom edge up and over filling. Pinch edges to seal, pressing out any air bubbles. Arrange pastries, 2 inches (5 cm) apart, on greased baking sheets. Pierce each pastry several times with knife. Brush tops with remaining egg wash.

Sprinkle sanding sugar over each pastry. Bake in 400°F (205°C) oven for about 15 minutes until golden. Makes 18 puffs.

1 puff: 153 Calories; 8.9 g Total Fat (2 g Mono, 4.9 g Poly, 1.3 g Sat);
12 mg Cholesterol; 16 g Carbohydrate; 0 g Fibre; 2 g Protein; 82 mg Sodium

Pictured below.

Measurement Tables

Throughout this book measurements are given in Conventional and Metric measure. To compensate for differences between the two measurements due to rounding, a full metric measure is not always used. The cup used is the standard 8 fluid ounce. Temperature is given in degrees Fahrenheit and Celsius. Baking pan measurements are in inches and centimetres as well as quarts and litres. An exact metric conversion is given on this page as well as the working equivalent (Standard Measure).

Oven Temperatures

Fahrenheit (°F)	Celsius (°C)	Fahrenheit (°F)	Celsius (°C)
175°	80°	350°	175°
200°	95°	375°	190°
225°	110°	400°	205°
250°	120°	425°	220°
275°	140°	450°	230°
300°	150°	475°	240°
325°	160°	500°	260°

Spoons

Conventional Measure	Metric Exact Conversion Millilitre (mL)	Metric Standard Measure Millilitre (mL)
1/8 teaspoon (tsp.)	0.6 mL	0.5 mL
1/4 teaspoon (tsp.)	1.2 mL	1 mL
1/2 teaspoon (tsp.)	2.4 mL	2 mL
1 teaspoon (tsp.)	4.7 mL	5 mL
2 teaspoons (tsp.)	9.4 mL	10 mL
1 tablespoon (tbsp.)	14.2 mL	15 mL

Cups

1/4 cup (4 tbsp.)	56.8 mL	60 mL
1/3 cup (5⅓ tbsp.)	75.6 mL	75 mL
1/2 cup (8 tbsp.)	113.7 mL	125 mL
2/3 cup (10⅔ tbsp.)	151.2 mL	150 mL
3/4 cup (12 tbsp.)	170.5 mL	175 mL
1 cup (16 tbsp.)	227.3 mL	250 mL
4 1/2 cups	1022.9 mL	1000 mL (1 L)

Pans

Conventional Inches	Metric Centimetres
8 x 8 inch	20 x 20 cm
9 x 9 inch	22 x 22 cm
9 x 13 inch	22 x 33 cm
10 x 15 inch	25 x 38 cm
11 x 17 inch	28 x 43 cm
8 x 2 inch round	20 x 5 cm
9 x 2 inch round	22 x 5 cm
10 x 4 1/2 inch tube	25 x 11 cm
8 x 4 x 3 inch loaf	20 x 10 x 7.5 cm
9 x 5 x 3 inch loaf	22 x 12.5 x 7.5 cm

Dry Measurements

Conventional Measure Ounces (oz.)	Metric Exact Conversion Grams (g)	Metric Standard Measure Grams (g)
1 oz.	28.3 g	28 g
2 oz.	56.7 g	57 g
3 oz.	85.0 g	85 g
4 oz.	113.4 g	125 g
5 oz.	141.7 g	140 g
6 oz.	170.1 g	170 g
7 oz.	198.4 g	200 g
8 oz.	226.8 g	250 g
16 oz.	453.6 g	500 g
32 oz.	907.2 g	1000 g (1 kg)

Casseroles

Canada & Britain

Standard Size Casserole	Exact Metric Measure
1 qt. (5 cups)	1.13 L
1 1/2 qts. (7 1/2 cups)	1.69 L
2 qts. (10 cups)	2.25 L
2 1/2 qts. (12 1/2 cups)	2.81 L
3 qts. (15 cups)	3.38 L
4 qts. (20 cups)	4.5 L
5 qts. (25 cups)	5.63 L

United States

Standard Size Casserole	Exact Metric Measure
1 qt. (4 cups)	900 mL
1 1/2 qts. (6 cups)	1.35 L
2 qts. (8 cups)	1.8 L
2 1/2 qts. (10 cups)	2.25 L
3 qts. (12 cups)	2.7 L
4 qts. (16 cups)	3.6 L
5 qts. (20 cups)	4.5 L

Recipe Index

Recipe Index ■ 187

Recipe Index ■ 189